Jolly Della Pringle

Jolly Della Pringle
Star of the Western Stage

Charles E. Lauterbach

McFarland & Company, Inc., Publishers
Jefferson, North Carolina

LIBRARY OF CONGRESS CATALOGUING-IN-PUBLICATION DATA

Lauterbach, Charles E.
　　Jolly Della Pringle : star of the western stage / Charles E. Lauterbach.
　　　　p.　　cm.
　　Includes bibliographical references and index.

　　ISBN 978-0-7864-9891-8 (softcover : acid free paper) ∞
　　ISBN 978-1-4766-2123-4 (ebook)

　　1. Pringle, Della, 1870–1952.　2. Actors—United States—Biography.
I. Title.

PN2287.P7337L38 2015
792.02'8092—dc23
[B]　　　　　　　　　　　　　　　　　　　　　　　　　　　2015009750

BRITISH LIBRARY CATALOGUING DATA ARE AVAILABLE

© 2015 Charles E. Lauterbach. All rights reserved

No part of this book may be reproduced or transmitted in any form or by any means, electronic or mechanical, including photocopying or recording, or by any information storage and retrieval system, without permission in writing from the publisher.

On the cover: Della Pringle about 1890 (courtesy of the National Society for the Preservation of Tent, Folk and Repertoire Theatre at the Theatre Museum of Repertoire Americana, Midwest Old Threshers, Mt. Pleasant, Iowa)

Printed in the United States of America

McFarland & Company, Inc., Publishers
　Box 611, Jefferson, North Carolina 28640
　　www.mcfarlandpub.com

To the women in my life:
 my wife Margaret
 my mother Emma
 my sister Ann

Table of Contents

Acknowledgments   ix
Preface   1
Prologue   3

1. Curtain Up: Child Star, Novice Actress   7
2. Della's Wedding and the Comedy Ideals   12
3. Della Pringle and G. Faith Adams   20
4. Prosperous Seasons and the Great Loop   34
5. Western Star on Eastern Stages   47
6. West to the Coast   58
7. To Court and to the Altar   68
8. Seasons of Challenge   80
9. Rough Road to a New Home   98
10. Running Before the Wave   111
11. Off the Stage and Onto the Screen   126
12. Biding Time in Boise   142
13. "The working old fool"   154
14. Curtain Coming Down   172

Epilogue: A Summing Up   183
Chapter Notes   187
Bibliography   201
Index   205

Acknowledgments

Several individuals and institutions aided in the research and completion of Della Pringle's biography. The author is indebted to and expresses gratitude for the contributions of the following persons and organizations.

The Idaho State Board of Education awarded a sizable grant to fund research. Lesser grants came from Boise State University and the Idaho Humanities Council.

Claudia Scott and the interlibrary loan staff of Boise State University obtained countless rolls of microfilmed newspapers which greatly facilitated research. Gwyn Hervochon and the staff of the Special Collections Department of Boise State University's Albertson Library secured rights to reproduce the photograph of Cecil Van Auker. Historical society personnel in Utah, Wyoming, Iowa, South Dakota and Idaho examined their collections and sent photocopies of relevant items. Steve Woodhouse, editor of the *Knoxville Journal-Express*, deserves credit for granting permission to quote at length from the archives of his newspaper.

A few articles, including several letters to Della Pringle and almost all of Della Pringle's photographs, came from her scrapbook preserved by the National Society for the Preservation of Tent, Folk and Repertoire Theatre at the Theatre Museum of Repertoire Americana in Mt. Pleasant, Iowa. Special appreciation is owed to Dr. Joe Mauck who arranged for duplication of photographs from the scrapbook. David Ripper, Grace Davis and Sue Mitchell deserve credit for arranging permission to reproduce photographs from the Theatre Museum's Della Pringle collection. Martha Hayes, the museum's collection supervisor, supplied information on the career of Grace Eagle, Della Pringle's only relative. A museum member, Florence Darling of San Antonio, Texas, was kind enough to write a letter commenting on the late stages of Grace Eagle's career.

The late Dr. Jere C. Mickel planned to write a book about Della Pringle and his papers located in the Special Collections Library of Texas Tech University contained valuable information about Della Pringle's later years in Boise, Idaho. Randy Vance, Dr. Monroe and Donna Ortega of the Texas Tech University Special Collections Library were instrumental in supplying photocopies of Dr. Mickel's papers.

Kathleen Smith and Carl Nollen, connected with the Marion County Historical Society in Knoxville, Iowa, have aided in local research and securing additional photographs of Della Pringle from the society's collections.

Thanks to Sally Burke of the University of Rhode Island for her patience in editing my Della Pringle article for the September 1996 edition of *The American Transcendental Quarterly.* It greatly improved the publication.

Several people and institutions in Boise, Idaho, contributed to or gave support to the creation of Della Pringle's biography. Dr. Kent Neely and the staff of the Boise State University Department of Theatre Arts encouraged and supported the project. *Idaho Statesman* columnist Tim Woodward wrote an entertaining article about Della Pringle and the research into her life. A portion of Betty Penson-Ward's book on women in Idaho history was dedicated to Della Pringle and served as an early guide for research. The Boise Public Library's microfilm and online copies of the *Idaho Statesman* greatly facilitated research. Jim Maguire of Summer's Funeral generously provided the records of Della Pringle's funeral details.

Although they did not specifically contribute to my research, I owe so much to those teachers and mentors who guided my education and development as a theatre artist. High school teacher Willis Lloyd "Jerry" Turner introduced me to the wonder of theatre and later was my colleague at the University of California, Riverside, before he left to became the artistic director of the Oregon Shakespeare Festival. At the University of Colorado, Boulder, I was the student of and participated in the play productions of Dr. Jack H. Crouch (founder of the Colorado Shakespeare Festival), Dr. Albert Nadeau and Anthony Lawrence Kadlec. I also had the privileged to take dramatic literature courses from Shavian scholar Dr. E. J. West. In the doctoral theatre program at Michigan State University I worked with Dr. John Dietrich, Dr. James Brandon and Dr. Frank Rutledge. Aside from formal education, I learned from and enjoyed working with hundreds of students who enrolled in my classes and participated in plays under my direction.

On a personal level, I would like to thank James and Stella Schneider for putting up with my frequent reports of research in progress. Jim also aided in genealogical research about the Van Winkle family and digitally retouched some photographs. My wife, the *Idaho Statesman* gardening columnist Margaret Lauterbach, has allowed me to carry on an academic affair with Jolly Della Pringle for two decades and deserves both my praise and gratitude for doing so.

Preface

Numerous biographies of American actresses performing around the turn of the twentieth century exist. Most are of major stars who appeared on the Broadway stage and on tour to other major metropolitan centers. Less attention has been paid to actresses such as Nellie Boyd, Phosa McCallister, Katie Putnam and Margaret Fischer who starred in the traveling "ten, twent, thirt" repertory theatre productions that provided entertainment to the inhabitants of smaller American towns and remote communities. Such a star was Della Pringle and this book relates her eventful life and long career as she toured with her own company to farm communities, mining camps, military forts, cow towns and logging camps in the American West and Midwest in the decades before and after 1900.

In view of the relative rarity of studies about repertory theatre actresses, this biography expands the knowledge of the field. Pringle's life is interesting in itself. Employing her beauty and natural talent in acting, singing and dancing, she rose from obscurity to become a major star in the repertory theatre industry in the West and Midwest, performing in tours that extended from coast to coast and border to border in a thirty-year career. She even appeared in a few silent films, amassed a considerable fortune and became acquainted with a significant number of recognized stars in the show business of her time. Also important, her experiences as a performer provide insights into the conditions and practices of the touring repertory theatre movement, the nature of its entertainments and its appeal to diverse audiences west of the Mississippi River.

I first encountered the name Jolly Della Pringle in the early part of the 1970s in Boise, Idaho, when, as a newly-hired theatre professor at Boise State University, I agreed to be a judge in a junior high speech competition. The school principal, knowing of my interest in theatre, asked if I had ever heard of Jolly Della Pringle, a supposedly famous actress who had once resided in Boise. I had not, found the name rather amusing and mentally dismissed her as a person of local reputation only. Then in the late 1980s I became involved in research into the theatre history of Boise. While examining the city's newspaper archives, I encountered numerous items regarding and references to Della Pringle and it became clear that she had not only been a dominant figure in Boise's theatrical world from 1908 to 1915 but had a long career before arriving in the city. A laborious reading of theatrical trade papers (*New York Clipper* and *New York Dramatic Mirror*) provided information on the touring routes of Pringles' theatre companies from 1890 to her long stay in Idaho. This led to an intensive use of interlibrary loans to obtain microfilm copies of newspapers from the scores of cities and towns where she had appeared. Information from these varied sources was compiled into a seventy-page chronology which served as an outline for this biography.

Della Pringle made it a practice to correspond frequently and at length with both the theatrical trade papers and her hometown newspapers in Knoxville, Iowa, and Boise, Idaho. The correspondence, printed by the newspapers, has been employed extensively in the biography to give a firsthand commentary about Della Pringle experiences, observations and opinions. She also maintained a scrapbook of articles, photographs and ephemera that ended up in the repertory theatre museum at Mt. Pleasant, Iowa. With few exceptions, the photographs included in this biography are from that scrapbook.

Years of research have uncovered only a handful of commentaries that mention Della Pringle and there appear to be no comprehensive works devoted to her life and career. It is hoped that this biography will demonstrate her importance in the history of American repertory theatre in the West. It is too good a story not to be told.

Prologue

It is unlikely that anyone living today would recognize the name of repertory theatre actress Jolly Della Pringle and, yet, in the decades before and after the turn of the twentieth century thousands of American theatre-goers knew and loved her. Although she was not a national celebrity, there was not a town of any consequence in the West or Midwest where she was not a welcome visitor and a household name.

Della, called "jolly" because she loved to laugh and provoked so much merriment in her audiences, led a life as dramatic as any play she ever presented. Like a female Horatio Alger, she rose from teenage hotel maid to become a lady of wealth, clothed in the latest Paris fashions and traversing the continent in her own private palace Pullman car. She faced sudden death three times, survived railroad and stage coach accidents, escaped from burning theatres and endured both freezing winters and searing summers. In an age when divorce was rare, she married and divorced a "sinful" five times!

Jolly Della Pringle never appeared on Broadway or ever claimed to be a great actress. She had no formal training in the craft. Yet, her natural talents in acting, singing and dancing, her small, well-formed figure, her long golden hair, her well-featured face and her witty, vibrant personality made her a star in her realm, the small towns, mining camps, logging camps, military outposts and cow towns of Western America. In spite of her modest claims about her talents as an actress, she earned critical acclaim when she did appear in larger cities like Denver, Salt Lake City, Des Moines and Los Angeles. On her only tour through the Northeast and New England the press found her to be the equal of any eastern repertory actress. Critics aside, audiences crowded theatres to see her shows, making her a fortune.

On occasion Della Pringle settled in place to operate a permanent stock theatre company, but for most of her long career she was on tour. She traveled from coast to coast (Portland, Maine, to Portland, Oregon), border to border (El Paso, Texas, to Canada), from the heights of Colorado's Rocky Mountains to the depths of an Arizona gold mine. Audiences in thirty-two of the then existing forty-eight states attended her shows. Except for one season in the Northeast and brief forays into Wisconsin and Illinois, Della performed west of the Mississippi River.

It may be an exaggeration, but it has been said that Della Pringle knew almost everybody in the show business of her time. Certainly, scores of actors and actresses had been members of her various companies during her thirty-year career. She often visited with other touring groups when their paths crossed. Della spent two years in the California movie industry and appeared in a dozen films. While there she made friends with such celebrities as Charlie Chaplin, Fatty Arbuckle, Douglas Fairbanks, Ben Turpin and Gloria Swanson. She acted for Mack Sennett in his classic Keystone Kops slapstick comedies. Della knew Buffalo Bill Cody and Annie Oakley and visited with Cody on several occasions through 1915. Through her marriage to her first husband she became a virtual stepmother to silent screen idol John Gilbert. Her correspondence and pictures frequently appeared in the theatrical trade papers and twice her photograph was featured on their front pages.

In Della's era many repertory theatre companies bore the name of their leading ladies, but the troupes were managed by and the shows directed by men. Della was not only a leading lady, but produced and directed her own shows. Through experience she became accomplished in all aspects of show business on and off stage. She knew what audiences wanted and supplied it in abundance. Della was resourceful, hard working, inventive and persistent in all her endeavors. In addition to acting on stage and in films, she pursued farming, real estate investment, rooming house management, millinery, running a costume rental business, education and dog breeding.

Examination of Della Pringle's acting career also provides some insight into the American repertory theatre movement and its practices. In the days before motion pictures, radio and television, the American public outside of major cities relied on touring theatre productions for entertainment. A network of railroads, developed after the Civil War, brought shows to towns and cities across the nation. Larger cities attracted tours of single Broadway shows that might play for days, even weeks, before moving on. These were referred to as "road shows" since they traveled by railroad or as "dollar shows" because that was usually the cost of admission. Smaller or remote towns were served by regional traveling repertory companies like Della Pringle's which usually played several evenings, presenting a variety of older, low royalty comedies and melodramas for the admission price of ten to thirty cents. Such troupes were termed "ten, twent, thirt" companies because of their low cost tickets.

Like similar repertory troupes Della Pringle often employed eight to a dozen actors and actresses who appeared as stock characters: leading man, heavy or villain, ingénue, juvenile, character woman, etc. In the days before stage unions, performers were also expected to do double duty, filling in as stage hands, prop masters, wardrobe mistresses, projectionists— whatever was needed to mount and run a show. Often company managers hired a small orchestra (piano, violin and one or two brass or woodwind players) to play before performances and between acts. Sometimes the musicians were hired locally, but many troupes carried their own orchestra to ensure the quality of the music. Musicians, too, pitched in to set up scenery and sometimes left the pit to play minor roles on stage.

In addition to presenting a play, an evening of repertory theatre entertainment included the performance of "specialties" by members of the company between the acts of the play. Quite often this involved a variety of singing, dancing and playing solo instruments, but could include comic monologues, short skits, magic tricks, trained dog acts, etc. Here, the actors doubled as vaudeville performers. The more performance skills an actor or actress possessed, the more valuable they were to the company. Some were employed because of their "specialty" and then integrated into acting roles. One common specialty was the illustrated song in which song lyrics were projected on a screen and an actor led the audience in song accompanied by the orchestra.

In addition to all their other duties, the entire troupe of actors, specialty artists and musicians participated in promoting performances by parading and playing down a town's main street either in the afternoon or just before show time. There may have been glamour in repertory theatre, but mostly it was hard work.

To a leading lady in a repertory company her wardrobe was almost as important as her talent. Women attending plays expected to see a display of elaborate and fashionable gowns usually not available in the community. Della Pringle's collection of costumes did not disappoint expectations. She claimed to have the finest, up-to-date wardrobe of any leading actress on the western stage. Early in her career she used her sewing skills to create her own costumes, but by 1900 she made it a practice to purchase imported Parisian fashions from major clothiers in New York and Chicago. For one season alone, she spent $5,000 on Paris gowns, the equivalent of $100,000 in today's money. She saw to it that her supporting actresses also had impressive wardrobes.

Della Pringle's productions excelled in scenic display, too. Traveling companies commonly used the stock scenery available in the theatres where they performed, the same interiors and exteriors providing the same backdrop for every play by every troupe. Della's shows differed in that she traveled with thousands of dollars worth of scenery designed for particular productions. Most of the scenery came from the best scenic studios in Chicago, but from time to time Della purchased settings from Broadway shows after they closed in New York. With such investment and attention to production details, newspaper critics quite often praised her "ten, twent, thirt" shows as equal in quality to Broadway "dollar" shows on tour.

While the plays presented by Della Pringle and other repertory troupers provided entertainment for a vast, general public, few survived beyond the age or came to be regarded as significant dramatic literature. Repertory theatre companies like Della's presented few classic plays; most specialized in roaring farces, thrilling melodramas, southern romances and soap opera domestic dramas. Della, like so many other managers, repeated some older, standard works such as *Uncle Tom's Cabin*, *East Lynne*, *Little Lord Fauntleroy* and *Camille*. However, most of her plays were the standard dramas of the day with formulistic plotting, obvious stock characters of little or no dimension, uninspired dialogue and shopworn themes. They were intended to be merely entertainment vehicles for an immediate audience and, because of their lack of literary merit, demanded more from performers to be effective.

In 1952 an author in Boise, Idaho, interviewed Della Pringle and then published an article entitled "The Saga of Jolly Della Pringle," an apt title for a long story with dramatic events. A better term to describe Della Pringle's life would be "odyssey," a long, wandering, adventurous voyage marked by many changes in fortune and notable experiences ranging from hardship to triumph. For, truly, Jolly Della Pringle lived an extraordinary life in interesting times.

1

Curtain Up:
Child Star, Novice Actress

Jolly Della Pringle, a popular actress and entertainer who performed before audiences in the smaller communities of American West and Midwest for the three decades of her professional career, came into the world as Cora Della Van Winkle on August 20, 1870, in Trenton, Missouri. Her mother, Nancy Ellis, who had married James Van Winkle in Illinois sometime in 1858, gave birth to eight children before her husband passed away in 1878. The family appears to have moved about in Illinois and Missouri (with a possible visit to Fishkill, New York) before settling at Knoxville, Iowa, about 1884.

Tuberculosis claimed most of Cora Della's siblings before she reached adulthood. William lived only one year, John died at age three and Mary passed away at seven. Allie and George attained the age of twenty-three before passing on. Cora Della, brother James Elmer and sister Sadie survived, the latter two still alive as Cora Della began her adult professional career on stage.[1] After seven years of widowhood, Nancy Van Winkle remarried, her wedding to Ira Hendrick taking place in Attica, Iowa, on October 18, 1885.

There is little information about Cora Della's younger years, but based on her demonstrated ability as a writer and her skills as a theatre manager during her adulthood, she apparently received a good basic education, sufficient enough to qualify her at one time for a school teaching position. There is evidence that she worked to help support her family by taking jobs as a baby sitter and later as a hotel maid.

Three events in her early life influenced her choice of a career in acting. Like many children of the time she took part in local amateur productions, appearing in such shows in Missouri and Iowa as early as eight or nine. Later in her career she would claim to have appeared as one of the village children in a Fishkill, New York, performance of *Rip Van Winkle* starring the legendary Joseph Jefferson.[2]

Next, as a result of being employed as a baby sitter at age eleven for a family in Rich Hill, Missouri, she came in contact with the manager of the Robert Neff Chicago Comedy Company who took her into the company. She may have been hired primarily as a companion for the child star of the troupe, but she did appear on stage from time to time in roles such as Little Eva in *Uncle Tom's Cabin*, Willie in *East Lynne* and Mary Morgan in *Ten Nights in a Barroom*.[3] Later she would cite her one-year engagement with the Neff Company as the beginning of her professional career.[4] Her tour with the company began at Butler, Missouri, on June 6, 1881. During the rest of June and all of July the Neff troupe appeared in small Missouri towns. After halting the season temporarily at Kansas City, Missouri, in late July of 1881, the reorganized company played one-week stands in Missouri and Kansas to the end of 1881. The tour resumed in 1882 at Fairbury, Nebraska, and continued in that state until early April. By April 20, 1882, the Neff troupe entered into Iowa and ended the nearly year-long tour at Sac City, Iowa, on May 13, 1882.[5] Cora Della then returned to join her family in Knoxville, Iowa.

Finally, she was influenced by the actors and actresses who performed in Knoxville from time to time. She not only saw them on the stage in Knoxville's theatre (which also served as the community's roller skating rink), but she met with them personally when they rented rooms at the city's Linden Hotel where she worked as a maid beginning at age fourteen. Surely the performers with their fashionable suits and attractive dresses, their larger-than-life personalities and riveting tales of life on the road greatly impressed this small town girl who labored under challenging family circumstances.

As soon as she reached the legal age of eighteen in August of 1888, the joy and excitement of her early theatre ventures led Cora Della to leave her mother's home and seek employment as an actress. Her mother objected mightily, crossing out Cora Della's name from the family Bible and writing in despair, "Gone on the Stage."[6] This would not be the last time Della faced the prejudice against actors and actresses which viewed them as sinful creatures involved in the devil's work. Allegedly, when the minister of the local Methodist Church denounced Della for being an actress and banned her from the church, she responded by grabbing a horsewhip and chasing him all the way down the street.

No longer under her mother's thumb, Della worked her way in and out of several stock companies. She traveled difficult routes from town to town, lived in walk-up rooming houses and often had to battle the company paymaster for her wages. Top pay was ten dollars a week, including board, as available, and rooms, not always first class. And the pay many times was not there.

From what can be discerned from occasional brief items in the theatrical newspapers of the time—the *New York Clipper* and the *New York Dramatic Mirror*—Della met with uneven success in pursuing a career as a professional actress. How soon Cora Della joined her first troupe is unknown, but by November 19, 1888, she had changed her name to Della Van Winkle and was a member of the Callicote Comedy Company then appearing in Marysville, Missouri.[7] After leaving Missouri the company toured to Iowa towns of Bedford, Calendra and Hamburg before crossing into Nebraska to appear in Nebraska City and Lincoln, all this during the end of November and all of December. Callicote planned to play in Geneva and Harvard, Nebraska, in January of 1889, but went broke at Lincoln, Nebraska, about January 6. Like many small repertory companies of the time, the Callicote troupe had a perilous existence, depending on making enough money on one engagement to make it to the next. One bad stand with small audiences, inclement weather or competition with another troupe might doom a theatrical enterprise. This seemed to be the case with Della Van Winkle's tenure with the Callicote troupe. Prior to the company collapse, manger Callicote had not paid his troupe of fourteen for three weeks and attempted to skip town without paying a board bill for which he was sued. After all this, he absconded with the remaining money and left the actors stranded.[8]

While Della may have secured a position with another troupe soon after the Callicote collapse, records indicate that nine months passed until she became a member of the J.G. Pringle Chicago Comedy Company at Birmingham, Iowa, sometime in October 1889.[9] During part of this nine-month period, she may have performed along with old time friend Charles Archer in a company managed by Charles Horn, information not revealed until twenty years after the event. The engagement with Pringle lasted barely three weeks before he disbanded the company about November 16 and became an advance man for the Spooner Comedy Company in Des Moines.[10] Due to Pringle's financial problems, he did not pay Della during her time with the company.

Della may have also joined the Spooner Comedy Company at this time; however, her name does not appear in any reviews or notices. If she were a company member, she would have performed with fellow actor Corse Payton—a man destined to later become a successful actor-manager in New York. A few years later, when Payton became head of his own troupe in Iowa, he hired Della for an extended engagement. Then in 1902,

Della at age 20 in Knoxville, Iowa, with unidentified children (courtesy the National Society for the Preservation of Tent, Folk and Repertoire Theatre at the Theatre Museum of Repertoire Americana, Midwest Old Threshers, Mt. Pleasant, Iowa).

as owner of his own theatre in Brooklyn, New York, he would feature Della as star of his comedy company which made an extensive tour of the eastern United States.

How long Della may have remained with the Spooner organization is unknown, but by July 26, 1890, trade papers reported that she was spending the summer with her parents in Attica, Iowa. Evidently Della's mother had come to accept her pursuit of an acting career. After a few weeks of relaxation Della teamed up with the Pringle-Kellog Company at Keokuk, Iowa, about August 11, 1890.[11] The troupe, managed by her former employer, Johnny Pringle, starred Nettie Kellog during a tour of small Iowa towns. For reasons unknown, Della only remained with the troupe for about nine weeks before leaving to join the Simms' *Modern Dromio* company at Mt. Pleasant, Iowa, about October 15.[12]

Della's transfer to the Simms' troupe appeared to be a step up in her career on stage. Simms himself enjoyed a reputation as a comedian and his present show had received fine reviews from appearances in Toronto, Detroit and Grand Rapids As an added appeal for Della, *Modern Dromio* was scheduled to be presented in her hometown of Knoxville, Iowa, on October 24 where she would have the delight of performing before her family and friends. Unfortunately for the aspiring actress and the Simms' company, a poorly attended performance at Oskaloosa, Iowa, on October 20 failed to earn enough money to pay for transportation to the next engagement and Simms disbanded the stranded troupe.[13]

Following the *Modern Dromio* debacle, Della does not seem to have procured another theatre engagement. Discouraged by a series of short run engagements and irregular paychecks, Della decided to give up show business at age nineteen. Three months later, on February 1, 1891, she is reported to be visiting her parents in Attica, Iowa, and, as of April 29, was still there assisting with house cleaning.[14] Facing the fact that after almost two years she had little to show for her attempt to earn a living as an actress, Della resigned herself to becoming a school teacher. About this time she became engaged to a local young man who worked for the railroad.

Then Johnny Pringle came a courting.

2

Della's Wedding and the Comedy Ideals

John "Johnny" Preigel, a son of German immigrants, changed his name to John Pringle—an English-sounding name more acceptable in the acting profession—because he thought his original name sounded too Prussian. His grandfather had been a circuit-riding Methodist clergyman who claimed to have ministered to train robber Jesse James and his brothers.[1]

Born sometime in 1865, nothing is known of his childhood and only a little about his early stage career. There are hints that he had acted in Canada at some time. His name began to appear in theatrical newspapers after about 1888 in connection with performances in the Midwest, particularly in Iowa and Missouri. He functioned in a variety of theatre jobs as actor, manager, advance agent, singer and even as playwright. Scattered references note his singing talent and his skill as an actor in farces.

Physically, he was a slender handsome man of average height with dark, piercing eyes. Interviewed late in her life, Della said that when she first acted in a company with Pringle all the girls in the troupe had a crush on him, but none took him seriously for he was too vain and conceited.[2]

Della may have not taken Johnny seriously, but he had some serious thoughts about her. Late one night near the end of June 1891 Pringle appeared at the home of Ira Kendrick in Attica, Iowa, where Della was staying with her mother and stepfather. She recognized him as a member of a troupe she had performed with but was surprised at his sudden reappearance.

The young actors talked nearly till dawn, during which time Pringle managed to make her see him in a new and positive light. He confessed he had kept her in his mind after the show they had been playing in suddenly folded. He revealed that while performing with the Issac Payton Company in nearby Centerville, Iowa, he had lost no time in hiring a livery rig and driving to Attica after the first evening's performance. He pleaded with her to marry him at once. Promising to make her a great star, he declared that in no time at all they would have their own company.[3]

In spite of earlier reverses in pursuing an acting career, the starstruck Della still yearned for the glamour of the theatre. Thoughts of her railroad fiancée faded away and she accepted Pringle's marriage proposal. Before Pringle left to return to his company in Centerville, a wedding date had been set.

Understandably, Della's mother and stepfather were upset with her abrupt change of grooms, but they pitched in to arrange the new wedding. Della's wedding gown (a rose-colored voile dress, gathered full with a demi-train) although meant for a different wedding, served for her marriage to Johnny Pringle on July 1, 1891. The band that Johnny borrowed from the Issac Payton troupe furnished wedding music and even the jilted railroad man joined in blessing the newlyweds.[4]

Johnny's promise that in no time he would make Della the star of their own theatre company was not fulfilled as quickly as planned. Della spent the rest of July with her parents and on July 25 she officially changed her stage name to Della Pringle.[5]

On August 1 both Pringles joined the Spooner Payton Company at Hamburg, Iowa.[6] They toured with this troupe in a series of one-week stands in Iowa, Nebraska, Kansas and Missouri through the end of October 1891. At this time,

Only photograph available of Johnny Pringle (printed in the *Wenatchee World* [Washington], June 30, 1906).

Corse Payton, who had starred along with Etta Reed in the Spooner Payton Company took over as manager and renamed the troupe the Corse Payton Comedy Company.

Both Johnny and Della remained with the re-organized company for over five months as it performed one-week engagements in Iowa, Missouri, Kansas, Nebraska and Illinois. In early May of 1892 the Pringles left the Corse Payton troupe to at last form their own company as Johnny had promised.[7]

During the months spent with the Payton companies, Della and Johnny seldom earned mention in newspaper items and reviews. Johnny did win some recognition for his singing ability as a member of the troupe's Hawkeye Quartet. While most reviews centered on stars Corse Payton and Etta Reed, for the most part they found the supporting players to be engaging and excellent support.

Della did receive some special mention about her acting from time to time. The January 15, 1892, edition of a Trenton, Missouri, paper noted that Della scored a great hit as an old maid character.[8] The Chillicothe, Missouri, newspaper reviewer on January 26 stated that Della Pringle deserved special mention for her portrayal of Mary Marshell.[9]

After leaving the Corse Payton Company, Johnny Pringle wasted little time in forming his own troupe for Della. After forty weeks of employment with the Payton companies he and Della had saved enough money to finance their own troupe. This initial attempt met with little success. In the May 28, 1892, edition of the *New York Clipper*, a major national theatre newspaper, Pringle advertised for actors.[10] What the response was is not known, but by June 15 the Pringles were reported to be going to Lovilla, Iowa, to fill an engagement.[11] For a month nothing appeared about their tour and then on July 15 they ended the tour because of Della's bad health. She rested for two months at the her parents' home in Attica during which time it was reported that Johnny Pringle had supposedly accepted short engagements with the Spooner Comedy Company and the Ben Warner Company.[12]

The Pringle's had better luck with their second attempt at creating their own company that they named the Comedy Ideals. In early September they went into rehearsals to prepare for a tour and on September 21, 1892, began their season with two satisfactory performances in the roller skating rink that served as Knoxville, Iowa's, theatre.[13] The "company" consisted of just four performers—Della, Johnny, pianist Grace Barrett and a juvenile, Little Toots Barrett.[14] With such a small troupe, Johnny and Della had to play multiple roles during a show. Quick costume changes created new characters in no time at all. While Della would be behind the curtain changing into a new disguise, Johnny entertained the crowd with his "specialties" which included singing, dancing, juggling, yodeling, telling jokes and doing impersonations. When Johnny needed to change characters, Della would charm the audience with her fine soprano voice and "skirt" dancing.[15] At times even the troupe's pianist turned stage performer to fill small roles.

Even in rural America during the gay nineties, female audience members expected actresses to display fashionable gowns of the latest style. For this reason, Della spent what little spare time and money she had in creating dresses for her wardrobe. She was handy with a needle and used her purchases of satin and velvet fabric to craft fancy dresses decorated with the buttons and bows so fashionable at the time. She also made her own hats—gorgeous Lillian Russell affairs with willow plumes.[16] Her wardrobe would be one of her strongest assets for the remainder of her long professional career.

For five weeks after opening in Knoxville during September nothing appeared in print about the Comedy Ideals. Then their itinerary began to appear regularly in the "Dates Ahead" columns of the *New York Clipper*. They jumped from town to town in the Midwest in three-night stands beginning at Cainsville, Missouri, on November 2, 1892. From there they toured through southwestern Iowa into Nebraska where they played in almost twenty towns through early January 1893. Available newspaper reviews from the Nebraska towns visited by the Comedy Ideals praised them for entertainment that made audiences both laugh and cry. Johnny was cited for his mirth, humor and wit displayed in jokes and songs. Della pleased with dancing, an attractive and beautiful wardrobe and a pure soprano voice that could be heard distinctly all over the house. With few exceptions, they drew sizable audiences and profited at the box office.

Next they entered into South Dakota to play in mining camps such as Deadwood. Except for one off-night performance in Rapid City, the Pringles continued to earn flattering notices. Sometime near January 21 they added Louis Bishop, a violinist of some fame, to their small troupe.[17] After a brief foray into Wyoming at New Castle on February 15, the Comedy Ideals returned to South Dakota to complete five months on the road.

The Pringles returned to Knoxville, Iowa, by late March of 1893 and purchased a fine home with the profits from their successful tour. By late April they announced a summer tour to commence on May 10.[18]

This summer tour of Iowa towns lasted only about eight weeks and ended at Knoxville on Independence Day. While resting in their new home after the brief tour, they may have taken time to journey to Chicago and take in that city's World's Fair.[19] In the last two weeks of July they prepared for yet another season to begin on August 2 with intentions to travel to the Pacific coast via the Black Hills and northern states.[20]

The Pringles strengthened their troupe by adding two performers, Olive "Ollie" Ackerly and Frank Hillecker, and retaining violinist Louis Bishop of the Boston Quadrille as musical director.[21] Their former pianist, Grace Barrett, began the tour with them, but in late August was replaced by Miss Lillian Dyer, late of the New York Symphony Club.[22]

The new tour covered roughly the same territory as the previous year with stops in southwestern Iowa through August 12 before entering Nebraska where they performed through October 14. Notices remained supportive with compliments to all in the company, especially for violinist Louis Bishop. One review stated that Bishop's playing alone was worth the price of admission. Another noted that Bishop's vocal imitations of squealing pigs, crowing roosters and braying donkeys brought down the house.[23]

Two incidents marked the tour of Nebraska towns. On the dark side, illness in the company forced cancellations of shows in Central City on August 18 and 19.[24] On a happier note, Olive Ackerly and Frank Hillecker got married by a local minister on the stage of Broken Bow's Northside Opera House on August 24.[25] This would not be the last onstage marriage for a Pringle company.

By October 16 the Comedy Ideals left Nebraska and began a tour of South Dakota's Black Hills starting at Edgemont. During this part of the tour the Pringles drew good crowds and frequently displayed a "Standing Room Only" sign before performances in such locations as Rapid City and Deadwood. Newspaper items included praise for the company's entertainment which for only ten or twenty cents admission equaled that of larger companies that charged fifty cents or more. Additional praise came for an absence of vulgar or objectionable material and actors who conducted themselves as ladies and gentleman off stage and on.[26]

Up to November 8, 1893, the Pringles had generally repeated the pattern of their 1892–1893 extended tour. After this date they opened up new territory in Wyoming and Colorado. Between November 9 and 12 they zigzagged between towns in eastern Wyoming and western South Dakota before heading west for two engagements in Nebraska, Alliance and Crawford.

From there they re-entered Wyoming and remained there through December 9 having performed to large houses and earning flattering revues in the towns of Douglas, Glenrock, Casper, Lusk and Cheyenne. Performance notices were few, but a Cheyenne paper declared that "Della Pringle is a natural actress who continuously delights an audience."[27]

Heading south the Pringles began touring in Colorado starting at Loveland on December 13, 1893.[28] Their engagements to the end of the year were east of the Rocky Mountains in such towns as Longmont, Lyons, Louisville and Lafayette. The troupe spent Christmas in Denver then headed for the hills in a five-month tour of mountain towns, mostly mining camps. At this time the Pringles engaged Harry Englund and Nellie Neilson to fill the places of Olive and Frank Hillecker.[29]

While there are few local sources remaining to document the Pringle's Colorado tour, the "Dates Ahead" columns of the *New York Clipper* and the *New York Dramatic Mirror* reveal an almost complete record of engagements. Mainly they performed at mining towns in the interior of Colorado's Rocky Mountains as far west as the Montrose area and as far south as Alamosa. The tour proved profitable as the company did not play a losing week during the season.[30]

During the Colorado tour the Pringles played to a lot of rough looking characters in the mining towns. To the end of her days Della could still recall seeing tears streaming down the painted faces of prostitutes in Leadville, moved by her death scene in *Camille*.[31]

The Pringles had intended to end performances by June 16 at Pueblo, Colorado, but major flooding in the area brought the tour to a halt a week early. They returned to Iowa by June 10 and visited her parents in Attica.[32]

Della and Johnny enjoyed a one-month vacation at their Knoxville home. During this time they entertained the members of the *Ole Olson* company when they played at Knoxville on June 29.[33] By July 29, 1894, the Pringles opened yet another season with four shows at the Knoxville Opera House.[34]

Although they generally covered the previous season territory, they did not book theatres in a more or less linear fashion as they had done in two previous tours. Instead, they jumped back and forth between engagements in the states of Iowa, Nebraska, Missouri, Wyoming and South Dakota. While they still played some one-night stands, one-week engagements became more common. This was due a larger repertory of plays made possible by another increase of performers in the company. Including the Pringles, the company roster stood at ten including actress Franc Barrett and Lillian Dyer from the previous season and new performers Frances Owen, Lester Walker and Minnie Huffman.[35] As the tour progressed some performers either quit or were let go and replacements were hired, but the total remained about ten.

For unknown reasons, Della advertised herself "at liberty" in the October 13, 1894, edition of the *New York Clipper*.[36] Such an ad would indicate that she was seeking a new position as an actress. In spite of this she remained with the company through the end of the year. This act may have signaled some difficulties in the Pringle marriage, a matter that was resolved on New Year's Eve of 1894.

From what can be discerned from newspaper reviews, the repertory for the Pringle's third major tour retained hits of previous tours and mounted three new works including a play written by Johnny Pringle. They repeated *Eccles Girls*, *Married in Haste* and *Is Marriage a Failure*, added *Tangled Up* and *Angel* and introduced Johnny Pringle's *Miss Nobody* at Douglas, Wyoming, sometime in late November or early December of 1894.

Sometime during this same period the Pringles played an engagement in Sheridan, Wyoming, that was attended by a very special guest. At this time the legendary Buffalo Bill Cody managed a hotel in Sheridan. Cody took his grandchildren to see a matinee performance of *Little Lord Fauntleroy* and after the show came backstage and introduced them to Della and her company.[37]

As in her past tours, Della earned golden opinions from the local press. A Shenandoah, Iowa, paper declared her one of the handsomest soubrettes on the road.[38] The Hamburg, Iowa, press reported about the well-merited applause that she received for both her skirt dance (in which she wore an oriental silk robe made up of seventy-five yards of material) and her display of versatility in voice and facial expression.[39]

All seemed to be going well for the Pringles until an engagement at Rapid City, South Dakota, at the end of the year when Della abruptly left the Comedy Ideals. As she revealed in a later interview, her marriage to Johnny had never been a happy one and that he had often physically abused her, leaving her black and blue from his actions.[40] In addition, he had not remained true to her and had been guilty of adultery.[41] Clearly she had had enough and though it might cost her financially, she elected to divorce the man, who after promising her so much, had abused and betrayed her.

Della fled to Omaha, Nebraska, and took up temporary residence at the Baker Hotel on January 4, 1895.[42] From there she placed an ad which appeared in the January 12 edition of the *New York Clipper* announcing herself "at liberty" for theatrical engagements.[43] Apparently from the ad she made contact with the manager of Rentfrow's Jolly Pathfinders and joined that organization in Denver at the Curtis Theatre before the end of January.[44] She toured with Rentfrow's troupe through Colorado until she left the troupe at Grand Junction on April 14, 1895,[45] after which she returned to her home in Knoxville, arriving there before the end of April.

Della filed for a divorce from Johnny Pringle on April 30, 1895, on the grounds of adultery and other causes. The divorce became final on May 4 and on the fourteenth she advertised in the local paper that she would sell or rent her home of seven rooms on East Marion Street.[46] Although now divorced from Johnny Pringle, she did retain Della Pringle as her professional stage name and would do so for the rest of her life and through four subsequent marriages.

3

Della Pringle and G. Faith Adams

Not wasting any time in re-establishing her acting career, Della placed another "at liberty" ad for the 1895–1896 season in the *New York Clipper* of June 8, 1895.[1] About that time she left Knoxville for an extended stay with a friend, Mrs. Harvey Goddard, in Decorah, Iowa.[2] Her notice in the *Clipper* resulted in a contact with Nelson Compostan of the Compostan Dramatic Players who hired her for the coming theatre season.

On August 17, 1895, Della left Decorah to join the Compostan troupe in Chicago to begin a tour of Illinois, Indiana, Iowa and Wisconsin on the nineteenth.[3] Della remained with the company until late October at which time she and a fellow actor in the troupe, G. Faith Adams, departed to form their own company, the Della Pringle Company, as it would be known in its various manifestations for the next two decades.

As the head of her own company at last, she opened a season at Dodgeville, Wisconsin, on November 8, 1895.[4] The next day her ad seeking dramatic people for her troupe appeared in the *New York Clipper*. After appearing in Wisconsin towns through mid–December, she mainly appeared in Iowa except for two engagements in La Cross, Wisconsin, and Austin, Minnesota, before ending her season at Mason City, Iowa, on February 15, 1896—an end dictated by Della's ill health.[5]

Even in this early part of her career Della Pringle impressed audiences and critics with her acting ability. A writer at Nashua, Iowa, commented on February 6, 1896:

> Della Pringle is one of the most versatile of actresses, her conception of child characters and impersonations of strong emotional parts are remarkable for their individuality, their artistic delicacy, and their fidelity to nature. She makes you laugh with the joys of childhood, or weep under the interpretations of sorrowing womanhood: but through all runs a fine vein of naturalness and power that is rarely seen. She runs the gamut of human emotion, and is a true artist.[6]

Studio photograph of Della taken at Monroe, Wisconsin, in 1896. At age 26, Della for the first time was head of her own company (courtesy the National Society for the Preservation of Tent, Folk and Repertoire Theatre at the Theatre Museum of Repertoire Americana, Midwest Old Threshers, Mt. Pleasant, Iowa).

On the very same day that Della received such praise in the press, she and G. Faith Adams were married on the stage of the Nashua, Iowa, theatre—the date, February 6, 1896.[7] Although Adams would be an important part of Della Pringle's personal and professional life for the next decade, little is known about him. There is some indication that he was the adopted son of a famous circus family,[8] but that is all. He appears to have been a competent actor, especially in comedies, and a fair singer. Pictures reveal him to be a lean-faced tall and slender man with a full head of hair and a prominent jaw.

Della's season ending illness did not prevent her from returning to Knoxville by February 23 at which time she announced her retirement from the stage.[9] She felt well enough to attend the wedding of her brother, James Elmer Van Winkle, at Melrose, Iowa, on February 26.[10]

Della's "retirement" did not last long. She recovered after resting at Knoxville for the better part of three months. On June 13, 1896, she announced plans to begin a fifth annual tour on August 26 and placed ads in theatrical trade papers seeking actors and actresses for the season.[11] In the time before the tour began Della spent time attending to personal and professional matters. In early April she and Adams participated in a local talent show to raise funds to buy a town clock. During the following weeks they worked with and coached Knoxville amateurs to prepare a minstrel show for another clock fundraiser. To further the town's clock project, they offered to present a benefit performance of one of their own plays in May.[12]

An attempted burglary of their home on May 11, the third attempt

George Faith Adams, 1903 (printed in the *Alliance Semi-Weekly Times* [Nebraska], September 1, 1903).

during the spring months, disturbed their hiatus and created unwanted excitement. That evening the sound of someone walking up from the basement stairway awakened Adams. As the intruder entered the bedroom, Adams grabbed a gun, fired at a fleeing burglar and missed. Then he saw a second felon's face in the window and fired his gun, again missing. Shortly after this failed robbery attempt, Adams joked that he would ask the commander of a local army company to guard the premises until he could mount a cannon in his backyard.[13]

Della entertained members of the Rentfrow family at her home on June 17—the owners of the Jolly Pathfinder Company that she performed with in 1895 after leaving Johnny Pringle.[14] On June 30 she attended another family wedding, that of sister Sadie Van Winkle to Harry Smith at Attica, Iowa.[15]

Professionally, Della and Adams accepted a two-week engagement at the Roof Garden in nearby Des Moines beginning about July 15. Billed as Adams and Pringle, they did not present plays, but performed between act specialties (songs and dances) from their regular season.[16]

This vaudeville engagement was the outgrowth of a need for cash after a failed "get rich quick" scheme involving raising chickens for profit. Della and Adams saw that eggs were selling for a quarter a dozen and decided to start raising chickens in a big way. They invested in seventy hens and seven roosters. When the hens began to lay, Della was overjoyed and gathered up a large basket of eggs while Adams joyfully calculated their profits. Unfortunately, when Adam's got to the grocery stores, the cost of eggs had dropped to a literal dime a dozen, making their investment worthless.[17] So they were forced into vaudeville to fill empty purses.

During the engagement in Des Moines a critic falsely accused Adams and Pringle of stealing material from another act, writing that Della had bribed musicians for the music and that she had taken down the lyrics in shorthand. In answer to this accusation, she wrote a letter to the Knoxville paper saying she had no skills as a stenographer and that the songs in question were already easily available from music publishers. She ended the letter with "We attend to our own business, let other people alone and give a good show."[18]

Della and Adams ended their long vacation in August to prepare another season of touring. After opening in Knoxville on August 19, 1896,[19] they began retracing the routes of previous seasons, first performing in Iowa before entering Nebraska on their way to the Black Hills of South Dakota. In October they made a change and played in the eastern part of the state at Yankton, Vermillion, Parker and Sioux Falls. By November they returned to Iowa, but for unstated reasons were forced to disband before opening at Estherville about November 22 after which they returned to Knoxville.[20]

During the abbreviated season, Della and Adams enjoyed financial success, frequently playing to standing room only crowds and mostly favorable reviews. They mainly appeared in plays from the previous season, but did add two shows of note. One was *Humpty Dumpty*, a work for children and presented only for Saturday matinees. The other was an original nautical drama, *Wrecked*, written by a member of the company, James H. Martin, that featured a third act sensation scene in which a schooner filling half the stage exploded into pieces followed by a daring lifeboat rescue of the survivors from the fiery wreck.

Having lost bookings due to the early closing of their season, Della and Adams took time out to re-organize their theatrical enterprise and to make another contribution to the town clock fund by offering yet another benefit, this time with James Martin in his creation, *Dixieland*, on December 17.[21] About this same time they met with members of the Neuville Company then performing in Knoxville and made arrangements to tour with that organization beginning in Chicago on December 30.[22]

The engagement with the Neuville Company lasted for only two weeks and by January 16, 1897, Della and Adams returned to Knoxville with plans to present a local show in the near future.[23] In just three weeks they organized a new company, acquired rights to several new plays and purchased new scenery.

The route for Della and Adam's first theatre season of 1897 covered familiar ground beginning after opening at Knoxville on February 6. After a week's engagement at the Bijou Theatre in Des Moines,[24] they journeyed through Nebraska for a month before spending six weeks in western South Dakota. Following a tremendously successful season in the Black Hills, they spent the last three weeks of the tour back in Nebraska, ending the season at Lincoln on May 22. Except for some small houses in Broken Bow and Alliance, Nebraska, they enjoyed a highly profitable season.[25]

Two incidents during the tour marred an otherwise fine season. During early April actors and audience suffered through extremely cold weather in Deadwood, South Dakota.[26] In early May, after performing at Fort Robinson, Nebraska, the Pringle company had to travel in wagons for a four-mile ride to catch a train at Cranford. During the wagon trip, the horses in the lead wagon, startled by a sudden sand storm, ran away, smashing the carriage and injuring four of the performers. Violet Marsden suffered back injuries and her husband, Richard, had three cuts on his hip. James Godey sprained his wrist and arm and was bruised about the body. His wife, Geraldine, was badly hurt by a blow to the head. The company laid off for a few days at Cranford while the injured recovered before resuming the tour.[27]

The four injured actors made up half of the company with Della, Adams, character actor James Martin and an excellent pianist, Lizzie Smith, completing the troupe. Martin, a familiar stage figure in the Black Hills since 1876, received a warm reception from all the old timers in the Dakota mining towns when he appeared on stage. He also authored several plays, at least one written especially for Della Pringle. Unfortunately, Martin had a problem with alcohol that forced him to leave the company before the end of the season.[28]

The repertory of plays presented during this first 1897 season consisted originally of seven works, all new to the touring area. Della and Adams paid higher royalties for the rights to perform these more recent plays. This set them apart from rival companies that saved money by repeatedly presenting time worn dramas and comedies year after year. It also made a hit with audiences who were tired of such familiar fare.

Della began the season with *Dangers of Greater New York* with its sensational burning tenement house scene, *A True American Girl* (an original script written for Della), *The Dancing Girl*, *Pawn Ticket 210* (for which Della had secured an exclusive contract to present this hit show in the West), *In Cuba* (a topical play dealing with the Spanish American War) and *Rags and Tatters*. Later in the season Della added a children's play, *Humpty Dumpty*, and the popular drama of *Trilby* presenting a girl under the hypnotic spell of the villainous Svengali.[29] Only a few performances of *The Girl from Cripple Creek* and *Our Girls* were offered at the end of the tour.

The tour gained generous critical commentary in the local newspapers. Adams won notice for his skill as a comedian, but as befits the leading lady of her own troupe, Della elicited most attention. Several newspapers regarded her as one of the best actresses to have appeared in their town with a popular priced company. Reviewers noticed a marked improvement in performances over previous seasons, finding her to be cute, jolly and entertaining as ever. They praised her for bravely performing when severely ill. She received plaudits for creating both laughter and tears in her portrayals, especially in *Trilby*. Once critic went so far as to state that Della and Adams were "decidedly irresistible"[30] and another described them as the "Ringling" of repertory troupes in the West.[31]

After closing their first season of 1897, Della and Adams, as usual, retired to their Knoxville home for the summer. While there Della welcomed her old friend from Decorah, Iowa, Miss Franc Barrows, who had been her pianist in the days of the Comedy Ideals.[32] She had her usual visits with relatives.[33]

Out of curiosity, Della and Adams on June 9 attended a performance at the Knoxville theatre by the outrageously untalented Cherry Sisters, an event Della would remember over forty years later. She recalled how the four tall, old, scrawny sisters would march around the stage beating a drum and singing "Ta-ra-ra Boom De-ay." The sisters' act was so terrible that audiences brought tin pans, cowbells, horns and other noisemakers to the theatre to drown out songs and recitations by the sisters. Some patrons even threw ripe tomatoes at them. In spite of all such demonstrations, the Cherry Sisters went right on with their wretched act. Della felt so sorry for them that she went backstage after the show to talk to them. Although pleasant, the sisters never said a word about their offensive presentation. Later the sisters resorted to playing behind a protective net to protect them from fruits and vegetables hurled at them from the auditorium. On the way home Della asked her husband, "Do you suppose they think they are clever or do they know they are rotten?" Adams replied, "I'm damned if I know."[34] Clever or rotten, the Cherry Sisters made enough with their untalented displays to pay off the mortgage on the family farm.

Even during this vacation period Della and Adams spent some time preparing for their second tour of the year to commence in late August. Della renewed her rights to perform *Pawn Ticket 210* in communities west of Chicago.[35] Adams chose to invest in new specialty acts for the troupe. He paid $500 for the rights and apparatus to reproduce Loie Fuller's famous grand and elaborate "serpentine dance."[36] In this dance the performer wore a voluminous skirt made up of as much as 150 yards of silk. In each hand the dancer held long bamboo rods that on the other end were attached to the hem of the skirt which enabled her to swirl the silk over her head and twirl it around her body in all kinds of patterns suggesting flames, birds in flight, blooming flowers, etc. As the dancer moved about and manipulated the silken skirt, shifting colored beams of light from calcium lights (lime lights) illuminated her and the billowing skirt. Depending on the colors of light employed, the dance could have several variations. Of course, the most popular was the "fire dance" with its red, orange and yellow colors with a touch of blue at the bottom.

In addition to the elaborate costume needed for the serpentine and fire dances, Della had purchased another spectacular costume to wear for performances of her dramatic roles. It was made of looking glass beads, tiny squares of glass sewn so close together that they covered her entire figure. As Della moved about the stage, the glass glistened and flashed in the light.

During one performance the glass beads created unintended hilarity in the audience and some embarrassment for Della. Although considered shapely, the slender Della did not possess the buxomly hour-glass figure so fashionable at that time. To achieve the hour-glass shape, she wore an inflatable rubber brassiere under her beaded costume. At some point during the show, some of the beads cut through their backing and into one of the rubber breasts. Air leaked out and down it went, leaving Della decidedly one-sided. The audience saw it and roared with laughter. Della quickly exited the stage to make repairs. Upon her re-entrance with a restored bosom, the crowd broke up again. Della went on with the show as if deflated and re-inflated bosoms were nothing at all![37]

Della in a dancing pose sometime between 1898 and 1902 (printed in a Knoxville, Iowa, paper, date unknown).

In addition to Della's special costumes, Adams purchased electrical equipment for the projection of illustrated songs that the audience could sing along with a performer. The equipment needed to produce the popular illustrated songs and spectacular dances required a skilled technician to operate and maintain it. So on August 18, Adams hired Jack Carson, an electrician and calcium light expert.[38] (Calcium or lime light, an early form of the stage spotlight, was produced by burning limestone with an electric arc resulting in an extremely bright light that was focused through a lens.)

Della and Adams made few changes in the repertory of plays for the fall season, repeating all shows from the previous season. This saved effort in learning new works and money in using existing scenery and costumes. Most of the tour would be through towns that had not seen last year's shows, so the plays would be new to the audiences.

Some of the plays were presented under alternate titles, a practice not unknown among repertory troupes. *The Yellow Kid, Paradise Alley, The True American Girl, Ragged Dick, Pawn Ticket 210* plus *Rags and Tatters* were all performed under their original titles. However, *Dangers of Greater New York* sometimes became *New York by Day and Night, In Cuba* at times changed to *Yankee Notions* and *The Dancing Girl* got a new title, *The Live Wire*. One review on the tour listed *Poverty Row*, but it is not clear whether this was a new play or a previous work under a new title. During the tour no mention is made of last season's children's play, *Humpty Dumpty*, but Della and Adams did offer matinees where children received elegant presents such as railroad trains, balls, bats, dolls and watches.

In addition to investing in new specialty equipment, Della and Adams improved their theatrical enterprise by adding more performers to their company. Richard and Violet Marsden returned from the last tour, he as stage manager and actor, she as actress and specialty dancer.[39] Nellie Wilson, last season's excellent pianist, began the tour, but at some point Mrs. Bartlett replaced her before it ended. Various reviews during the season mention other company members as William Ecols (juvenile lead), Mary Van Etton, Tracy and Nanette Maguire, J. Ferguson, G. Fredericks, John Young, Ted Bartlett and juvenile, Baby Thelma. Whether all of these performers were in the company at the same time is not known. Repertory troupes frequently changed personnel during tours. At the very least, Della and Adams had about doubled the size of their organization from last season.

Only the beginning of the fall tour resembled previous tours. As usual, Della and Adams celebrated the opening of the season at Knoxville with a four-night stand beginning on August 24.[40] Then they spent two and a half weeks performing in the Iowa towns of Mystic, Fairfield and Greenfield before filling one week engagements in southern Nebraska at Kearney, Hastings, Grand Island and North Platte during parts of September and October. About October 10 Della's troupe jumped into new territory, Colorado, to play for three weeks in towns on Peter McCourt's Silver Circuit. Except for a week in the mining town of Central City, the Colorado tour was most unpleasant. Heavy snows interrupted travel and at one point Della and her company were trapped in their hotel for twenty-six hours.[41] Escaping the frigid conditions in Colorado, Della took her troupe north to Wyoming on November 1 and played two one-week stands at Cheyenne and Laramie before returning to Nebraska to perform the week of November 15 at Fremont. From there she returned to Iowa to fill engagements in the new communities of Missouri Valley, Carroll, Marshalltown and Indianola. She ended the tour at Muscatine on January 1, 1898, due to illness in the company.[42]

The horrible weather in Colorado was not the worst that happened to Della on this tour. Sadly, her sister Sadie, married for only a year, died on October 8 in Iowa while Della was performing in North Platte, Nebraska, which made it impossible for Della to return to attend her funeral. Della received the telegram announcing Sadie's death at 4:00 p.m. and with an understandably heavy heart appeared before the audience that evening.[43] About this time and in marked contrast to the news of her sibling's demise, Della was entertained by a visit to Buffalo Bill's ranch near North Platte where she received souvenir deer horns.[44]

Except for the poor season in Colorado, Della and Adams did a tremendous business during the four-month tour. Their efforts for investing in Fuller's fire dance and the illustrated songs were well rewarded. Time after time in town after town they played to full

An example of Della's elaborate millinery (courtesy the National Society for the Preservation of Tent, Folk and Repertoire Theatre at the Theatre Museum of Repertoire Americana, Midwest Old Threshers, Mt. Pleasant, Iowa).

houses, often having to turn patrons away at the door or put out a "Standing Room Only" sign. Reviewers found their fine show at the bargain price of ten cents equal to fifty and seventy-five cent attractions. Even their "paper" (advertisement posters and banners) won praise for its quality from one reporter.

Della and Adams could not continue their season into the spring because Della had suffered from ill health for some time. It took her some six months to fully recover. While she recuperated in Knoxville Adams remained active in the community. As early as January 5 the local press reported him involved in raising chickens on his farm.[45] By January 22, 1898, he once again helped raise funds for the long proposed city clock.[46] The profits from his theatrical enterprise enabled him to offer small loans to Knoxville citizens, an opportunity he advertised in the paper on March 26.

"The Maples," Della's home in Knoxville, Iowa, in 1898. Della is at center with the dogs, her mother (Mrs. Ira Hendricks) is behind her and George Faith Adams is with the horse at left. The person at right is unidentified (courtesy the National Society for the Preservation of Tent, Folk and Repertoire Theatre at the Theatre Museum of Repertoire Americana, Midwest Old Threshers, Mt. Pleasant, Iowa).

By late June Della felt well enough to join Adams in preparing for new shows. They secured rights for an almost completely new repertory of plays. The selected dramas included a blood and thunder melodrama, *Way of the World* that featured depictions of the Brooklyn Bridge by moonlight, the New York Harbor and the Statue of Liberty.[47] Adams spent $1,000 on scenery billed as the *Palace of Gold*. The sets included electrical chandeliers and other striking effects.[48] Other plays performed during the tour were a Civil War epic, *The Volunteer, Greed for Gold, Mother and Son, Princess of Paris, The Last of Her Race, Warm Times* and *Police Inspector*. Only two plays were carried over from the last tour—*True American Girl* and *New York by Day and Night* or *Dangers of the Great City*.

The performing company consisted of returning actors and several new comers. Veteran actors Richard and Violet Marsden returned for a

The Jolly Della Pringle Company in 1898 posed on porch of "The Maples." Della and G. Faith Adams are with the dogs, bottom center. The identities of the other actors are unknown (courtesy the National Society for the Preservation of Tent, Folk and Repertoire Theatre at the Theatre Museum of Repertoire Americana, Midwest Old Threshers, Mt. Pleasant, Iowa).

third tour. New performers were James and Geraldine Godley, Van Barrett, Harry Sutton, Caddie Gail and her daughter Baby Gail, a nine-year-old with a fine singing voice.[49] There may have been four more since Adams alluded to a troupe of fourteen, but there is no record of them.

After opening at Knoxville on August 23, Della and Adams returned to an old touring route for the first leg of their fall season.[50] Until November 15, 1898, they booked shows for a month in Iowa (August 23–September 24), two weeks in Nebraska (September 26–October 9) and five weeks in South Dakota (October 10–November 14). They then journeyed further west for two weeks in Wyoming (November 16–27), three weeks in Montana (November 28–December 17) and a month in Colorado (December 19–January 18, 1899) before ending the season prematurely at Montrose, Colorado.

Until the Montana engagements at Butte and Anaconda, the tour had gone very well. Della and Adams grew their fortune a dime at a time as audiences on their route crowded into theatres and opera houses, attracted by new and entertaining plays, numerous between the acts specialties (including last year's spectacular fire dance) and illustrated songs—all for between ten and thirty cents. The Jolly Della Pringle Company frequently broke box office records for a single performance in venues that seated from up to 1,000 patrons.

Paper after paper hailed her company as the best or one of the best repertory troupes playing in the West at popular prices. Some even deemed them equal to companies charging seventy-five cents to a dollar. With few exceptions, Della drew praise for her acting, singing and dancing talents. Adams earned his share of plaudits as a comedian and the rest of the company was regarded as excellent in support. The youngest of the company, Baby Gail, proved to be the greatest hit with audiences with her singing and dancing specialties. Reviewers were impressed by her versatility in acting, her graceful stage presence and the numerous encores she received for her efforts.

With an investment of $5,000 in scenery, costumes and lighting also contributed to the appeal of the Pringle company. Newspaper items described the $1,000 electrical *Palace of Gold* setting as a masterpiece of scenic art.[51] Della's new wardrobe, cited as the most expensive carried by a western star, was an attractive and pleasing feature for female patrons. Reports found the electrical and calcium light plant to be the best money can buy and the projections for the illustrated songs superb.

As a sidelight, Della bragged to be the first case on record of a Methodist minister traveling with a theatrical company. Her brother, J.

Elmer Van Winkle, an ordained Methodist minister, had been forced to abandon his congregation due to brain fever and nervous prostration brought about by overwork. His doctors advised rest and a western trip so Della invited him to be her guest during her tour of South Dakota. He joined her on October 6 just as she was beginning return engagements in the Black Hills.[52]

All the good fortune that Della's company had enjoyed changed markedly during engagements in Montana during December. The Montana stands began well enough at Billings during the week of December 5, but at the mining town of Butte the sulfur smoke from the gold smelting operation affected the health of all the performers. Della lost her voice and couldn't sing. Another actress suffered greatly from pleurisy. The general poor condition of the company led to the loss of three evenings of performance at Anaconda the following week. Facing such poor environmental conditions, Adams canceled all the remaining Montana dates and jumped to Grand Junction, Colorado, where the afflicted actors met with pure air and beautiful weather.[53]

While most of the company regained their health during the late December tour of southwestern Colorado towns (Ouray, Telluride and Durango), some did not which caused Adams to halt the current season's tour at Montrose on January 18, 1899, when only six of the actors in the eleven-member troupe were well enough to perform. Illness may have been only part of the reason for ending the season. Comments in the Montrose paper of January 19 allude to internal dissentions among the actors and the narrow averting of free for all fights on three occasions.[54] Whatever the reason, Adams paid his company a week and a half salary and saw them off to St. Joseph, Missouri. He and Della set out for their Knoxville home, arriving there on January 23, 1899.[55]

4

Prosperous Seasons and the Great Loop

Upon reaching Knoxville, Della and Adams took a fourteen-week break from performing, but were far from idle. On February 8 they entertained her brother, the Rev. J. Elmer Van Winkle, who had regained his mental and physical health and returned to his ministry. During late February Della and Adams increased their Knoxville real estate holdings. They engaged carpenters to build cottages on the eight city lots Adams had purchased opposite his home.[1] The same crew remodeled and painted their home which they christened "The Maples" and built a new barn on their farm.[2]

With all the building underway, Della and Adams departed for Chicago and points east via Des Moines to gather material for the next season and to sign up the finest specialties available.[3] Although not reported, it is assumed they visited Adams' relatives in the East. They returned to Knoxville on April 29.[4] About this time an issue of the *New York Clipper* reported on their efforts to form a company and Della's return to full health.[5]

An ad Adams placed in the April 20, 1899, edition of the *New York Clipper* revealed what Della and Adams expected of performers in their troupe. They sought versatile actors who could double in other capacities, such as character actor who also served as stage manager. They also wanted a stage carpenter who was not only a practical electrician, but could handle stage props and scenery. Adams made clear that he would not pay for board for the actors, but did pay regularly in cash. He stated that "all must be thoroughly experienced and capable in every respect, with a first class wardrobe." Finally, he warned, "Drinking or incompetency means instant dismissal."[6] This ad and other contacts attracted a group of actors that included F.C Huebner, Harry Ellis, the Miller sisters, Frances Owens, Ed Settle, Frank Patton and Minnie Hoffman.[7]

For the 1899–1900 season Della and Adams offered all new plays with the exception of three shows repeated from the previous season—*Police Inspector, Pawn Ticket 210* and *True American Girl.* These plus ten new plays made up the extensive repertory.

As the tour progressed reviewers had little or nothing to say about the content of *A Wonderful Woman, For Hire, Slave for Honor* or *The Prisoner.* Brief items characterized *The Irish 400* as a laughter-provoking sketch, a strictly Irish comedy. The main feature of *Old New Hampshire Home* (also presented as *Blue Jeans*) was a functioning sawmill. Two popular railroad melodramas, *The Midnight Alarm* and *The Midnight Express*, provided thrilling situations and sensational scenes for patrons. In the first a train passed over the stage and a full fire brigade raced to battle flames. The other abounded in excitement as a train headed for disaster at an open drawbridge.

A well-known drama, *Camille*, provided opportunity for Della Pringle to display her talent as a dramatic actress and her expensive wardrobe. In fact, the costumes drew the most comment. Reporters found them magnificent and were duly impressed that some came from Paris at a cost of $125 to $200. Headed by "A Fine Wardrobe," the *Rapid City Daily Journal* of October 27, 1899, carried the following lengthy item:

> The ladies in the different towns where Della Pringle has appeared this season have gone into ecstasies over her imported Paris gowns. A great many actresses advertise fine wardrobes, but when you come to see them closely they are made up in cheap satins and velvets and made in a cheap way. Miss Pringle has two tailor made suits which she will wear in Camille that cost over one hundred dollars apiece, being made up in the latest style and lined throughout in the finest of taffeta silk. The black dress worn in the fourth act is a very elaborate affair of black satin with overdress of Brussels net spangled in black sequins in lover's knots and vines, line throughout with lavender taffeta silk, the skirt alone costing sixty-six dollars. These are only a few of her nice gowns of which she is justly proud.[8]

Of all the plays in the season, *Faust* drew the largest audiences and the most attention in the press. The play, adapted from Geothe's masterpiece by English star Sir Henry Irving, replaced the poetry and philosophy of the original with sensational scenic effects and scene chewing sentimentality. The work had been presented for several years before Della and Adams added it to their repertory with Lewis Morrison's production recognized as the best American version.

Irving's popular edition of *Faust* contained as many sensational scenes as most melodramas. Press comments about Della Pringle's production mention an "electrical duel" and an "Electric Garden," but the greatest scenes were titled "Brocken in Hades" with its "Revels of Demons" and "The Transformation of the Golden Realm" in which the heroine Margurite dies and then ascends to Heaven. In the Brocken scene snakes crawl, owl's eyes glare, crows dine on carrion, departed souls wail, trees take on grotesque human form, bolts of lightning strike and fire rains down. One reviewer requested that the audience remain seated until the final fall of the curtain to see the beautiful and moving ascension of Margurite to the Golden Realm.[9]

All the sensational extravaganzas of *Faust* still demanded acting talent to make a successful presentation. Della Pringle received several rave reviews for her portrayal of Margurite, a role requiring the actress to grow from an innocent peasant girl into a tragic figure who gives up her life to save the soul of Faust from eternal damnation. G. Faith Adams also earned critical approbation as the devil, Mephisto, appearing to good advantage in the role. One Missouri paper declared the Pringle production of *Faust* a worthy rival to that of Lewis Morrison.[10]

With repertory chosen and company members acquired Della and Adams set off on a thirty week season beginning with the usual opening performance at Knoxville on August 17, 1899[11] and ending at New Sharon, Iowa, on March 24, 1900. This tour was divided in two parts. The first part began, according to Pringle tradition, in her hometown and ended there in December to celebrate the holidays. During this part of the tour, the Pringle company, after performing at fairs held at towns in southern Iowa and northern Missouri, returned to Knoxville for Fair Week on September 11.[12] From there they jumped to St. Joseph, Missouri, then back to Oskaloosa, Iowa, before revisiting towns in their familiar path through Nebraska, South Dakota and Wyoming—drawing large crowds and golden opinions in the press at almost every stop. Della had planned to appear in Salinas, Kansas, the week of December 18, but cancelled the engagement and once more returned to Knoxville, this time to celebrate the holidays.[13]

Della had a splendid time over the Christmas season as she explained at length in the January 6, 1900, issue of the *Clipper*.

> We spent our first Christmas at home in many years, and to say we enjoyed it is putting it mildly. We were surrounded by friends and relatives and every comfort, with a splendid dinner and plenty of nice presents for everyone. As this has been the most prosperous season we have ever had to our credit, we felt as though we could afford to have a pleasant two week's vacation.... These are some of the nice presents [the

Pringles] received: $45 steel range, bird's eye maple dressing table, steel carving set, China dinner set, fountain pen, silk muffler, $16 pattern hat, silver curling iron and other trinkets too numerous to mention.[14]

Even during this vacation Della and Adams had to attend to theatre business. They placed an ad in the *Clipper* on December 30, 1899, an ad that possibly reveals the reason for cancelling Kansas engagements in December. In the ad they stated that they wanted "thoroughly experienced people who could act in all lines of business and had a good wardrobe." In effect, Della and Adams sought to reorganize their entire company. The ad concluded with this declaration: "You must attend strictly to business and work for the manager's interest. We have just cleaned out a batch of boozers and disorganizers. We will not tolerate such people for a minute."[15]

While Della and Adams awaited the results of the *Clipper* ad, they took in a show and attended to personal business in Knoxville. They celebrated the new year by going to Des Moines to see famous actor Lewis Morrison perform in *Frederick, the Great*.[16] They added to their considerable real estate holdings by purchasing an eighty-acre farm two and a half miles from Knoxville for $4,500, the profits from the season up to Christmas. After buying the new farm, they went about stocking it with fine cattle.[17]

Actors responded to the *Clipper* ad and by January 15, 1900, when the Pringle company renewed touring the new organization included some members from previous Pringle tours (Richard Marsden, Van C. Barrett, Caddie Gail and Baby Gail) and people new to the troupe (Robert Kieley, George Rush, Lou and Gertie Harrington and Jessie Brink).[18]

The second leg of Della Pringle's 1899–1900 season began with a performance of *The Dangers of a Great City* before a local standing-room-only crowd at the Knoxville Opera House on January 15.[19] The troupe next appeared at Rich Hill, Missouri, the week of January 19—the very same town where Della began her career at age eleven. After that the company spent most of February touring through Arkansas at Fort Smith, Texarkana, Little Rock and Newport in the only southern season undertaken by Della Pringle.

Even in new territory, Della and her merry makers attracted full houses and received sterling press notices. The paper in Fort Smith reported standing room only for Pringle's *Faust* and declared it a performance surpassing that of the renowned Lewis Morrison in some particulars by one of the best companies on the road.[20] A Little Rock writer judged Della Pringle in *The Princess of Paris* as an actress of the first class and found Babe Gale, the child star, a delight.[21] Other editions reported an audience well rewarded for braving rainy weather to attend *Faust* and marveled that half of the audience had attended the previous show—a tribute to the quality of productions offered at bargain rates. *Pawn Ticket 210* received particular praise, the reporter observing that most repertory companies presented that play the Pringle version surpassed all in stage settings and acting.[22]

Only one, somewhat amusing, incident marred the Little Rock engagement. When the audience members for a performance of *Pawn Ticket 210* sensed that the play was almost over, many—loudly and rudely—began to head for the exits. Della broke character and above the racket called out, "Sit down until we finish."[23] And they sat down.

In early March Della and her company played in Alton, Illinois, where several hundred people could not secure seats to a performance of *The Princess of Paris* and 250 patrons stood in the aisles and back of the theatre. Sleet and snow challenged audiences on their way to take in *Faust*. Still, large crowds turned out for the entire Pringle engagement in spite of the worst weather ever experienced in Alton.[24]

Bad weather continued to hamper Della and her troupe at their next stop, Clinton, Iowa, and temporarily halted the tour when illness in the company, brought on by the rain and cold, made it impossible to fill an engagement in Dubuque, Iowa, the week of March 11.[25] The tour resumed at New Sharon, Iowa, on March 19 but closed permanently on March 24 when Della was severely injured when she fell over a broken chair in her dressing room—the first of several accidents marking he career.[26]

Della and Adams returned to their Knoxville home and began their annual vacation on March 26. Della spent the first few weeks recovering from her injury in New Sharon and after that she and Adams devoted their time to mundane tasks at home and on the farm. Happily, the farm yielded additional revenue when a vein of coal was discovered on the property in late April.[27]

In early May the local paper revealed that Adams had been initiated into the Elks Club in Oskaloosa, Iowa, and that he would stow away the company's scenery before taking a trip to New York to arrange rights for more plays and to purchase new scenery.[28] On June 8, he and Della left Knoxville for a month to visit Buffalo, Niagara and New York before going to Atlantic City to take a saltwater plunge in the surf. On their way back to Iowa they spent some time with Adam's mother in Philadelphia.[29]

Upon their return to Knoxville on July 4, they began preparations for the 1900–1901 theatre season which would be their most ambitious tour yet. They would be on the road for thirty-six uninterrupted weeks. It would be the longest with plans to cover territory to the Pacific coast. Although it turned out that they did not reach the coast, they did perform as far west as Utah and Idaho. It would be the most expensive season ever with new scenery from both Seavery Studios in New York and Sosman and Landis in Chicago, royalties for new plays and additional specialty performers.

While Della still performed the popular fire and serpentine dances, Adams noted that people called for even more dancing and added several dancing specialty artists to the Pringle company. He hired Robert "Bobbie" Burgess (a prize-winning cake-walker), Alfred "Alf" Allen (the great rubber-legged comic dancer) and the Sisters Allen—petite dancers and singers.[30] During his trip to the east Adams had also secured rights to the latest, up-to-date musical selections.[31]

Adams made his biggest investment to secure the talents of Baby Estelle, the seven-year-old daughter of Alfred Allen. Billed as the "Greatest Child Actress of the Age," she came direct from principal eastern theatres and was acknowledged to be the highest salaried vaudeville act with a western company.[32] For his money Adams had a cute little child who sang ragtime songs, danced in wooden shoes with her father in an act titled "Big and Little Dutchman" and acted the lead role in performances of *Little Lord Fauntleroy*. In addition to receiving a handsome salary (undetermined), she garnered enthusiastic reviews wherever she performed.

After improving and expanding the dancing components of his theatre offerings, Della and Adams incurred more expense when they employed a Keith Vaudeville Circuit comedy act known as "Big and Little Tramps"—a sketch reported to be highest priced act before the public.[33] Actor C.B. Archer, friend of Della since her first days in show business, was hired to play his signature role in *The Silver King* and probably also merited a salary befitting his reputation.[34]

The Della Pringle Company payroll at the beginning of the season also included William Echols, Frank Patton, Fred Bates, Marcie Van Etten Echols and Margurita Allen.[35] Mattie Burgess served as pianist and musical director but was replaced in November by Gustave Kline. At the same time, E.M. Crane, playing character leads, seems to have been hired when C.B. Archer left the troupe.[36] Other changes in the company roster occurred when Georgie Ryan joined in February of 1901 and Eck Osborne a month later.

All in all during the 1900–1901 season Della Pringle's troupe offered a variety of plays, sixteen specialties, illustrated songs and over $5,000 in stage settings, costumes and "Bewildering Electrical and Calcium Light Effects."[37] All of this for as little as ten cents. Small wonder that press item after press item repeated that Della Pringle's aggregation was the best company for the money on the road.

With all the expenses included in mounting productions, it appears impossible that Della and Adams charging only ten to twenty cents for admission grew rich from their tours. The answer lies in the change of value of a dollar since 1900. Estimates of the value of a dollar at that time range from twenty-two to twenty-eight dollars of modern value. Given an average of twenty-five dollars, the ten cents charged for Della's shows is the equivalent of two and a half dollars. When Della opened the season at Knoxville, the paper reported that she took in a record $190,[38] a paltry sum by modern standards, but equivalent to just under $5,000 in current money. And the Della Pringle Company more often than not played to full houses—sometimes with standing room only!

Della promised, except for *Faust*, all new plays for the 1900–1901 tour. *Faust* continued to be in demand by patrons and she saw no need to disappoint them. She and Adams also revived *The Midnight Alarm* from the 1889 season, but the remainder of the repertoire was indeed new for the communities visited during the current tour. The royalties for some of the new works could be as high as fifteen dollars per performance. Including *Faust* and *The Midnight Alarm*, Della's company presented thirteen plays overall. Only a few were described in performance reviews.

The Heart of Arkansaw, set in the mountain region of Arkansas, depicted the lonely, half savage, life of persons involved in strong love, hate and bitter feuds. *The Silver King*, a famous ten-year-old melodrama by Henry Arthur Jones, dealt with a man accused of murder in England fleeing to Nevada and striking it rich in the silver mines. Returning to England in disguise, he exposes the real murderer and is reunited with his wife and family. *The Struggle for Life* drew reviewer's attention for a lurid scene in an opium den. Papers dismissed *Soldier of the King* simply as a romantic drama.

The remaining plays (*The Cross of Gold* or *The Fatal Card*, *Dad's Girl*, *A Race for Congress*, *Among the Pines*, *The Boy Tramp* and *Alone in New York*) drew little or no comment in the press. The story of *Little Lord Fauntleroy* was too well known to merit comment, but when the work was offered at Saturday children's matinees reporters emphasized the pleasing performance of Baby Estelle in the title role.

Della Pringle's 1900–1901 tour, a mixture of familiar and new routes, began with a single performance before hometown fans at the Knoxville

Fair on August 26.³⁹ For the next six weeks she and her "Merry Makers" performed at various Iowa fairs in such locations as Des Moines, Oskaloosa, Marshalltown and Council Bluffs. By October Della began to cover familiar territory in Nebraska during which time her troupe enjoyed the honor of opening a new opera house in Sidney on October 5.⁴⁰

After performing at Alliance, Nebraska, on October 8–11, Della did not head north to the Black Hills as she had done on several previous tours. Items in the Alliance paper hint at problems with a new booking agent for the Black Hills whose mistakes had disrupted the usual theatre business for that area. For whatever reason, Della abandoned her established route and instead headed across Wyoming where she first performed at Laramie on October 15–20.⁴¹

Della and Adams, who usually diligently informed the theatrical trade papers of the location and dates of their performances, sent such information only sporadically from late October 1900 to mid–January 1901. With such little information all that can be discerned is that Della and her troupe performed somewhere in southern Wyoming from late October to late November. She then went to northern Utah, playing to small crowds in small towns such as Heber City, Park City and Lehi during December.

Both business and communication with theatre newspapers improved after the Della Pringle Company reached St. Anthony, Idaho, on January 14 of 1901. Here G. Faith Adams wrote a long letter to the *Knoxville Express* extolling the beauty of eastern Idaho, the impressive agricultural irrigation system and the friendliness of the people. He stated that his company was making big money and leaving a fine impression among the people. He revealed that he had just spent a hundred dollars to purchase a black bear skin measuring seventy-seven inches from head to foot to be mounted for display in his Knoxville home.⁴²

After two weeks in Idaho Della journeyed to Butte, Montana, for an unusual two-week engagement beginning January 27. She played one week at Sutton's New Theatre and the next at the Grand Theatre.⁴³

After spending two weeks crossing eastward through Montana, Della reached the very familiar towns of South Dakota's Black Hills where she again drew full houses and enjoyed the adulation of her admirers in a period between February 21 to March 11. Continuing on this familiar path, Della took her troupe south into Nebraska, playing in such established stops as Alliance and Broken Bow before ending the thirty-six week season at Lincoln on April 4, 1901,⁴⁴ and returning to Knoxville.

Upon reaching home, Adams added his Idaho bearskin to the other valuable furs, skins of wild animals. Indian relics and expensive gold specimens gathered on his theatrical tours that decorated his elegant home, the Maples.⁴⁵ In between visiting relatives, hosting them on return visits and making improvements to their home and farm, Della and Adams worked on plans for their next theatre season.

As early as May 1, Adams announced that he would add a uniformed brass band to the next tour. Shortly after, he placed an ad in the *New York Clipper* seeking musicians. Two weeks later he revealed plans to visit Cuba during the summer to see if a tour there could be arranged,⁴⁶ but evidently scrapped the plan for nothing further about it appeared in the local press. Instead, he and Della attended the Pan American Exposition in Chicago sometime in June, meeting there with Adams' mother and brother.⁴⁷

Della and Adams added two new and important elements in their plans for the upcoming season—the aforementioned band and the acquisition of a "Palace" Pullman railroad car.⁴⁸ They wished to form their own band and orchestra to insure that they would have quality musical accompaniment for their performances on tour and avoid having to employ local music groups of questionable and unreliable skills. In a *Clipper* ad of May 11, they sought an "A1" leader who has plenty of up to date music and preferred musicians who could double as actors. The same ad asked for dancers who could also double in the band. The ad also requested a property man who could act and play in the band. The ad assured theatre managers that the addition of the band would not weaken the strength of the acting company.⁴⁹

By the beginning of the season, Della and Adams had assembled a sixteen-piece band with Fred Philips as its leader and a seven piece "operatic" orchestra under the direction of Douglas Crawford. In order to save on salaries and transportation costs, there had to be much doubling up between band and orchestra. Except for the two conductors, no other musicians are mentioned in newspaper items.

On tour both musical groups wore magnificent, expensive made to order uniforms. The band marched in a street parade every day before a performance to attract the attention of prospective patrons. The orchestra entertained before and during the performance and accompanied song and dance specialties. Generally, both band and orchestra drew praise for their contributions to the Pringle company's full evening of entertainment. While some critics remarked that the musicians alone were worth the price of admission, a Salt Lake City paper described the orchestra as "poor."⁵⁰

Even more important to the operation of Della's troupe was the investment in a "Palace" Pullman railroad car. Della and Adams were among the first theatre managers to tour in their own private car. Such a vehicle provided great convenience for the performers on the road and saved enormous amounts of money in transportation and housing for the managers.

In late June Adams first announced his intentions to buy the Pullman car that would be manufactured in Chicago and completed in a month.[51] Around August 2 Adams returned to Knoxville from Chicago aboard his new and opulent Pullman sleeper/diner car.[52]

On August 11, Della invited the public to make a tour of her Pullman car between 2:00 and 5:00 p.m. During this time Della's old friend, Colonel William F. "Buffalo Bill" Cody, and sharpshooter Annie Oakley (in town with his famed "Wild West" show) dropped in to visit with Della and complimented her on the finely equipped car. At Cody's invitation Della and Adams spent the evening in his private car.[53]

The Pringle Company's new private car weighed sixty-eight tons and measured sixty-seven feet long by ten feet wide with an interior that contained an office, three state rooms for married couples, a ladies' room, a kitchen plus a washroom and a coat room. The interior was finished with the finest of hardwoods—walnut, oak and maple—and featured several French plate mirrors. It also included a twenty-six foot cellar for the storing of scenery and equipped with automatic brakes and steam heat. This handsome and convenient home for the actors rolled on two six-wheel trucks.[54]

The Jolly Della Pringle Company's repertoire for the 1901–1902 season mixed new plays, previous season hits and two old works performed by almost all theatre troupes. Two of the new plays, *The Diamond Breaker* and *The Pulse of New York*, were melodramas with sensation scenes. The main feature of *The Diamond Breaker* depicted a monster coal breaker in operation. At the climax of the drama, the hero is rescued just as he is about to be ground up in the giant wheel crushing the coal. *The Pulse of New York* offered two scenic sensations—a great elevated railway with a train running at full speed and a pile driver in operation at the pier on the East River. There may have been another new play, *The Opium Fiend* (also listed as *The Opium Ring*); however, the plot suggests it may have been from the last season's *The Struggle for Life* which also dealt with opium addiction. The final new play, *The Bowery Girl*, was also performed under the title of *The Bowery After Dark*.[55]

The Pringle troupe continued to offer its crowd pleasing rendition of *Faust* from the past two seasons. *The Princess of Paris* was also repeated from the previous season.

Della and Adams chose to complete their repertoire by mounting productions of *East Lynne* and *Uncle Tom's Cabin*, both long established favorites with the American public. *East Lynne*, a Victorian tear-jerker, afforded Della great emotional scenes to act and the opportunity to wear her fine wardrobe of gowns from Chicago's Marshall Fields Company.[56] Although on the stage for some forty years, *Uncle Tom's Cabin* never lost its audience appeal and fitted in well with the company's roster of crowd pleasing, theatre filling attractions.

Except for rehiring E.M. Crane from the previous season, Della and Adams employed a completely new company of performers. Perhaps because of the cost for creating the new band and orchestra, fewer specialty acts were signed. The Mandevilles (sisters Daisy and Enola) performed an acrobatic dancing and contortion act as their specialty and doubled as actresses in the plays. Montrose Howard, a baritone from the minstrel stage, also doubled as an actor. Little Marjorie, "a wonder for a child of her age," replaced Baby Estelle, the star of last season, as the juvenile attraction. She sang, danced and did impersonations of the celebrities of the time.[57] George Wright, William H. Roberts, Louisa Roberts and Fred Mason made up the remainder of the troupe.[58]

With preparations completed, the Jolly Della Pringle Company began a 1901–1902 tour which turned out to be a huge clockwise loop covering the northern half of the American West and Midwest. As in all previous tours, Della started her season at Knoxville, this time the week of August 20.[59] A week's engagement at Des Moines followed[60] after which Della's troupe spent most of September performing in Iowa towns of Fairfield, Chariton and Ottumwa.[61]

Then the troupe skipped through Nebraska between late September and early October, appearing only at North Platte and Alliance. While performing in Alliance the actions of cool-headed patrons averted a panic when a fire broke out in the gallery. Quickly extinguished, the fire did little damage.[62]

Crowds in the southern Wyoming communities of Cheyenne, Rawlins, Rock Springs, Green River and Evanston, greeted Della's company during the rest of October. At Laramie on October 11 patrons filled the theatre to witness *The Pulse of New York* after fighting their way through an unseasonable snowstorm.[63] Later at Green River, Wyoming, a new member joined the Jolly Della Pringle Company when a gentleman of the town gave Della a Great Dane dog which she named Flossie.

All during November and December Della and company appeared in various small Utah communities (Heber, Springfield) except for a December 9–11 stand in Salt Lake City. Here the troupe received an unusual negative reception that savaged both actors and musicians.[64]

On top of doing poorer business in Utah than last year, engineers in a Utah railroad switchyard bumped Della's prized Pullman car into another car, doing severe damage to the cellar storage area under the car that carried all the company's scenery. Inside the Pullman furniture was overturned and Della's china broken. After the accident, Della and Adams had to tour with two railroad cars—the Pullman for actors and a rented baggage car for scenery and costumes.[65]

In January of 1902 Della found better luck in Idaho while touring along the route of the Oregon Short Line Railroad between Pocatello and Boise. At some time while performing in Boise the week of January 13, Della entered her dog, Flossie, in a local dog show. Flossie, reported to be the largest Great Dane in America, won a first prize.[66] Flossie also appeared on stage as one of the "ferocious" bloodhounds in Della's production of *Uncle Tom's Cabin,* but instead of pursuing Little Eva across the ice flow, she wandered into the Columbia Theatre auditorium and fell asleep in an aisle. Before leaving Idaho, Della and Adams visited with some Knoxville natives now living in Boise and Caldwell.[67]

Della's tour covered eastern Oregon in early February with stops at Sumpter and La Grande before heading north to perform in Washington State. After engagements at Walla Walla and Waitsburg plus a week in Lewiston, Idaho, this lap of the tour culminated with a performance at Spokane on February 24 in that city's impressively appointed Auditorium Theatre.[68]

Next day the Pringle company went to western Montana with a first stop at Libby where Della wrote a letter to the *Knoxville Express* in which she extolled the scenic wonders of Washington and Montana, voiced her opinion that Spokane was the best of western cities and revealed the cost of transportation by rail. She stated that her company had to play to full houses at advanced prices (fifty to seventy-five cents) because it cost $750 per month to move her Pullman car from town to town. She went on to contrast theatre facilities in Libby with those in Spokane—from the finest of theatres to a "tall timber" town hall with a hundred chairs, a platform and "not a stitch of scenery." To make the hall fit for a performance, the men in the troupe had to construct a stage and scenery. Della concluded her letter with news of a wedding in the company. Dancer Daisy Mandeville had married baritone Montrose Howard while in Spokane.[69]

During the first two weeks of March, Della quit sending information about her engagements to the trade papers. Generally she traveled east across Montana on the Great Northern Railroad. After appearing in Williston, North Dakota, on an unspecified date, the troupe ended up in Devil's Lake, North Dakota, on March 15 amid a horrendous blizzard that stranded the performers there for three days. Snow drifted three feet deep around Della's Pullman car in the worst storm in fifteen years. The actors struggled to get to the opera house and, to their surprise and delight, performed to a large audience whose members had fought the elements to attend the show. Adams wrote of sickness in the company and the lack of heat in the Pullman car, adding, "Oh, it is lovely traveling in the northwest!"[70]

Escaping the snow, Della led her company to Barnville, Minnesota, where the long and arduous season came to an end on March 22 instead of completing the tour at St. Paul in April as originally planned. Adams paid the performers for transportation to Chicago from where he and Della returned to Knoxville by March 26 thus completing the great loop of touring.[71] In spite of hardships and setbacks, it had been another profitable season that added to the solid reputation of the Jolly Della Pringle Company.

5

Western Star on Eastern Stages

Shortly after returning to Knoxville in the spring of 1902, Adams sold the company's Pullman car. He and Della had enjoyed a profitable season, but had endured considerable difficulties with the special car. It had been knocked off the tracks by switch engines and loose cars. Because the Pullman lacked steel wheels, some of the railroads in the West would not carry the car on passenger trains. The troupe was forced to make "jumps" of 200 and 300 miles hooked up on freight trains.[1] Della regarded the car as a necessary evil for her large company since it saved a great deal on hotel bills. By April 19, 1902, the Pullman car was sold for $2,200. At the same time Adams sold off the special scenery and electrical effects for his production of *Faust* plus the sets and full drops used in *The Palace of Gold*.[2]

After taking care of business concerns, Della and Adams spent the beginning of their vacation by visiting her brother in Des Moines. Back in Knoxville, on May 9, they won the gratitude of townspeople by directing a fundraising entertainment sponsored by the Cemetery Aid Society for maintenance of the Graceland Cemetery.[3]

Adams stated that he would give Della a long vacation from performing and not send out a troupe for the 1902–1903 season. On May 10 they left Knoxville for the beginning of what was supposed to be an extended vacation in the East.[4] First they went to Chicago, spending two days seeing *Flora Dora* and other theatre productions. Then they boarded the Lake Shore Limited for a twenty-four hour trip to New York and arrived there about May 14.[5]

Della and Adams stayed in Brooklyn as guests of Corse Payton and his wife, Etta Reed, old friends and theatre colleagues from the 1891–1892 season in the Midwest. Payton, who had begun his career in Iowa and Missouri and for many years maintained a summer home in Centerville,

Iowa, had since achieved great success as manager of two theatres in Brooklyn, his own stock companies and two road show troupes.

The Paytons dazzled Della and her husband with their display of wealth—a beautifully decorated house, four servants, champagne parties and a pair or imported automobiles, one of which Etta Reed used to chauffer Della around New York and New Jersey. When not being entertained by the Paytons, Della and Adams spent their time at Broadway shows and in fashionable shops purchasing Della's expensive Paris and London wardrobe for next year's theatrical season.[6]

After several weeks of relaxing with the Paytons at Rockaway Beach, Della and Adams drastically altered their vacation plans. Although they had not intended to resume their theatrical tours until the 1903–1904 season, on July 6 they entered into a fifty-fifty partnership with Corse Payton to head one of his road show companies on a tour through major cities in New York, New England and New Jersey. Della was to be the leading lady and to furnish her own elaborate wardrobe; Adams was to manage the troupe and play major character roles. Corse Payton furnished sets, furniture, rugs and properties as well as engaging the remainder of the company including specialty artists.[7]

Della Pringle began rehearsals for the upcoming forty-week season at Payton's Lee Avenue Theatre in Brooklyn on August 1. In addition to Della and G. Faith Adams, the company consisted of twenty-one performers including Baby Estelle, a noted juvenile star who had been in Della's troupe during the 1900–1901 season.[8] In just over two weeks this company prepared ten plays for production, enough to fill an entire week of a repertory engagement. The shows included *Friends, Frou Frou, Dangers of the Great City, A Harmless Flirtation, Faust* (W.G. Will's adaption), *Held by the Enemy, A True American Girl, Only a Farmer's Daughter, Little Lord Fauntleroy,* and *Over the Hills to the Poorhouse.*[9] Later in the season the troupe added *A Midnight Folly* to its repertoire.

This selection of productions, made up of rather familiar and often aged plays, was well fitted to the skills of the performers and the resources of the managers. There was no attempt to mount a cheaper version of current hits, a practice that usually disappointed audiences. Payton and Adams never tried anything they would not result in a good performance. Corse Payton had offered many of the plays during previous eastern tours and Della Pringle had presented several of the same works on her western tours between 1896 and 1902, notably *Friends* (also titled *The Struggle for Life*), *Dangers of the Great City, Faust, Little Lord Fauntleroy* and *A True American Girl,* a play written especially for Della Pringle by veteran western actor, James. M. Martin. Most audience members had probably seen most, if not all, on several occasions over the previous decades and could compare the talents of Della Pringle and her supporting players with those of other repertory companies' actors. The plays also afforded great opportunities for Della to display her talents and wardrobe in a wide variety of roles and emotions—a southern belle in *Held by the Enemy*, a wealthy beauty wooed by two brothers in *Friends*, the dramatic intensity and pathos of the adulterous wife in *Frou Frou*, both a nun and a Bowery girl in *Dangers of a Great City*, the love and sacrifice of Marguerite in an adaptations of Goethe's *Faust* and the love-smitten, father-defying young lady in *A True American Girl*.

These and the lighter comedies in the repertory allowed patrons so see a leading lady in scenes ranging from tear-inducing pathos to farcical hilarity. While the appeal was quite broad, presumably the women in the audience enjoyed the emotional aspects of these theatrical pieces more than the men. None of the plays, except *Faust*, could be considered great drama, but they supplied the melodramatic thrills, the hearty laughter and the sentimentality so desired by the audiences who attended the bargain-rate theatre of the traveling repertory companies.

In addition to the plays, Corse Payton like most other managers offered "specialties" or "polite vaudeville" performed between the acts of the dramas. In Della's company these "specialties" included Laura Comstock and a boy's choir presenting Southern plantation songs, Harry McKee, a lightning change artist, a sextet, the Rutherford sisters in songs and dances, Arthur Moxon leading the singing of illustrated songs and young Baby Estelle with her hit songs and dances. All these plus Mannie and Brownie, trained dogs who jumped, did tricks and boxed with a punching bag. Even Della and Adams appeared in singing specialties from time to time.

With a bill of familiar repertory plays and a strong roster of refined vaudeville specialties, Della Pringle began her season in the East as leading lady of the Corse Payton Road Company at Schenectady, New York, on August 18. Prior to this date she may have appeared in some preview performances between August 8 and 16 in one of Corse Payton's Brooklyn theatres. In later years she alluded to playing night after night to adoring audiences in Brooklyn; however, no other evidence of such performances has surfaced.

Friends, the opening performance in Schenectady, made a tremendous hit with its impressive costumes and scenery. Specialties between the acts "simply took the town by storm." Della and company played to

Della in New York in 1902 with her punching bag–boxing bulldogs and wearing her stylish wardrobe and hat (courtesy the National Society for the Preservation of Tent, Folk and Repertoire Theatre at the Theatre Museum of Repertoire Americana, Midwest Old Threshers, Mt. Pleasant, Iowa).

sold-out matinee and evening performances for the entire run of eleven shows and broke the house attendance record for an opening repertory company, taking in a total of $2,564 for the week.[10] Following the Tuesday matinee Della, Baby Estelle and other members of the company gave a "pink tea" on the theatre stage and shook hands with over 1,000 women and children.[11]

Della Pringle's offering of "pink teas" continued a practice Corse Payton had originated at his Brooklyn theatre some years earlier. As the women and children stepped onstage, Della personally shook hands with each one. Pink-gowned ladies of the troupe served pink lemonade punch and ladyfingers to their female audience who were seated at tables placed around the stage. If effect, it was a theatrical presentation in itself which afforded women patrons and their children an opportunity for close personal contact with the glamorous creatures of the stage. French gowns, delicate lace and other details of elaborate costumes worn by the leading lady and her supporting actresses could be examined and admired. For a short while the matinee audience shared the life and the "glitter" of the stage. Patrons had come to see the actresses and went away feeling they were "friends" of the performers.

The Payton-Pringle pink teas were serious business in spite of their informality. Pink teas, usually offered early in a week's engagement, were obviously great public relations events and helped stimulate ticket sales for the balance of the run. Della's company presented some such post-matinee activities as often as three times a week, but not all were pink teas. Some featured giveaways of bonbons, others pictures of Della Pringle and still others a metal pin tray impressed with Della's likeness.

Following a rewarding opening engagement Della and company appeared the week of August 24 in Poughkeepsie before less than ideal audiences. In a letter to her hometown paper Della complained: "The audiences are very enthusiastic over here, in fact a little too much so, the galleries being very noisy, and they won't stand for very much love-making on stage. It would take about forty policemen to keep order in some of these galleries."[12] She further related that, with the audience in tears at the end of her pathetic death scene in *Frou Frou*, a youngster yelled out, "More work for the undertaker," which evoked laughter in the house and broke everyone up onstage, too.[13]

Smart-aleck boys were not the only audience problems for Della Pringle and her troupe. While still in Poughkeepsie, the management established a policy banning babies at performances. As a newspaper item disclosed, due to cheap admission for the Pringle shows, "an unusual number of women with infants in arms attend and there is more or less crying and disorder throughout the house; so much so, in fact, that is very often disturbs the actors."[14] For the good of the performers and the public, from that time forth no woman with a baby in her arms was allowed to witness a performance.

Della's troupe filled four one-week engagements during September at Newburgh, Binghamton and Kingston, New York, and Paterson, New Jersey. While the local press at Newburgh praised the troupe as "one of the best popular priced companies ever seen here" with specialties that "have caught the town,"[15] papers in other cities printed little critical commentary. In all these cities Della continued to spend her leisure time sightseeing, even though Paterson had little to offer but miles of ruins, the result of a major fire the previous year.

During her engagement at Yonkers, New York, the week of September 29, Della had part of her wardrobe stolen when stagehands let some young ladies into her dressing room. She lost $200 in costumes, one skirt alone worth forty dollars, and had to go to New York City to replace the lost items.[16] Despite this thievery, Della must have enjoyed the hearty endorsement of the Yonkers' press. Reviews found her "at her best" in *Dangers of the Great City* in which she acted two contrasting roles—a nun and a Bowery girl—and added that she "showed great talent" in her portrayal of Marguerite in *Faust*.[17]

Della toured on to Trenton to appear the week of October 6. In addition to acting in the usual twelve plays a week (six evenings and six matinees), the company had to work additional hours to rehearse a new production, *A Midnight Folly*, under the direction of George Hoey, stage director of the Corse Payton Stock Company in Brooklyn. The troupe added the new production to the performance repertory at Wilmington, Delaware, during the following week.[18]

After an excellent week of business at Trenton, Della, Adams and fellow performers arrived at Wilmington on October 13 for a week of shows. Houses "packed to overflowing" greeted opening performances and by the end of the engagement the press declared it one of the most successful stands in many seasons. As for Della Pringle's particular contribution to the company's success, a local reviewer commented that in *Little Lord Fauntleroy* and *The Struggle for Life*," Della Pringle in the leading roles proved herself to be a capable and accomplished actress" and that in *Dangers of the Great City* she "did excellently in the numerous characters she portrayed."[19]

More crowded houses greeted the troupe when it played Hartford, Connecticut, the week of October 20. Press notices remained favorable, even though the vaudeville specialties performed between the acts tended to receive more attention than the major performances. Nevertheless, a local commentator wrote: "Miss Della Pringle ... is an actress of merit and is fairly well supported."[20]

The Lyceum Theatre at New London, Connecticut, featured the Corse Payton Road Company from October 27 through November 1. The combination of popular prices, solid acting, fine scenery and lively vaudeville acts drew large audiences. Notices said little or nothing of Della's talents as an actress; her wardrobe elicited more comment. As the local reviewer declared, "Miss Pringle's gowns are a revelation and to the ladies are alone worth the price of admission."[21]

Comments regarding Della Pringle's wardrobe appeared frequently in performance reviews during the tour and not by chance. Her wearing of Paris gowns and other garments of high fashion was calculated to attract a heavy volume of female patrons who, by attending the theatre, could see the latest expensive fashions in all their splendor rather than mere illustrations of them in popular women's magazines of the time. Whatever the specific part in a given drama, Della's stage demeanor and wardrobe most often emphasized her role as a glamorous lady of high society, an ideal, poised and desirable woman of distinction. In effect the elaborate wardrobe greatly aided her in portraying herself as a romantic role model for an audience largely made up of the rather ordinary wives and daughters of common mill workers, shoe makers, fishermen, store clerks and merchants.

Given her own origin and experience, irony lay behind Della Pringle's portrayal of fashionable, romantic upper class ladies. Lengthy letters sent to her hometown newspaper reveal her to be a rather ordinary woman who seemed to be homesick for Iowa people and Iowa food. She viewed easterners as rude in manner and appeared uncomfortable among the east's large populations with their ethnic and national diversity as well as their foreign accents. The society gulf between middle and upper classes in the east was of great concern to her; she felt she would never be at home in such conditions, conditions that did not seem to exist in her native Iowa.[22]

As for the particulars of Della's stunning wardrobe, a reporter at Salem, Massachusetts, wrote that Miss Pringle wore a gown "that sparkled as if studded with diamonds" which the largely female audience appreciated highly and which would "likely be the topic of conversation in many places about the city for several weeks."[23] Similarly one of the Lewiston, Maine, papers noted: "Miss Pringle has, without exception, the finest gowns that have ever seen on our stage."²⁴ A Lawrence, Massachusetts, a paper carried a detailed description of some of Della's Paris and London gowns. First there was a thousand dollar court gown with a "long train of shimmering pink velvet" decorated with embroidered "ascension lilies" and "beautiful Irish point lace." Another gown was a "negligee of faille silk with overdress of daintily painted bolton cloth and a profusion of filmy lace" contrasted by a black velvet bow fastened at the bust "with long loops falling to the bottom of the skirt." Still another was made of "white duchess satin with a train of turquoise blue panne velvet, embroidered with seed pearls and silver threads [worn] over a petticoat of white satin and ... lined with cloth of silver." Finally, the reporter described "a duchess gown of pink faille silk, on the skirt of which are embroidered in black pearls and cut steel three Prince of Wales plumes."²⁵

While her acting and her wardrobe brought good fortune during the early months of the eastern tour, some bits of bad luck haunted Della and her husband in early October. Adams lost a valuable diamond stud while on a quick visit to Payton's Brooklyn theatre. Then Della learned her stepfather back in Iowa had become very ill and was likely to become an invalid. She also incurred heavy losses on her Iowa farm where several valuable stock animals died. In addition, heartless thieves killed her prize winning Great Dane, Flossie. Back in the East, a dressing room maid broke Della's electrically wired makeup glass into a thousand pieces. Adams and Pringle, while they regretted their losses, let a theatrical trade paper know that "as long as business keeps up the way it has so far we need not worry, as we can buy more."²⁶

Three engagements filled the itinerary of the troupe during November, the first week in Fall River, Massachusetts, the second at Norwich, Connecticut, and the final week at Brockton, Massachusetts. Since Della had been accustomed to traveling great distances by train in the West, she found it remarkable that in New England she could take a trolley car for just fifty or sixty miles and in that distance pass through three states to fulfill engagements.²⁷

At the Academy of Music in Fall River, crowded houses greeted opening performances and Della "established herself as a favorite from her first appearance."²⁸ During a two-week engagement in Brockton, a reviewer responded favorably to her in *Held by the Enemy*, finding her to be "a pretty and agreeable actress, whose methods are refined and natural, and who never yields to the temptation to rant and seize the center of the stage by force." Two nights later her portrayal of Marguerite in *Faust* was judged to be "tender and sweet."²⁹

Della Pringle began two weeks of performances at New Bedford, Massachusetts, in early December then took the week of December 14 off to return to Knoxville for a brief rest and to visit family and friends.[30] After her week's vacation in Iowa, she resumed performing on December 20 at Lowell, Massachusetts, where her company would remain through January 3, enjoying good business during its almost-three-week stand.[31]

Starting on January 5, 1903, Corse Payton's Road Show Company played through Massachusetts into Maine in four successive one-week stands. During the first engagement at Lawrence, the paper's reviewer devoted one entire column to the French dresses worn by Della Pringle at the opera house, describing them as "dreams of loveliness ... aristocratic gowns full of the conscious pride in their own greatness."[32] The following week at Lynn, Massachusetts, the theatre editor of the paper noted Della's fine costuming as well as the troupe's acting ability and the abundance of specialties, saying of the opening performance: "No better staged production at popular prices has been seen in Lynn this season."[33] Audiences must have agreed, for the company did good business all week.

Weather curtailed attendance somewhat during Della's week in Salem, Massachusetts, and the local critic took exception to the quality of a few plays, faulting the authors rather than the actors. On Friday of the run all women in attendance at the matinee received a souvenir portrait of Della Pringle. Payton's troupers finished January's engagements at Portland, Maine, where they enjoyed great patronage for the entire run. On opening night a local critic praised the management abilities of Adams, the "talent, beauty and experience of Della Pringle" and declared her wardrobe to be "one of the largest and finest ... possessed by any American actress." Following a performance of *Held by the Enemy* the same critic wrote that she "was full of life and jollity and also did some very clever acting in her serious scenes."[34]

During the first half of February Della's players performed in Maine, drawing capacity crowds in spite of heavy storms. Bangor's theatre critic, who devoted an entire column to the company's bag-punching bulldogs, also found some space to comment on the excellence of the troupe, writing that it was a "very considerable distance above the average [of the] twenty or more companies now touring the New England Circuit."[35] He added: "The abilities of Miss Pringle are too well known to need extended comment, while her gowns are something which are quite beyond the range of masculine ingenuity."[36]

Patrons filled the Music Hall in Lewiston, Maine, during the week of

February 9 and once again Della won favorable comment in the press where she was described as "a ladies favorite [who] acts natural and wears the finest wardrobe we have seen in a long time."[37] Della ended her tour of Maine with a single performance at the Soldier's Home in Togus with a guarantee of $250.[38]

Payton's company finished out February with week-long stands back in Massachusetts. Of the opening night at Haverhill's Academy of Music, a local critic wrote, "Miss Pringle, the leading lady, is pretty, wears magnificent gowns and is an actress of great ability."[39] Fitchburg press representatives commented on almost everything but acting skills, choosing rather to describe the Tuesday matinee pink tea, the bonbons presented to the ladies at the Wednesday matinee and the aluminum pin tray engraved with Della's likeness given as a souvenir to the women attending the matinee on Friday.[40] The vaudeville acts also drew more attention than the plays. The critic went so far as to state: "It was something of a question from the first whether the specialties were incidental to the play or the play to the specialties. The entertainment opened with a performance by four trained dogs and their performance alone would have been called value received for the money a few years ago."[41]

Della Pringle's acting troupe spent all of March and the first week of April in New England. The week of March 1 the performers appeared at Taunton, Massachusetts, and played to large, enthusiastic audiences in spite of the Lenten season. During her engagement at Newport, Rhode Island, the week of March 9, Della took a night off and boarded an overnight boat to New York City to attend a performance of Tolstoy's *The Resurrection*, starring noted actress Blanche Walsh. Of the experience, Della Pringle wrote: "I never suffered so in my life. I cried until I had the sick headache, and my eyes were almost blind, and yet I never enjoyed a performance so much in my life."[42]

After rejoining her company following the Newport engagement, Della played a week at New Britain, Connecticut, and another at Holyoke, Massachusetts. There Della had an interview with a local reporter, an item later reprinted in the Knoxville paper. The interviewer referred to her as Jolly Della, "as she is known all through the profession," and asked her what she was doing in the East, to which she replied:

> I am acting and sight-seeing at the same time. This is an outing for me in a way, as I have never played in the east before, and of course every city I play in is new to me and I explore it thoroughly. I have been frightfully extravagant on this account as I may not play through here again and I want to get a good idea of what your wonderful east looks like.[43]

The interview, which included a description of several gowns in Della's wardrobe, concluded with the writer's assertion that "Miss Pringle and her husband are wealthy."[44]

At Meriden, Connecticut, for the week of April 6 the touring troupe received the only negative press reception for the entire season. While not mentioning the company by name, press notices referred to the shows in the Pringle repertory and voiced the opinion that shows presented in Meriden during Holy Week. Objections seemed to be more on religious grounds rather than artistic.[45] Having opposed the idea of even presenting plays at this time, the press just ignored the rest of the company's efforts.

Following the snub in Connecticut, the Payton Road Company went to Cohoes, New York, for the week of April 13, then played a return engagement at Paterson, New Jersey. The Paterson performances packed the house twice daily and audiences were enthusiastic, receptions being given to all the company, and bouquets for Miss Pringle and other favorites. From Paterson the company went to Peekskill, New York, where the forty-week season ended on May 2.[46]

Della Pringle's tour of northeastern states had been satisfying in most respects. Based on attendance, profits and encouraging critical reception in the local press of the cities she played, Della Pringle proved that she was at least the equal, if not the superior, of leading ladies in the repertory companies of New York and New England. She might well have established a reputation there, but she was an Iowa woman, a western woman, and in that direction lay her future. While Jolly Della Pringle had enjoyed success as an actress on eastern stages, she must have found a territory where a troupe could travel from engagement to engagement on a trolley car a bit limited. After all, this Iowa actress had enjoyed, and would enjoy, trouping across two-thirds of the American continent that spread free and open west of New York and New England.

6

West to the Coast

The theatrical season of 1903–1904 saw many triumphs and a near tragedy for Della Pringle and G. Faith Adams. As much as they seemed to have enjoyed their artistically and financially successful tour of the East, they lost no time in returning to Knoxville. There, a near-disaster occurred that threatened Della's life.

On the first day after they reached their home, May 7, 1903, a horse dealer brought them a new horse for trial, but it ran away a half hour after it was harnessed to a buggy. With Della in the driver's seat, the racing horse pulled the buggy under a low-hanging tree limb that knocked her out of the trap, senseless, and caused severe injuries to the left side of her head and shoulder. Twenty hours passed before she fully regained her senses.[1] Happily, within a few weeks she completely recovered and began to plan with Adams for the 1903–1904 tour of the Jolly Della Pringle Company.

The new season and supervision of the construction of a large addition to their already spacious summer home occupied most of the couple's time.[2] Early in July Della took time out from all activities and rested for a short time at the Iowa Sanitarium in nearby Des Moines.[3] Rejuvenated, she returned home and on July 24 hosted a housewarming party to celebrate the completion of the addition to her home. Guests included family, friends, several prominent people from Des Moines and many of the show folks spending their summer west of Chicago. The royally entertained guests saw a beautifully decorated house and a lawn illuminated with a perfect maze of colored Chinese lanterns.[4]

During the three weeks following the impressive housewarming, Della and Adams concentrated on the details of the new season. They did not have to spend much effort on assembling a company since they hired most of the performers that had been in last season's Corse Payton Road Company tour in the east.

Baby Estelle and her parents, Alf and Marguerite Allen, would join

Della for the third time. Charles Archer served as lead actor and stage director. Frank Lynch, a noted dancer, also filled the roles of singer for illustrated songs, operator of motion pictures and stage manager. Music director and pianist Edith Martinot, a sister of the famous Broadway star Sadie Martinot, provided music for productions and specialties. Horsford Plowe, a baritone from the Boston Opera Company, appeared in singing specialties and doubled as a supporting player. William Echols, W.M. Sheldon and Marie Van Etten had been members of earlier Pringle companies. Maude Livingston and Fred Mason began the tour as part of the company.[5] After late January, 1904, Fred Wilson, his wife, Louise Perine and Nettie Prescott replaced some members of the troupe. At the same time, a juvenile, Little Trixie, took over the Baby Estelle's place in the company. Although only seldom mentioned in press items, the Shepard Sisters appear to have been in the troupe late in the season.[6]

An additional singing specialty was performed by Adams and Pringle and Della revived her "fire dance," now re-titled the Kaleidoscopic Dance in which colored calcium lights illuminated her costume with its 125 yards of swirling silk.[7] Another specialty featured Professor Genter and his canines starring Bill, the bag-punching bulldog.

With few exceptions Della offered a repertoire of works new to her troupe and its audiences. Several were recent plays commanding a high royalty payment. Since Della had been so moved last year when seeing Tolstoy's *Resurrection* on Broadway, she added it to her productions.[8] She balanced this heavy drama by selecting a roaring farce, *The Sultan's Daughter*. For melodramatic offerings she chose *Circumstantial Evidence* and a detective drama, *The Mansion of Aching Hearts* or *Caught in the Web*. Taking advantage of the popularity of a novel about a Norwegian princess, Della selected a stage adaptation of *Thelma* with its realistic ship scene. Other plays in the season's original repertoire were *The Guilty Wife, The City of Sighs and Tears, A Soldier to the King* and a repeat production of *Little Lord Fauntleroy* to be performed for children's matinees. Sometime around March of 1904, Della added fresh shows which included revivals of *Dangers of the Great City* and *The Princess of Paris* plus new productions: *The Pace That Kills* and *Wealth and Poverty.*

At the beginnings of at least two previous seasons, Adams had declared that Della's troupe would play to the Pacific coast. In these instances the tours went no further than eastern Oregon and Washington. For the 1903–1904 season he once again announced plans to reach California and this time he reached the goal. The Pringle company not only followed the familiar path through Iowa, Missouri, Nebraska, South

Dakota, Wyoming, Idaho and Utah, but opened new territory in Nevada, California, Arizona, New Mexico, Texas and Oklahoma.

Following custom, the Della Pringle troupe opened the 1903–1904 season at Knoxville on August 12 with a pleasing performance of *The Sultan's Daughter* which brought in $215 at the box office. The four performances of this initial engagement earned a total of $785, a grand beginning for the season.[9]

Travel and performances were routine as Della's merry makers journeyed through western Iowa, northern Missouri and made the usual stop at Alliance, Nebraska, the week of August 31.[10] Heading north the company was welcomed at the South Dakota towns of Lead City, Deadwood, Rapid City and Sturgis.

When things did not go well at Lead City and Deadwood, Della attributed it all to an incident on September 7 in which a company actress, Marguerite Allen, accidentally broke a dressing room mirror, a sign of bad luck among theatre folks. That same evening a fire broke out in the opera house. Film from the troupe's movie projector fell against an electrical device and burst into flame. Although the fire was quickly extinguished, it caused a near panic during which two ladies fainted. Only quick action by manager Adams and some cool-headed patrons quieted the frightened audience. The fire destroyed fifty dollars worth of film and a set of illustrated songs.[11]

Bad luck continued as the worst storm in years dropped eighteen inches of snow on Lead City. Della lost a night of performance and the snow adversely affected business for the whole week. Finally, actor William Echols became ill with typhoid fever and had to be taken to the hospital in Deadwood. Della said it all the trouble began with the broken mirror.[12]

Poor luck appeared to follow Della's troupe at Deadwood the following week. Here the actors found no regular theatre but a damaged skating rink which the men in the company had to transform into a playable venue.[13] After all their work, stormy weather and freezing temperatures kept patrons from turning out. The actors performed before sparse audiences in a frigid rink where they could see the sky through the roof.[14]

After much more pleasant weather and better business at Rapid City and Sturgis, Della and company journeyed on to a return engagement in Alliance, Nebraska before entering Wyoming for October performances at Cheyenne, Laramie, Rock Springs and Evanston. Performances were well and enthusiastically received by substantial audiences. Della's only complaints were about Wyoming town's lack of good hotel accommodations and the poor quality of food.[15]

6—West to the Coast

After playing short, successful stands in the eastern Idaho towns of Montpelier, Pocatello, St. Anthony and Idaho Falls the last of October and the first eleven days of November, Della arrived at Ogden, Utah for a two-night engagement ending on November 13. In view of the rather poor business in Utah in two earlier seasons, Della and Adams elected to travel to new territory in Nevada.

On November 16–19 at Winnemucca, Nevada, Della wrote and sent a long, folksy letter to the Knoxville paper. She briefly described the path of her tour to date, revealed that business had been good and that she had enjoyed eight weeks of good weather. As she put it: "Weather so good you could love your enemies."[16] The letter related how she had met with Knoxville people who had moved to Idaho and Utah. She said that the train trip across the desert had been tiresome and then made good-natured comments about fellow passengers which included a western millionaire and the Virginia Harned Company on its way to perform in San Francisco. Della marveled at how heavily the Harned actors drank and how lavishly they dined.[17]

Della found time to pen another long letter to the Knoxville when she played the week of November 23 in Reno, Nevada. She wrote:

> I thought I would write a few of the experiences of the Jolly Della Pringle Company, enroute in the wild and wooly West. We have certainly been on the frontier this season and seen life in all its phases. This state of Nevada is all new to us, this our first trip in this direction. The public have taken kindly to us, and I can really say I like the trip through here, although it is filled with hardships and poor accommodations in the way of theatres and hotels, but the weather is so glorious and the air so invigorating, the people so nice and friendly, so delighted with our entertainments we give them for "75 cents a throw," that we can't help liking them.
>
> We see thousands of Indians all through the state, the Pinto and Washoe tribes. They are quite civilized, the squaws do washing for the white people and earn a little money for the men to spend at Winnemucca. Two Indian men hauled our baggage.... It is nothing to look out the back of the hotel and see 50 or 75 of them sitting flat on the ground in a round ring playing couch. They are all great gamblers, squaws and all.... All their work is very high. They come to the show and seem to enjoy it immensely.[18]

Della wrote of the "wild west," a term that well fits events in Wadsworth, Nevada, on November 20–21. Della's letter vividly described those events.

> We had quite a scare at Wadsworth. We were playing a matinee and had Rochester lamps [kerosene lamps] for footlights. The stage was small

and just as George [Adams] finished his announcement he accidently upset one of the lamps. In a second oil ran all over the front of the stage and caught fire. The house was all decorated with red tissue paper for some ball and it caught fire and the flames were leaping and spreading all over the stage. The people became panic stricken and stampeded for the doors. Large men ran over small children in their haste to save themselves. The actors tore down the tissue paper and a cool headed man in the audience threw the lamp out the window. They finally put it out without much damage, but I tell you it was a scare.[19]

Della reminded readers that this was the second fire of the season, referring to the motion picture fire in Lead City. She went on to describe the deplorable conditions in Wadsworth.

This same town of Wadsworth was the limit in every way for poor accommodations. It is only a small [railroad] division with only one hotel: they charge $2 a day straight. They can't get girls to stay there, the town is so unattractive, so all their help was Chinamen. Imagine having a Chinaman having to come into your room to do a chambermaid's work. Cooks, waiters and all. I couldn't eat anything: there was a dirty, greasy smell and look to everything. We paid our little old four dollars just the same. Some of the people. in sheer desperation, bought alcohol stoves and cooked light lunches in their rooms—enough to hold body and soul together. It was the toughest town I ever saw, being the division point, all bums going east and west get off there, and we saw some of the most desperate looking characters—they would just as soon knock you over and rob you as to look at you. We had to cross a high viaduct over the tracks to the opera house and climb about a hundred steps, and dark— not a light! We were all scared to death to go over there. I had several hundred dollars on my person and we had no protection, only the bulldogs. One of our men was going across there alone and a couple of drunken men stopped him and asked him to take a drink. He was afraid to refuse so he took a drink although he is not a drinking man.[20]

In the same letter, Della has something to say about train travel in Nevada and the housing situation in Wadsworth.

The trains are very uncomfortable. They are packed full all the time with people going to the coast and so many immigrants and children galore. It is impossible to get a seat. It is lovely to take a mid-night train and get into one of those coaches; the stench that greets you, and then to have to sit in a seat with a consumptive who is going to Colorado for his health and they cough and expectorate all night, and 40'leven babies crying. Oh, this travelling is not a fairy dream! ... We arrived there [Wadsworth] at 4 a.m., only one hotel in the town and they only had one room. George and I got that, as the others didn't care to pay $2. The town was asleep, only one place open and that was a saloon and all-night lunch counter. They had some benches out in front and our people sat there until daylight, waiting for places to stop.... Fortunately is was warm weather and they were comfortable in that way. But it must have been a ridiculous sight to see those poor troupers, tired out and sleepy, sitting there so disconsolate. They have laughed about it since, but it was far from funny at the time.[21]

After the miserable days in Wadsworth, Della and company had a glorious time in Reno, Nevada, the week of November 23. In her letter to Knoxville she characterized Reno as "the greatest western town I ever saw" and continued her observations: "It is thoroughly a western town, finest mirror front saloons and some of the noted gambling places of the world are here. Hundreds of men in the streets at all times and all nations represented."[22] Della had a fine carriage ride on Sunday and was impressed by the number of beautiful and elegant homes in Reno. She found her hotel "a positive delight after some of the bad ones we have had since we left Ogden."[23] Della and Faith Adams entertained all the company members at a Thanksgiving dinner after the matinee—a dinner that was more than excellent. She was impressed that wine was served with dinner free of charge, a custom in California at the best hotels. Della ended her Reno letter with "This is one of the best show towns on the coast. We will play to about $1,400 on the week, seven performances."[24]

Della completed her tour of Nevada with one-week stands at Carson City (November 30–December 5) and Virginia City (December 7–12). She found the latter town to be a relic of the past. Once the "mining camp of the world" with its fabled Comstock mine that produced millions in silver, Virginia City's population had fallen from 40,000 to only 1,500. Two miles of once prosperous store buildings stood vacant. Della described it as "magnificent in its day, but now a morgue."[25]

From Virginia City the Pringle group next crossed over a mountain divide into California. In yet another letter to the *Knoxville Express*, she recounted this leg of her tour.

We went through 40 miles of snow sheds. Anyone who thinks this is a pleasant experience doesn't know. They close up all the windows and transoms and light a couple of dim coal-oil lights, and there you sit in the dark, breathing this horrible coal smoke from the engine; you can't see out or see to read, and all you can do is grumble and be thankful after it is over.[26]

After the ordeal in the snow sheds, Della found it too good to be true to see the green vegetation at Grass Valley and Nevada City, California, where she completed two three-day stands between December 14 and 19. A week of rain, however, dimmed he enthusiasm for the California climate.[27]

Della and her company took a break from performing and rested at San Francisco during Christmas week. She found the vacation to be a success in every way. Her actors attended the city's fine theatres to see other performers and dined on fine food at the Poodle Dog Restaurant. On December 22, six in the company rented an automobile and drove through Golden Gate Park down to the ocean where they wrote their names in the sand and had a grand view of ocean liners steaming out of Golden Gate Harbor. The ended the auto tour with a spin through the Presidio.[28]

Shortly after the jaunt through San Francisco, Della and her troupe resumed performances at San Jose on Christmas Day. Full houses for matinee and evening presentations of *Thelma* brought in over $600, but earned the troupe one of the most savage and brutal newspaper reviews a Della Pringle company had ever received.

San Jose critic P.H. MacEnery began his nasty review with a sub-heading: "Wretched Production By Aggregation of Amateurs." After citing pre-production publicity extolling the excellence of Della's production of *Thelma*, MacEnery declared it a hoax. He attacked the actors as "the most unsuccessful that have ever inflicted themselves on the San Jose public." He said of Della: "She stalked lazily around the stage a la somnambulist.... She drawled lines with lungless cadence and leisurely strode about the boards as if she were memorizing a couplet from a dressmaker's novelette." Even Della's wardrobe, so often praised by several other critics, was trashed: "The elaborate costumes were cheap, gaudy garments, the refuse probably of some Italian huckster's clearing sale." On the only positive note, MacEnery wrote that the performance "was relieved by a few specialties." He concluded his diatribe with "No doubt every member of the cast believed he or she is a star of the first magnitude. Their disdainful nonchalance was evidence of this."[29]

Della and her performers had left town before the release of the corrosive review. She never alluded to it and only had memories of San Jose as a place where displaced Knoxville natives dropped in after a performance to visit in her dressing room.[30]

The Pringle company next stopped at beautiful old Monterey, mainly to go sight-seeing. Della felt that "a lovelier place could not be imagined" and contemplated moving to the city except for the fact that one had to "have a big income as all costs a lot of money." While in Monterey Della took part in an excursion on Monterey Bay in a glass-bottomed boat and wrote that she had "never seen so many fish in my life."[31]

6—West to the Coast

Della Pringle summed up her feelings about her adventures in California in one of her long letters to the Knoxville public. She wrote:

> California is a beautiful state, but you want lots of money, and you don't want to depend on making a living in the state; it is all overdone and the people one meets traveling through are all "grafters." It is a case of "throw up your hands!" all the time: you finally get so disgusted after you have been robbed by the hotels, railroads, restaurants, bus men, and in fact everyone else you have any dealings with, that you are glad to escape with your life. They have a system of robbing you, and, no matter how wise you think you are, they are just a little wiser. You make rates at a hotel and they give you a room without a bit of heat; it gets cold in the evenings and mornings; you ask for a fire, they charge you 25 [cents] for a little bucket of coal, about three chunks in it, or if they have a fireplace you get about four sticks of pine that only last about a half an hour. George [Adams] and Mr. Bates went into a restaurant, ordered two plates of chicken hash and two cups of coffee, and the bill was $25. So it goes; I paid $5 a dozen for my washing. You get so you hate the people in California and want to get away for that one reason. We were only in the state for three weeks; business was only good in spots, so we decided to take a jump; we couldn't afford to waste our time and money.[32]

Della and Adams paid $800 for railroad tickets to Phoenix, Arizona. They boasted that few companies could afford the cost of such a jump. Fortunately, they only lost one performance night in making the long trip.

The sudden relocation to Arizona pleased Della and her actors. The climate, especially, impressed them and Della felt "the climate is much better than California, no damp weather, all sunshine." She could "sit on the veranda of the hotel every day in a summer shirt waist and do fancy work."[33] All enjoyed the abundance of fruits, grains and vegetables grown in the state.

The great climate, so praised by Della, with its dry, clean air afforded a healing environment for the many people afflicted with tuberculosis and other lung diseases. Della viewed these unfortunates with conflicting emotions—compassion and revulsion. She described the situation in a letter from Jerome, Arizona, in late January of 1904:

> It is terrible to see the poor consumptives in this state. Everywhere you go you can hear that terrible cough, and in Phoenix are about 5000 of them. All the hotels and rooming houses are packed with them. I was scared to stay there, as it is contagious, and so many are coughing and expectorating around. I lived out of doors as much as I could and used a disinfectant. The call them "lungers," and treat them like lepers. It is a sad sight to see the poor things out with their overcoats on early in the morning, getting the fresh air and sunshine, and through the middle of

the day while it is the warmest the streets will be packed with them....
The town of Phoenix depends on its invalids in the winter for support.
Everything is very high; you can't rent a room under $1 a day in the commonest kind of rooming house. They have settlements of consumptives out on the mesa in tents; they sleep out the year round. This is the better way to get well, as the fresh air and sunshine do the work; but the death rate is appalling, so many wait until it is too late.[34]

After performing in Phoenix between December 27, 1903, and January 4, 1904, Della's company appeared at Mesa for one show on January 5 and then returned to Phoenix to complete the week. The troupe moved on to Congress to play January 11–13. Della said of this Arizona mining camp:

I thought I had played some tough towns, but this is the worst in the world. It was after pay-day, and there are 17 different nationalities in that camp..., and they are the lowest class of people on earth; a little bad whiskey and they would just as soon kill a man for $5 as to look at him. Fights, shootings and stabbings affrays are so common they don't pay a bit of attention to it. The first night we were there [January 11] the fire alarm sounded and our landlady screamed that it was in the house next to us and that we would all be burned alive. Well, to make matters worse we could not find matches and in the dark we couldn't find he door, and after that terrible fire in Chicago [the Iroquois Theatre fire, December 30, 1903, killed 600] you can imagine how nervous we were at the thought of fire. We found, though, it was farther away. The business part of the town was on fire, and the wind blowing at the rate of 60 miles an hour. It was a terrible sight; ten stores, two saloons and several other buildings burned. The next morning they found the charred remains of one poor drunken fellow who had burned to death. The wind being in the direction it was saved the town. We were all very nervous and were very glad when our engagement ended.[35]

Before leaving fire ravaged Congress, Della and all went down in a 3,750 feet deep mine. It was a novel experience, but not one that Della wanted to repeat very often.

Della didn't think much of the next town on the tour—Jerome, Arizona—where she and company appeared on January 14–15, 1904. In a letter written from this location she wrote:

The town of Jerome is one of the wonders of the world. We came over one of the crookedest roads in American to get here. It is 22 miles from the Junction, and it has 39 curves that outdo the famous Horseshoe curve. The richest copper mine in the world is here, owned by Senator Clark of Montana; they refused $90,000,000 for it.... The town is located on top of a volcanic eruption, and right below the main street is the crater, and it looks like hell with the fire pot out—that is the best description I can give of it. The company owns the town, stores, hotels, opera house and all the dwelling houses. It is a very good show town.[36]

As Della left Arizona to play a week at Albuquerque, New Mexico, she summed up her stay in the state: "The traveling is very hard in this country; the jumps are long and the towns are small and accommodations rather poor. Business is pretty good, and would be much better but all the shows are bunched up here at this time of the year, trying to escape the cold weather of the north."[37]

After closing their only date in New Mexico, Della's company crossed over into Texas to play the week of January 26, 1904, at El Paso, the first stop of what was known as the Greenwall Circuit. At the end of the El Paso stand Della and Adams took a flying trip into Mexico, but reported nothing of the visit.

Unfortunately, Della abandoned the practice of writing to the Knoxville paper while she toured Texas. Except for short notices in theatrical trade papers, there is little information on her Texas travels although Della performed in the state from late January to April of 1904. She played at Abilene the week of February 15 where local members of the Elks Club attended a show and after the performance treated Adams (a fellow Elk member), Della and the entire troupe to a "a social with a hop."[38]

Performances at Cleburne, Brownwood, and Temple followed before arriving at Corsicana on March 14. While there Della's husband invited the twenty-two players from the St. Louis American League team in spring training to a show.[39]

Leaving Corsicana on March 29, Della's troupe filled final Texas engagements at Sherman, Dallas and Fort Worth. Shows at Ardmore, Oklahoma, on April 9 and Oklahoma City the week of April 10 closed out the Jolly Della Pringle Company's 1903–1904 season.[40] Bridging the two seasons of 1903 and 1904, Della had traveled across the breadth of America—from the Atlantic Ocean to the Pacific Ocean. She played as far north as Portland, Maine and as far south as the Mexican border at El Paso, Texas. She had also been to the summit of California's Sierra Nevada mountains and to the depths of an Arizona gold mine. To say the least, it had been an epic tour.

7

To Court and to the Altar

In spite of the rigors of the 1903–1904 coast to coast tour, her husband pronounced Della never to be in better health when he returned to his Knoxville home on April 20, 1904. Still she had stopped off at Hot Springs, Arkansas, for almost a month of rest, relaxation, hot baths and therapeutic treatments for her stomach trouble.[1]

In the meantime G. Faith Adams had stored company baggage and scenery in Iowa before going to Chicago to supervise the refitting of a new fine Pullman car. Ever an opportunist, he bought it as a business speculation to be leased for parties traveling to the World's Fair in St. Louis.[2]

Della finally returned to Knoxville on May 18 in time to join Adams in hosting a visit by his mother beginning on May 25. Mrs. J. Faith, at age eighty, made the long trip from Philadelphia alone. On June 10, Della changed from host to guest and called on her brother and his family in Des Moines.[3]

Five days later, under the management of G. Faith Adams, Della Pringle chaperoned a party of enthusiastic and congenial young people on an excursion to the St. Louis World's Fair aboard Adams' new Pullman car which had been named "The Della" in honor of his wife. As she had done from time to time while on tour, Della wrote a lengthy letter to the *Knoxville Express* about the excursion and the attractions at the Fair.[4]

The party left Knoxville on Thursday, June 15. According to Della, no one got much sleep on the first night due to all the noise and confusion and the strangeness of the surroundings. Della's car had been hooked up to the Iowa governor's car with his staff from Des Moines. Some people in Della's group knew a few staff members and they visited back and forth between the two cars passing time in a most pleasant fashion on the way to the Fair.

Seeing the many attractions and exhibits at the Fair itself both excited and exhausted Della. She saw the Liberty Bell in the Pennsylvania building, a preserved ninety-seven foot whale at the Smithsonian institution, a

$12,000 sable coat at the Russian exhibit, a collection of unique Pullman cars in the Transportation building plus beautiful furniture, vases and embroidery work at the Chinese and Japanese exhibitions. Of course, Della had to see the stunning gowns in the French section of Manufacturer's Hall. She wrote that they were not only worth going to see, but that all dressmakers in America should see them.[5]

On one evening Della and several of her party went to see a big stage production of *Louisiana* at the Odeon Theatre. As Della wrote, "It was grand, they have 400 people in the cast. The play is historical, based on the purchase of the Louisiana territory, set to music. They have a fine orchestra of 25 pieces, a grand pipe organ, and the scenery and costumes are beautiful; lots of pretty girls, fine dancing, etc."[6]

Della and her young people spent several evenings strolling up and down the Pike, the main thoroughfare at the World's Fair. Again, Della wrote:

> Imagine a street nearly a mile long and thousands of lights, beautiful buildings of all sorts and colors with all the nations of the earth represented. You can see and hear more in one week at the world's fair about the different nations than you could in a lifetime of study. We saw all the real good shows on the Pike: "Creation," Hagenback's animal circus (no one ought to miss this—it is great), "Hale's Fire-Fighters," "Under and Over the Sea," "Galveston Flood," "Hereafter," "The Alps," Ferris Wheel, and last but not least, a ride on Thompson's Scenic railroad. This last made the biggest hit with our crowd of anything. Some of them rode as many as five times.[7]

Della ended her World's Fair letter with a description of how her party spent late evenings on The Della:

> Our car was so near the grounds we could sit in the observatory and see the Alps, the fountain playing, and the beautiful electrical effects, hear the bands playing, see the people coming and going to the fair, which alone was a great sight, and yet at night it was wonderfully quiet—not a train or engine to disturb us.... About twenty private cars were sidetracked by ours—some big railroad officials and their families. My brother, Mr. Van Winkle's car was just back of us, with thirty-two people. We all would get out on the platforms in the evening and visit or sing. We had pretty good singers in our crowd. One of the cars had a piano, and the porter was a great rag-time player. We had music "to eat by" and sleep by.[8]

After Della's trip to the World's Fair, her husband and brother, with his own Pullman car, continued the business of taking parties on weekly trips to the fair. In the meantime, Della busied herself with upkeep on home and farm. She did take time out in mid–July to travel to her friend

Corse Payton's hometown of Centerville, some fifty miles south of Knoxville. She sent a long letters about the trip to the *Knoxville Express* in which she complained about poor conditions on the railroad, reminisced about her early career in Iowa with the Payton and Spooner companies, compared Centerville with Knoxville, shared news about Corse Payton's achievements in his Brooklyn theatre and commented on her visits with various Centerville residents.[9]

Back in Knoxville on July 23, she entertained her sister-in-law, Mrs. J.E. Van Winkle, during a short visit. During the previous week Della had looked after the Van Winkle daughter, Grace, while he mother was in a Des Moines hospital.[10] This child, when mature, would follow Della into the theatrical profession.

On July 30 a sizable picture showing the observation end of her new Pullman car, The Della, appeared in the pages of the *New York Clipper*. According to the caption under the picture, the car had staterooms, a bathroom, an observation parlor and a Pullman standard sleeping section together with kitchen, toilets and other amenities. It accommodated twenty-nine passengers. The caption also revealed that the travel business to the World's Fair had been such a success that G.F. Adams would wait until November to take the Jolly Della Pringle Company on tour, thus giving Della a good long rest. The caption concluded with "The car has proven to be one of the best paying enterprises in which these people have invested."[11]

With the success of the excursions, the considerable financial gains of previous theatre seasons and the possession of a fine home and prosperous farming operation, the eight-year marriage of Della Pringle and G. Faith Adams seemed ideal. However, it came as a great surprise to Knoxville citizens to read in the paper of August 25, 1904, that Della Pringle had filed a petition for divorce with the clerk of the district court.[12]

After stating the date of Della's marriage to Adams and that she had at all times been true to him, the petition said, "but the defendant [Adams] disregarding his marriage vows and marital duties has since said marriage become addicted to drunkenness and has been guilty of such cruel and inhuman treatment of the plaintiff [Della] as to endanger her life."[13] Ironically, these allegations echoed those that disbanded her previous marriage to Johnny Pringle.

In the petition Della sought half of the couple's assets and the right to be known by her former name, Cora Della Pringle. The case would not be heard until the court's October term.[14] On or before October 12, 1904, Della Pringle and George Faith [his real name] were legally divorced.[15]

The bare outline of Della's divorce proceedings, as sad as it is, masks the real reason for the separation. The truth is revealed in a September 20, 1904, edition of the *Washington Times* which repeated an article from a Des Moines paper of the same date. The item shows the divorce to be a contrived and rather cold-blooded affair.[16]

At a time just before the August filing for a divorce, Adams bluntly asked his wife, "Don't you think it would be a good time, Della, for you to get a divorce?" Because there had never been a note of discord in their relationship, Della thought he was joking. But Adams meant every word he said and to her protests that she loved him as tenderly as ever he said, "Maybe you do, but I don't love you as I did, and I am not contented. The plain fact is, Della, that you are no longer the woman I love."[17]

The disturbing dialogue continued with Della inquiring, "Who is the other woman? I never saw anything wrong." Adams responded, "There isn't anything wrong. It doesn't make any difference who the woman is. I don't love you any longer and we simply cannot live together." Della than pleaded, "Then what is the matter? We have always got along splendidly together and prospered. I hope I haven't done anything to offend you." He assured her, "Certainly not. You are all right, only we can't live together under the circumstances, and I want a divorce. I am willing to do whatever you think is right."[18]

Della countered with:

> But we haven't any grounds for a divorce. You can't accuse me of anything and a know nothing against you. We never had a cross word in our lives that is worth the name. You are not a drunkard and you've always behaved properly as far as I know. I hope you don't think I have done anything wrong.[19]

To this Adams said,

> Of course not; that's all right. But we must get a divorce and it will be a kindness to you to permit you to get it. I am willing to let you file any reasonable charge against me and will arrange the alimony in advance so as to satisfy you thoroughly. You might charge me with cruel and inhuman treatment for it's pretty cruel to tell your wife you don't love her anymore and want a divorce.[20]

Still in disbelief, Della pleaded, "Surely, George, you don't mean this. I must be dreaming." He replied:

> Not much, you are wide awake. This is no dream. I am willing to give you all our theatrical stuff, our home here in Knoxville and our farm besides. Yes, and I'll pay you $50 a month alimony, too, for two years. I should like to retain our private car, Della, and run excursions in it. I

trust you will be good enough to concede this much when I am giving you everything else I possess. It is handing you $150,000 in cold cash and paying alimony besides.[21]

Finally convinced that Adams wanted a divorce, literally at all costs, Della gave in and said, "It is mighty hard, George, but if you insist I suppose there is no other way out of this."[22] She heeded his advice filed for divorce citing the false accusations he had suggested.

Della had reason to be deeply hurt by Adam's coldness and the divorce forced on her, but from it she gained considerable wealth and became the sole manager of her successful theatrical company. In early October, even before her divorce was final, she announced she would open her fourteenth season at Knoxville[23] and on the thirteenth left for New York to visit, see new plays, look at the latest fashions and make contact with potential company members.[24]

After returning to her home, Della chronicled her eastern trip in a long, newsy letter to the *Knoxville Express* on November 16. Townspeople seemed interested in her travels so she promised to "give them an idea of what I saw and did in a few week's visit to the great metropolis of New York City."[25]

Except for visiting the Spooners and Paytons, friends from her early theatrical career in Iowa, Della had no definite plans for her stay in New York. She contemplated finding an engagement with an eastern stock company but found the good troupes already filled. Then she decided to spend her time visiting, learning new songs and getting new ideas for her own use and benefit."

Della found the theatrical situation to be bad in the East. Her status in the professional theatre was such that she gained access to managers and the editor of the *New York Dramatic Mirror* who informed her that the season was the worst in fifteen years. Some forty failures had already occurred, all attributed to poor plays and over production.[26]

During her time in New York, Della attended about a dozen plays, some on Broadway and others by the Spooner and Payton companies in Brooklyn. On Broadway she saw productions with two famous stars—the internationally acclaimed British actress, Mrs. Patrick Campbell and America's Dustin Farnum. She found the Brooklyn shows to be great and enjoyed them as much as the two dollar shows over in New York.[27]

When Della arrived to visit Corse Payton and Etta Reed, she found them in the middle of a move into a new flat. The new dwelling connected with Payton's adjacent theatre by means of a little covered bridge, enabling the Payton's to walk conveniently out of their apartment into the dressing rooms and on to the stage of the theatre.[28]

Della began her Payton visit by helping Etta straighten up her new home, hanging curtains, pictures and draperies. When finished the apartment looked so lovely that the Paytons decided to invite Della and the fifteen members of Payton's stock company to a house warming after an evening performance. As Della described it, "They spared no expense; all their beautiful cut glass and hand-painted china were brought out and we had a centerpiece on the dining table that cost $45."[29] The menu offered a dozen items—to be washed down by twelve quarts of Mumm's "Extra Dry" champagne. Della observed, "the house was 'warmed' in good style, wit and wisdom flew through the air" fostered by all the champagne that had loosened the tongues of the clever actors. By two in the morning, guests repaired to the parlor for a preview of some music from a new musical comedy that Corse Payton intended to present during Christmas week. To Della it all seemed to be so "bright and gay."[30]

Della's letter continued with an account of attending a play in Brooklyn starring former heavyweight boxing champion, Bob Fitzsimmons. She judged him to be a better actor than one would imagine. The play, *A Fight for Love*, had been written for Fitzsimmons and showcased his blacksmith and pugilistic talents. In the first act he pounded out a horseshoe on stage and then shod a horse with it. In subsequent acts he gave an exhibition of bag punching and engaged in a prizefight. Fitzsimmons' manager, a former associate of Corse Payton, treated Della to a box seat and arranged for her to go backstage and receive one of the horseshoes made by Fitzsimmons as a souvenir for her home. Della declared, "I'm going to gild it and hang it over my door for good luck."[31]

The last week Della spent in Brooklyn Etta Reed had time off and they went around together. They had several automobile rides through Prospect Park to see the leaves turning color with the approach of fall. They also attended an excellent production of *Fabio Romoni* at the Columbia Theatre that led to an interesting incident for Della.[32]

After entering the Columbia Theatre and taking her seat, Della opened her program and found to her surprise and delight Ida Adair Pringle's name listed in the cast. She was Johnny Pringle's second wife and the mother of a seven-year-old boy named Cecil. Johnny and Ida separated two years before and he had remarried. Della sent her card backstage, stating on it that Della Pringle would be pleased to meet Ida Pringle. Upon receiving the card, Ida sent out for Della to come right back to her dressing room. Della described the meeting, "I went and such a greeting she gave me! She laughed and kissed me, and called the other members into the dressing room and introduced me, it was like sisters meeting after a long separation."[33]

Although this was the first meeting with Ida and little Cecil, Della knew her parents from visits to their home in Logan, Utah when on tours in the West. Della thought Ida a beautiful woman and was "glad to see her succeed and prosper."[34] What Della and Ida could not know at the time was that Ida's boy Cecil would grow up to become the fabled silent film star, John Gilbert. The paths of Della Pringle and John Cecil Gilbert would cross again in 1917 when both were part of the California movie industry.

Before leaving New York, Della took a ride on the new subway, "one of the greatest undertakings in modern history." She was impressed to see 200,000 people emerge from the subway and streetcars on their way home in the evening. She also found the subway a bit frightening. "You go so fast you can't see out the window, the rate of 60 miles an hour, and when another train passes you jump like you were shot."[35]

Della left New York and stopped off at Akron, Ohio, for a two day visit with Daniel Ely, the now retired leading man in Della's 1902–1903 Corse Payton Comedy Company, on his recently purchased farm. After a lengthy description of Ely's dairy farm business, Della disclosed that she showed the ex-actor that she knew something about farming when she went out and milked one of his cows. With pride she wrote: "They didn't believe I could do it but I proved it."[36]

She left Akron for Chicago but due to a missed connection had to spend thirteen hours in Chicago. She spent the time window shopping and taking in a fine vaudeville bill at the Olympic Theatre.[37]

Della arrived back in Knoxville with some new gowns purchased in New York. She announced she had engaged some clever people for her company and expected to open a season at the local opera house sometime in December.[38]

The details are missing, but by November 25 Della had once again acquired her Pullman car, The Della, and began assembling her company. Since The Della could accommodate almost thirty people, Della decided to carry a band and orchestra as she had done once before.[39] She eventually had a complete company of twenty or twenty-two with about ten in the acting troupe and a like amount filling the band and orchestra positions.[40]

For her acting troupe Della, now the sole proprietor of her company, hired a business manager, T.O. Tuttle, who doubled as an actor. She brought back old Pringle favorites—William Echols, Charles Archer, Marie Van Etten and W.H. Bruno—and added Gracie Eloise as her juvenile star along with Gertrude Steele, Walter Scott and a comedian, Mr. Burns.[41] Late in her tour she replaced Echols with R.B. Scott and Van Etten with Edese Fowler.[42]

As for the musical half of the Pringle company, Professor J.B. Adams served as director of the "operatic" orchestra and Professor Charles Stevens led the band in noonday parades down the streets to drum up business for matinee and evening performances.[43] Seven other musicians participated in both the band and orchestra with some actors assisting when needed.

In addition to actors and musicians, Della's company had an advance man (A.J. Kahn), an electrician and prop master (R.W. Conant), a chef (Clarence Hubbard) and a porter (Joshua Price). Two bulldogs trained in high jumping and bag punching, an extremely popular specialty, completed the company.[44]

Della's troupe presented some ten productions during the 1904–1905 tour. From previous seasons she retained *Mansion of Aching Hearts*, *The Sultan's Daughter* and *Thelma*. New scripts included *The Christian*, *The Marriage of Kitty*, *When Her Soul Speaks*, *No Cross, No Crown* and a farce comedy, *The Little Detective*.

Della opened her season with a three-night engagement in her hometown on December 19. Pre-show publicity promised "a coterie of actors and actresses of the better class," an excellent band and orchestra, clever specialty acts and "tons of new scenery, mechanical and electrical."[45] Ladies were invited to view the magnificent costumes worn Miss Pringle in the opening performance—"Each beautiful creation of art imported directly from Worth the famous French costumer."[46] The production of *The Christian* displayed special scenery and duplicate costuming of that used by Viola Allen in her New York production of the drama.

Following a successful opening in Knoxville, Della and company completed the year playing three-night stands in the nearby Iowa towns of Hiteman, Milo and Chariton. All was rather unremarkable except for the final New Year's Eve performance in Chariton when Della Pringle once again became a bride!

The *Chariton Herald* described the event as follows:

> Miss Della Pringle ... honored this city in a peculiar and highly original manner at the close of her three nights' engagement last week. The last appearance was on Saturday night, and after the last act in that night's play, "The Christian," Della and her business manager, T.O. Tuttle, appeared on the platform in a sure enough wedding outfit, with two bridesmaids and two grooms men, with their own band and orchestra and their company of players and, with the aid of Mayor I.N. Bowman, were united in the bonds of wedlock. The wedding was not a part of the play, but was part of the show. It was the real thing, and whether it was consummated for purposes of economy in traveling, or merely because of burning affection between the leading lady and her manager, we do

not know. It was certainly something entirely new in the annals of showdom and not only brought Chariton into the limelight..., but swelled the door receipts for the show company in a most encouraging manner. Della was never bound much by the prosaic customs of society, and if she chose to be married in an armory hall on the last night of a half week engagement with the whole audience as wedding guests, it is nobody's business. And as often as she has tried matrimony and failed to make it stick, she still returns to it, we cannot but admire her grit.[47]

Little is known about Della's new groom. A Knoxville paper described him as "a gentleman of fine address, a pleasing actor ... [who] made a good impression upon all he came in contact."[48] Judging from his picture in a South Dakota newspaper, he was handsome and quite attractive.

Della and Tuttle had no time for a honeymoon as the company crossed over into Nebraska to spend the first ten days of the new year with three-night engagements at Broken Bow, Alliance and Chadron. During the stand in Alliance, the press observed:

> "Jolly Della" has played many visits in past years and the majority of our people can almost claim a personal acquaintance with her. Though she has spent many years on the stage, Father Time seems dealing lightly with her, and she appears in public apparently as young, gay and clever as ever.[49]

From Nebraska the Pringle company turned north for a series of performances in South Dakota during the rest of January and the first week in February. As they had done in many previous seasons, crowds filled theatres in the South Dakota towns of Hot

T.O. Tuttle, Della's third husband (printed in the *Aberdeen Daily News* [South Dakota], September 22, 1905).

Springs, Rapid City, Sturgis, Belle Fourche, Lead City, Deadwood, Spearfish, Central City and Custer.

During the stay at Rapid City, a reporter from the local press invited to go aboard the company's private car noted that "everything is provided for the comfort of the company, and they can live on the car with almost as much ease at home" and added that "a fine chef and porter look after the wants of the company and make traveling a luxury."[50] That same afternoon Della invited her friends to visit her in her private car—an invitation issued several times on the tour.

While the crowds were warm and friendly, the South Dakota weather was not. Della wrote in the *New York Clipper*:

> The company experienced some cold weather in January, the temperature registering forty degrees below zero for over two weeks in the Black Hills where we were playing at the time. The women came to the theatre bringing hot water bottles with them to keep their feet warm. It was so cold in some of the theatres that we actually suffered, but in spite of all this, we played to splendid business.[51]

While the public reception of Della's troupe in South Dakota was warm and cordial, sometimes enthusiastic, one reporter in Central City on February 8 objected to the actors' onstage behavior and to an attempt to "gold-brick" audience members. He admitted that the troupe "gave a fair performance" and "demonstrated they had the ability to put on a good show." However, he felt the actors "fell down in several instances on account of too much levity, probably stimulated by a superabundance of booze." Finally, he observed that it is "very annoying ... to see a serious portion of the piece marred by too much giggling." Such breaches in stage decorum might have been overlooked if the management hadn't attempted to charge and extra two bits for a "concert" after the performance. Ticket vendors passing through the house received a very chilly reception and patrons in the gallery gave such a "roasting" that the sellers hurried back to the stage and announced that the "concert" had been abandoned and money would be returned. The reporter ended his item with: "Central City people may not be used to metropolitan ways ... but they know when they are being "gold-bricked."[52] This questionable attempt to squeeze extra money from the audience doesn't seem to have been repeated during the remainder of Della's tour.

On a more positive note, a critic from the Deadwood paper wrote a rare and illuminating evaluation of Della's acting talents. After noting Della had appeared in Deadwood for at least ten years, he added:

> Those that have heard her during the time she has been coming to the hills have noted the improvement from year to year, and at no time has the advancement of her art been greater than during the past year. While she is still mistress of the light roles in which she won the title of "Jolly Della," she now excels in heavier parts and in the admiration of her interpretation of such as that she appeared last evening. One feels that she has outgrown the title of "Jolly." She is still jolly, and can do the jolly business better than any other person who makes the hills towns and she can also do the heavy emotional parts.[53]

After leaving the frigid conditions in South Dakota, Della's troupe spent the last three weeks of February touring through Wyoming with brief engagements at Edgemont, Cambria and New Castle before a week's stay in Cheyenne. After three performances in Laramie, Della's troupe played the week of February 23 in Sheridan which ended the sojourn in Wyoming.

Della, Tuttle and company moved on into Montana, opening for a week at Billings on February 27 followed by a week at Bozeman. From there Della abandoned early plans to play to the Pacific coast and led her troupe east into North Dakota by way of Glendive, Montana.

The three-day engagements of Della's troupe at Dickson and Mandan, North Dakota, elicited no critical press commentary related to its performances. However, shows at Bismarck during the week of March 27 drew praise in the local press which termed Della's troupe "an organization high class in all particulars" and observed, "Rarely do theatre goers have an opportunity to witness anything so good at popular prices."[54]

After a week of attracting increasingly fuller audiences in Bismarck, the performers spent the week of April 3 in Valley City and then closed the season's tour at Casselton, North Dakota, about April 16.[55] After the Jolly Della Pringle Company disbanded, Della and Tuttle set off on another entertainment venture.

In a letter from Spokane, Washington, dated April 25, 1905, to the *Knoxville Journal*, T.O. Tuttle revealed the particulars of the new venture. First, he reported on the close of a successful season and revealed the leasing of the Pullman Car Della to the Iowa Tourist Association for tours to Portland, Oregon, for the Lewis and Clark Exposition. Next, he commented that Della's troupe had opened up quite a bit of new territory with such excellent financial results that it would be included in regular future routes. Finally he revealed that he and Della were playing vaudeville houses in Montana and the Pacific Northwest presenting their bag punching bulldog specialty as part of a vaudeville bill. Tuttle wrote,

> While playing at Bozeman, Mont., a few weeks ago, the circuit manager happened to witness the bag punching act of Billy and Bob, the bulldogs, and immediately made an offer for the act for eight weeks over his circuit. When we closed our own season, we accepted his terms of $600 for the eight weeks and are now filling the time. The act is a big hit out here and is creating much comment.[56]

He concluded his letter, "We shall continue on to Vancouver, Seattle, Tacoma, Portland, etc., take in the [Lewis and Clark] Exposition and return home to prepare for the coming season."[57]

Della's first and only vaudeville tour ended abruptly after only two weeks. On May 1, 1905, she and the dogs appeared at Portland, Oregon's Grand Theatre for the first night of a week's engagement.[58] Here she received word that her mother, Mrs. Ira Kendrick, was gravely ill back in Knoxville, Iowa.

Della left Portland immediately and upon reaching Knoxville found her mother in a dangerous condition suffering from a stomach tumor.[59] By the end of May Della accompanied her mother to the Iowa Sanitarium at Des Moines. After a week at the sanitarium her mother was no better, in fact she was worse, and Della brought her home.[60]

8

Seasons of Challenge

Operating a theatrical enterprise had always been challenging, but Della Pringle's 1905–1906 season would present greater challenges than ever before. She had to see to the care of her ailing mother who, in addition to a stomach tumor, suffered with rheumatism and heart trouble. Then Della had to oversee the maintenance of her large home and the operation of her stock farm. In between these major responsibilities, Della, with the aid of her husband, carried out the usual tasks associated with forming a theatre company: recruiting actors and specialty artists, obtaining performance rights for plays, negotiating their royalties, purchasing or fabricating scenery, buying new wardrobe, arranging for the printing of publicity posters and handbills, contracting with theatre managers for performance dates and making travel arrangements with railroad agents.

For the new season Della signed two performers from the end of the last tour—Edese Fowler and William Bruno. Papers lauded Bruno as the greatest comedian in the West and a "man of infinite jest."[1] In addition to acting, the comedian doubled as stage manager and performed several specialties: parodies, monologues and comic songs. Unfortunately for Della, Bruno left the troupe in mid–December of 1905.

The remainder of the twelve-person troupe consisted of actors new to the troupe. As usual, Della featured a juvenile star and this year's "phenomenal child actress" was Baby Rossie Maclan. Miss Olive McConnell, who would be with Della for many seasons, was a Canadian actress from Toronto. Music director Katherine Stein also acted in supporting roles. The multi-talented Maude Donelly acted, led the illustrated song specialty and performed the "fire dance," a perennial specialty of Della's troupes. Eddie Lamont, sometimes billed Professor Lamont, brought several skills to the troupe. He was renowned as a world champion baton twirler and recognized as a skilled musician able to play many novel musical instruments. Lamont also acted and served as property master.[2]

Press notices and reviews reveal little about other company actors: Mr. and Mrs. E.C. Walck, Joe C. Berry, Joseph D. Herbert and George Hasbrook (who also served as advance agent). Of course Della and Tuttle acted major roles with Della also appearing in comedy sketches with comedian Bruno and Tuttle filling in as stage carpenter.[3]

Above all were the stars of the six specialty acts carried by the company, Bill and Bob, the bag-punching bulldogs. Hardly a review of a Pringle performance appeared that did not at least mention the canine act and most lavished much praise on their high jumping and bag punching abilities.

Della mounted some dozen productions during the 1905–1906 season. She held over some plays from previous seasons such as *The Christian*, the clean wholesome comedy *The Sultan's Daughter* and *The Little Detective* which was often presented for children's matinees. This play required Della to quickly change in and out of five disguises: a society belle, a ragged news girl, an old apple lady, a foppish dude and a Sister of Charity.

She added some new plays, some with enormous royalties. One was a Sherlock Holmes–like melodrama, *Sheridan Keene, Detective*. Della not only secured rights for *Adrift in the World*, but purchased the scenery from the Broadway production of the great drama of life in New England. This play may have been presented under the alternate title of *Way Down East*. Della chose *A Southern Romance*, a tale of the south during reconstruction days, for the opportunity to play the

Della Pringle around age 35 in her production of *The Christian* (courtesy the National Society for the Preservation of Tent, Folk and Repertoire Theatre as the Theatre Museum of Repertoire Americana, Midwest Old Threshers, Mt. Pleasant, Iowa).

challenging role of the blind Roanoke which fitted her style of acting and required depicting a range of emotions from the light hearted to almost tragic pathos.[4] Presentations of *Missouri Girl, In the Shadow of the Cross, Dora Thorne, The Little Mother* and *Wealth and Poverty* completed the season's offerings.

Della took the train to Chicago on August 5 to complete some theatrical arrangements and then returned to Knoxville to conduct rehearsals of plays for the new season.[5] As she had done for nearly a decade, Della opened her season in the Knoxville Opera House, an abandoned skating rink fitted up with a poorly appointed stage and common chairs for seating. Due to the summer heat, the manager made efforts to keep patrons cool and comfortable with electric fans and serving ice water between acts.[6]

The Jolly Della Pringle Company opened the season on August 14 with a performance of *A Southern Romance* and filled the rest of the three-day engagement with presentations of *Adrift in the World* and *Sheridan Keene, Detective.* All shows were well received and drew large audiences. The *Knoxville Journal* hailed the company as Della's best ever with "capable people" well up in their profession.[7]

The troupe moved on for a three-night stand in Walnut, Iowa, for August 17–19. On Saturday, the final day of the engagement, Della received a telegram informing her that her mother had passed away in Knoxville. She immediately left for home, arriving there that evening.[8]

Della's mother had been found dead in her bathtub by her husband at five-thirty in the morning. Exactly how she died was not certain. Although her body was submerged in a full tub of water with only the upper part of her head and nose above water, she had not disrobed and still wore her nightclothes. She had been suffering from severe headaches. It was surmised she sought relief by bathing and died of a convulsion.[9]

Della and her brother made arrangements for their mother's funeral which was held in her home at 2:00 p.m. on Sunday. After writing a note to the paper thanking the people of Knoxville for their expressions of sympathy, Della left and rejoined her troupe at Guthrie Center, Iowa about August 22.[10]

After playing at Glenwood, Iowa, on August 24, Della did not report her theatrical engagements in the trade papers during the period between August 25 and September 17. By the seventeenth of September her troupe began a week's stand at Madison, South Dakota. Although Della and her various companies had toured through South Dakota for at least a decade, this tour was the first east of the Missouri River.

8—Seasons of Challenge

Performances during the Madison engagement earned high praise day after day in the press. Before the closing presentation the local paper offered this summation:

> In reviewing their offerings during the current week it is impossible to say too many good things for Miss Pringle and [her] capable company. Each play presented shows careful attention to detail, scenic effects and costuming. Each individual member of the company deserves praise for careful, painstaking, conscientious work. A company evenly balanced, showing careful direction. Miss Pringle has succeeded in establishing herself firmly in the hearts of Madison theatre-goers on the first visit to the city, and her return engagements will be looked forward to with much interest. For a number of years a great favorite in the Black Hills, her reputation as an artist had preceded her and much was expected of her. No one has been disappointed and the engagement has been an unusually successful one.[11]

Della enjoyed another successful engagement at Aberdeen, South Dakota, the week of September 25. She received the usual praise in the press and proved so popular that a local socialite gave a reception in her honor. About a dozen ladies attended the afternoon event and consumed a two-course luncheon. A local woman joined with Della and Mrs. Walck of her company to entertain the ladies with a medley of songs.[12]

Leaving Aberdeen, Della's troupe next performed in South Dakota's state capital, Pierre, the week of October 2. During this stand Olive McConnell of the company took out her first naturalization papers at a local court. Born in Canada, she wished to become an American citizen in order to file a homestead claim. She joined a half dozen other performers, including Della and Tuttle, who filed claims for 160-acre homestead sites near Grindstone, South Dakota.[13]

The following week the Jolly Della Pringle Company played its last dates in South Dakota at Huron before heading up to North Dakota for a series of one-week stands at Mandan, Bismarck and Dickinson. Only the paper at Bismarck commented at any length about the troupe. In addition to positive reviews, the editor of the *Bismarck Daily Tribune* printed the following poem about Della and her troupers.

The Big Show
A few more days and then behold,
The scenery comes in paint and gold
Ten Tons of it, maybe more,
All new and never been used here before.
It outdoes any ever seen
Since Cleopatra ruled as queen.
What will there be? We haven't space

The different scenes herein we trace.
And the ladies fair and gallant men
Too fair and brave for any pen
To do them justice, even though
The quill was pushed by Cicero
And all the ladies and Greeks
Of whom prolific Pliny speaks.
And at night up on the stage
A drama or comedy is all the rage;
Holy Moses you must go
To see Della Pringle and her show.
Take your sweetheart! Take your wife!
Or hired girl, you bet your life!
Take the babies! Take them all!
For the Pringle show, it beats the ball!
You can't afford it? Go for grass!
You can't afford to let it pass!
Jar loose and take the big show in,
Enjoy the play, music, glitter and din!
Give all the folks a holiday,
For Della Pringle hip, hooray![14]

After Bismarck Della's troupe played the week of November 6 in Dickinson, located almost on the western border of North Dakota. From there Della turned around and jumped to the northeast corner of the state to fill a three-day stand at Devil's Lake. Then the performers moved westward again playing one to three-night stands in small towns such as Leeds, New Rockford and Rugby during late November and early December. The company finished the tour of North Dakota with week-long performances at Minot and Williston before Christmas.[15]

Next, Della's company entered Montana, playing the week after Christmas at Harve.[16] Della and Tuttle lead the troupe southward through the state for two weeks and exited with three performances at Dillon the first week of January 1906.[17]

In the middle of January the actors were performing in southeastern Idaho in Rexburg, St. Anthony and Blackfoot.[18] In the two weeks between January 23 and February 5 the whereabouts of Della's troupe is not known, but they could have visited more eastern Idaho towns or sites in northern Utah. Della's troupe did play in Evanston, Wyoming the week of February 5 and traveled to Rock Springs for its next engagement.[19] Della had planned to fill more dates in Wyoming on her way to the welcoming audiences in the familiar territory of South Dakota's Black Hills.

The 1905–1906 tour of the Jolly Della Pringle Company ended abruptly, almost tragically, in its twenty-seventh week at Rock Springs, Wyoming, about February 17.[20] The catastrophic event ending the tour began simply enough when Della, who had suffered from stomach trouble for a number of years, sought relief from indigestion and asked a local pharmacist for bicarbonate of soda. Instead of dispensing the harmless chemical, the pharmacist made a stupid mistake and gave her a corrosive prescription of carbolic acid which she unknowingly ingested. She immediately experienced searing pain in her throat and stomach and only timely action by a company member saved her from dying. Tuttle rushed his stricken wife to the Battle Creek Sanitarium in Des Moines.[21] After some two weeks of intensive treatment, Della and Tuttle returned to Knoxville in late February.

Due to Della's compromised health, she and Tuttle had no intention to resume a theatrical tour. Nevertheless, they traveled a great deal during the remainder of 1906. On March 14 Della, still recovering from her stomach trouble, left Iowa with her brother, his wife and daughter for California.[22] Due to flooding in the West, they stopped off in El Paso, Texas and remained there until early April. Her brother also had health problems that were alleviated by the warm weather and dry air in El Paso.

Meanwhile, T.O. Tuttle returned briefly to Knoxville and from there on March 22 traveled onward to visit the couple's homestead claim in North Dakota.[23] He went back to El Paso to join Della and in early April they went to California to explore possible places for relocation.

After visiting various coastal and inland resorts, Della and her husband arrived in Long Beach, California, about April 18. Finding the city to her liking, Della soon purchased a beautiful family hotel, the Ardmore, located at the corner of Elm and East Ocean. Rather rapidly Della and Tuttle gained recognition in local society. The *Long Beach Tribune* found them "charming people in their private life" and that they had paid the city a great compliment by locating there.[24]

There had been earlier reports that Della would retire from the stage. However, the Long Beach paper reported that she had not retired to private life permanently. She was taking a much-needed rest and would not re-enter performing this season.[25]

According to the paper of April 25, Della had made arrangements to ship her furniture from her Iowa home, the Maples, to take the place of the furnishings in the Ardmore Hotel. The paper also reported:

> Among other things Mrs. Tuttle will have all her beautiful imported gowns which she wears on stage sent here and her curios and souvenirs that she has accumulated. Among them are gifts from many great Americans as well as nobility. She prizes the collection given by Col. Cody or "Buffalo Bill" perhaps the most of all. They include some beautiful elk horns. She was often a guest in his home.[26]

As her health improved, Della became more involved in the social life of Long Beach. She had brought her performing bulldogs, Bob and Billie, with her to California and on April 24 she aided a benefit for the survivors of the San Francisco earthquake by performing with her dogs in their hilarious bag-punching act.[27] About this time she hinted to a reporter that if a theatre were built in the city she might be inclined to head a stock company. Later, in September, she took part in a masquerade party at the Long Beach skating rink and won opera glasses for the most picturesque lady costume, a graceful and elegant pink gown which made her a "conspicuous figure" amid those watching 300 skaters gliding and whirling about the floor.[28]

Less enamored of the social scene, Della's husband tired of being a hotel manager and sought a theatre position. By early July he joined the Frank Rich Company in El Paso, Texas, for an extended engagement.[29] Della remained in California and resumed her own theatre career.

Della returned to the stage in Oliver Morosco's production of *The Halfbreed* at Morosco's Burbank Theatre on July 16. Her role of Marianne Adair, a circus rider, was not a large one, but she assured manager Morosco she would make it a leading part if given the role which he did.[30] Although the play did not receive strong reviews, it drew turn-away audiences and ran for over a month. To appear in this minor role Della had to travel twenty miles to and from the Ardmore Hotel and the theatre on an electric streetcar. For her efforts she received notices in the Long Beach paper and had her picture displayed in the *Los Angeles Examiner* and the *New York Dramatic Mirror*.[31]

While her return to acting went well, her marriage to T.O. Tuttle did not. In a letter from El Paso to the *Knoxville Express* of August 26, 1906, Tuttle stated that he would seek a divorce from Della Pringle. He wrote: "Della and I have finally separated, she remains in Long Beach, California. Too much Adams to suit me—so we've decided to end a bad bargain."[32]

The cryptic "Too much Adams to suit me" refers to the re-entrance of George Faith Adams, Della's former husband, into her life. After an amicable parting from Della, Adams remarried, became a father and formed his own theatre company, Adams' Comedians. During one of her trips back to Iowa from Long Beach, Della met with Adams and his new wife. Della found the wife charming and the three became close friends.[33] Adams and Della established a professional relationship, perhaps to plan forming a stock company in Long Beach.[34] Evidently, Tuttle viewed the situation unfavorably which spurred him to seek a divorce.

Tuttle may have had "too much Adams," but Della had had too much Tuttle. She announced intentions to file a counter suit against him.

In early September, prior to returning to Knoxville from Long Beach, she wrote to the *Knoxville Express* that she intended to prosecute divorce proceedings against Tuttle upon her arrival in Iowa later in the month.[35] She defended her actions by stating, "When I am attacked in my home by a stranger and adventurer I think it only right I vindicate myself."[36] She said had hoped to continue the marriage but that Tuttle was bound to force a divorce and since her reputation and business interests were involved she had no choice except to seek a divorce.[37]

In her letter Della pointed out that she had closed last season's profitable tour not only because of her accidental poisoning, but because her hard work and business responsibilities were made even harder by Tuttle's abuse, quarrelling, demands to spend money unnecessarily and his deception in business and other matters.[38] Having married Tuttle just five weeks after they first met, she soon found she had made a mistake and took steps to rectify it. Della had already consulted local lawyers about the possibility of divorce earlier in March before her departure to California,[39] but evidently decided to give her marriage to Tuttle another chance.

Judging from Della's divorce decree filed on October 19, 1906, in Knoxville, matters with Tuttle had grown worse. The divorce petition alleged that Tuttle, even though Della had remained a "kind and loving wife" throughout their marriage, "treated her so cruelly and inhumanely as to endanger her life."[40] Specifically, Della charged that on several occasions in front of their troupe and friends Tuttle "cursed her, called her a whore" and other vile and indecent names.[41] Further, he had "struck her, kicked her, driven her from her room at night [and] threatened her life."[42] This inhumane treatment so impaired Della's health that she abandoned her work and sought help at a Long Beach health resort. She claimed her nervous system became so affected from Tuttle's mistreatment that doctors advised her life was in danger if the mental strain continued.[43]

After stating her case against Tuttle, Della requested an "absolute" divorce and the restoration of her former name. She also asked to recover her legal costs for the divorce action and that she be given "such other and general equitable relief as the court may think here entitled to."[44] Tuttle was not present to contest the divorce and gained nothing from it. In Knoxville on December 7 the divorced was granted and Della's third marriage formally ended.[45]

In view of Tuttle's abusive behavior, Della felt little remorse at his parting. It was a different matter when she endured the loss of her Boston bulldog, Billie. In Long Beach she mourned the death of her pet that a callous neighbor shot when the dog walked across a partially dried cement walk. Della had been given Billie four years before during her tour of northeastern states. He had often appeared before the footlights with Della. He did tricks like punching a boxing bag with his nose and running up an eleven-foot perpendicular wall to retrieve a handkerchief. He also carried his trappings in his own little suitcase and would not travel without it. Della felt his loss keenly and instituted a suit for damages against the man who killed her dog.[46]

In between the steps leading to divorce, Della began to sever her ties to Knoxville. She returned there in mid–October to arrange for the sale of her farm and her home. On November 3 she sold her "farm of eighty acres two miles southeast of town" for $7,600.[47] Within the same week, her home—The Maples—was listed as for sale.[48] Shortly before these Iowa transactions, she seems to have put her real estate holdings in Long Beach up for sale.

Having disposed of all Knoxville property, Della left town on November 13 to see her brother and family in Colorado Springs for a week. She returned on November 21 and began the task of organizing another theatre company.[49] She went to Chicago in early December to recruit actors and arrange bookings for a tour.[50] Before the end of the month Della was advertising her opening in Knoxville on New Year's Day, 1907.[51]

The opening of Della's 1907 theatre season was a first and a last. It would be her first appearance in Knoxville's new theatre facility, the Rigg's Opera House, which had just opened in September. The 1,000-seat, well-appointed, first-class theatre with its comfortable opera chairs was a decided improvement over the old converted skating rink that Della performed in for over a decade.[52] The January engagement would also be the last time Della would ever open a season in Knoxville or appear before a local audience. Her acting career would last at least another decade but her audiences would be those of the far West and Canada.

As she had done so often in the past, Della Pringle employed a mixture of familiar and new actors for her 1907 company. Counting Della, the troupe had thirteen performers. When a Knoxville reporter asked if she were superstitious about the number she replied that she had done some of her best business on Friday the 13th.[53]

Players returning from previous seasons were Mr. and Mrs. Ezra Walch, Mrs. Gertrude Steele, Maude Donnelly and Olive McConnell, Mrs. Steele was married to Fred Bates, the new business manager and Olive McConnell had married a musician, "Mac" McMinn, who performed in specialties for Della's company. Other members of the troupe were Al Gorrel, W.C. Weston, Fred Stevens and pianist Fred Martin.[54] Della originally announced that Baby Gorrel would be this season's child star, but soon replaced her with Laura "Babe" Laird, a petite adult actress who could be passed off as a child performer. The company experienced one change of personnel during the season when Claude Kelly took over as business manager in early March of 1907.

Of course, no Pringle troupe would be complete without an abundance of specialty acts. The one specialty act mentioned most often on the tour featured Olive McConnell and her husband, McMinn, billed as "Olive and Mac." She impressed audiences and reviewers with her ability to hit extremely high notes in her cornet solos. McMinn pleased with his violin playing, then switched to slide trombones to join Olive in a stirring brass duet.[55] Other specialties offered in previous seasons presumably continued in 1907 and included Della in songs and comedy sketches along with Marie Donnelly in dances and illustrated songs.

Reviews written during the 1907 season mention a dozen different plays presented by the Pringle players. *A Southern Romance* (which allowed Della to reprise her role of the blind country girl, Roanoke) and *Dangers of the Great City* were repeated from Della's last season. In a new play, *True American Girl*, Della played two contrasting roles: Twister, a simple country girl, and Miss Saratoga, a British stage queen. A melodrama, *The Lighthouse Robbery*, thrilled audiences with its scenic effects, and a farce, *Irish 400*, provoked prolonged laughter. *California, Belle of Richmond, The Chorus Girl, Her Mad Marriage, The Cowboy's Girl, The Man in the Case* and *Masquerade Ball* (presented at matinees) made up the remainder of the repertory.

Due to its late start, the 1907 Pringle season lasted only sixteen weeks, from early January to mid–April. Della did not play in any new territory, but mostly in towns visited in previous seasons for engagements ranging from three days to two weeks.

As was her custom for over a decade, Della opened her 1907 season at Knoxville before a hometown crowd with a three evening engagement beginning on New Year's Day.[56] This was followed by a week at Webster, Iowa's, Armory Opera House. Reviews there found the troupe "without doubt above the average of 'ten-twent-thirt' companies." One newspaper item pointed out that although surnamed "Jolly," Della "had the power to stir hearts in serious roles."[57] Such praise resulted in full houses for the week.

Della's company next performed for a week at Sioux City, Iowa, in the Lyric Theatre. The *Sioux City Journal* described the company as "one of the best and strongest of its class" with special acclaim for Babe Laird, Fred Stephen and Claude Kelly for their "ease of playing."[58]

The Pringle company traveled on to South Dakota, first appearing in Yankton the week of January 21[59] and then in a three-night stand at Huron ending on February 2. At Huron on March 31, Laura Laird and Fred Stephens were quietly married by a town justice. They thought they had kept their marriage a secret, but company members found out and interrupted that evening's performance in mid-scene by showering them with handfuls of rice and presenting them with a baby cradle, much to the delight of the audience.[60]

For the next three weeks Della's company performed in towns somewhere between South Dakota and Mandan, North Dakota, before appearing at Dickinson, North Dakota, for the week of March 4. Here the troupe played nightly to exceptionally large audiences. A social dance followed the Wednesday evening performance with music supplied by the Pringle "orchestra," probably the pianist, the violinist and the lady cornet player.[61]

Della and her actors jumped to Sheridan, Wyoming, to fill an unusual two-week engagement between March 11 and 23.[62] For the following two weeks, the troupe performed somewhere in Wyoming and Nebraska before closing the sixteen-week season at Broken Bow, Nebraska, on April 13.[63]

Della took a short break from theatre business and visited her brother and his family in Colorado Springs during the last three weeks of April. By May 1 she went to Long Beach where the papers announced she would construct an airdome theatre there, financed by the sale of her rooming houses.[64] Airdome theatres, popular in summer before the introduction of air conditioning, consisted of a covered stage, and open air seating area and a surrounding fence of wood or canvas.

Headlines in the *Los Angeles Herald* of May 23, 1907, proclaimed "Happy Family Going On Road" and "Theatrical Company To Have Queer Combination."[65] These referred to supposed plans for Della Pringle to go on the road under the management of her former husband, G. Faith Adams, with Adams' present wife serving as troupe pianist. At the end of the item, the paper quoted Della as saying, "We will not have any trouble, I am sure, because of the unusual combination. Mrs. Adams is a beautiful woman and is perfectly willing for her husband to accompany me as my manager."[66]

For unknown and unstated reasons the "Happy Family" did not go on the road and any arrangements with Adams and his wife evaporated. Della placed an ad in the June 1 edition of the *New York Dramatic Mirror* seeking a new manager for her next tour and on June 3 she left Long Beach headed for Colorado Springs.[67]

In the *New York Clipper* of June 22, Della sought actors and specialty performers.[68] She quickly brought a company together and within two weeks she opened her 1907–1908 season at Hiawatha Gardens in Manitou, Colorado, a town near Colorado Springs, because repairs and repainting of the theatre in Colorado Springs prevented her from opening there.[69]

Although Della had assembled a troupe in such a short time, reviews during the season describe the company as strong, talented and versatile.[70] Della had retained five performers from the previous season. Olive McConnell, a pretty brunette from Canada, excelled at playing cold-hearted villainesses. "Babe" Laura Laird, described as a pocket edition of a famous musical comedy star, played juvenile as well as adult roles. Her singing of "Waiting at the Church" was a heartily applauded specialty. Her husband, Fred Stephens, continued to contribute solid acting who also offered clever singing and dancing specialties. Good-looking Jack Benjamin played juvenile roles. The last returning performer, Claude Kelly, did not join the troupe until a Denver engagement in August. He played male leads and appeared with Della in comic songs and pantomimes. Their sketch, "At the Opera," was a favorite.[71]

Although new to Della's company, Gertie Dunlap and Lew Virden had appeared often in Colorado Springs. She acted and specialized in impersonations of celebrities. Lew played star parts and appeared in unspecified specialties. They did not stay with the company for any length. Both remained behind when Della departed for Denver. A married couple, Grace and Fred Hamilton, were also new members. Both acted in support roles and she offered clever singing, clog dancing and a "burnt cork" sketch as specialty entertainments.[72]

The other new talent included handsome M.F. Hogan who handled the "heavy" or villain roles, a fine character actor, John Hopkins, who had appeared in support of Shakespearean actors Daniel Bandman and Lewis Morrison and Ed Belliville whose specialties included dancing, parodies and illustrated songs. Harry Adler, an actor who did not join Della's troupe until late October 1907, performed parodies and impersonations of Hebrews as his specialties.[73]

During the 1907–1908 season, Della directed and produced sixteen plays. In previous seasons Della had bragged that she offered only new plays in her territory, but, since she was playing mostly in new territory, she included eight previous hit shows in her repertory for the upcoming season. Della repeated *The Little Detective, Irish 400, The Sultan's Daughter,*

Belle of Richmond, True American Girl, Dangers of the Great City and *A Southern Romance* (sometimes listed as *Roanoke*). Her new productions included a domestic tragedy (*Her Mad Marriage*), a melodrama (*The Galley Slave*), a comedy romance (*The Bachelor's Honeymoon*) and a comedy western (*Kentucky Girl*). She also added *The Lighthouse Robbery* which featured a second act sensation scene depicting an electric storm as sea. In addition, Della secured rights to *The Chorus Girl*, a very successful eastern musical melodrama abounding in music, comedy, sensation and pathos. Later in the season Della opened *The Village Peacemaker*, a drama of everyday life set in the mining region of Pennsylvania. The final new offering, *The Parish Priest*, gave M.F. Hogan, the troupe's portrayer of villains, a chance to play a kindly and compassionate clergyman, a role made famous by the noted Dan Sully. It was one of the most successful productions of the season and kept in the Pringle repertory for years.

Della and company opened the Hiawatha Garden's three-week engagement with a matinee and evening performance of *The Chorus Girl* on July 4. The show's review found Della "especially good," gave general praise of the troupe's acting abilities and described the specialties as "above the ordinary."[74] Attendance was good in spite of competition from many Independence Day attractions.

Della altered her pattern of play offerings for this long engagement. Instead of performing a different play every evening, she presented just two plays a week. The troupe performed every night including Sundays plus matinees on Wednesdays, Saturdays and Sundays. The first plays opened on a Thursday and played through Sunday and the second play filled Monday through Wednesday. She drummed up additional box office revenue by offering a "bargain matinee" on Wednesday when she reduced the usual admission price of twenty-five to thirty-five cents to ten cents. This proved quite popular as did Della's practice of giving free admission on Monday evenings to any lady accompanied by a paying partner.

Sometime during the run at Manitou's Hiawatha Gardens a visitor from Knoxville, Iowa, called on Della. He had seen her red and white show placards about the town and hoped she had not departed. He went in search of her and discovered her on the veranda of the opera house where they enjoyed a find chat. As the anonymous visitor wrote in a lengthy letter to the *Knoxville Express* on July 24,

> She was very much surprised to see me. She is looking well, and had a thousand questions about people in Knoxville. She says the stories of her going to finance an open-air theater in Long Beach, California, are mostly hot-air from the high pressure reporters, says she has made

money, and does not intend to tie it up and perhaps lose it. Thinks she has the best company she ever carried and expects to "make good" with it this season. She tells me that G. Faith Adams is still in the car business, buying, equipping and selling private cars and that he is doing well. She has some money invested in the business.[75]

At the end of the Hiawatha Gardens engagement the Colorado Springs Opera House was still undergoing repairs so Della improvised a tour of two central Colorado mining towns, Leadville and Salida. The Leadville performances began about July 21 and lasted ten days. They drew crowded houses and the local press printed detailed reviews of most of the productions, finding the company excellent in all respects.[76] A shorter stay in Salida between July 31 and August 3 also attracted large audiences, but only limited and positive reception in the local paper.[77]

Although not all the improvements to the Colorado Springs Opera House had been completed, there were enough to once again allow theatre productions. Della opened a two-week season there on August 5 with *The Chorus Girl*. She raised evening admission prices (ranging from twenty-five and fifty cents), but kept matinee prices at a dime for children and a quarter for adults. She changed bills three times a week. After the Thursday matinees she treated the ladies of the audience to a "pink tea" on stage. She also boosted attendance conducting a drawing for a diamond ring on Saturday evenings.[78]

Pringle's shows packed the opera house to capacity and the press remarked on the over-all excellence of the company. Local favorites Gertie Dunlap and Lew Virden drew special mention and Della drew deserved praise, not only for her own abilities, but for her handling of the troupe.

> Miss Pringle is in a class by herself, in the treatment of her company she, unlike a great many stars, wants her ladies in the company to be just as popular as she is and spares no expenses in the selection of her support. The other ladies are beautiful, fascinating and clever, and all the gowns worn by Miss Pringle and the other ladies are certainly wonderful creations of the dressmaker's art.[79]

The same item also hailed the company's specialties as the "best ever carried by a repertory show."[80]

Next, the Pringle troupe presented eight performances of *The Chorus Girl* at the Curtis Theatre in Denver the week of August 24. Reviews in two Denver papers gave laudatory comments about Della and her supporting players. The *Denver Post* stated, "The real star in the person of Della Pringle ... proved to be a satisfying young woman."[81] A later item in the *Post* reported *The Chorus Girl* to be put on in good style before packed houses. The *Denver Republican* rendered a more complete reaction to the opening performance:

> Della Pringle is a dashing, active and well favored young woman of the type that lets no dust lie on the stage while she is there. The part is that of a bouncing American show girl who keeps London up to a super-insular heat, as Miss Pringle has plenty of chances to display those particular attractions of which she is possessed. Evidently they were of the kind that found favor in the eyes of the galley yesterday.[82]

Claude Kelly, M.F. Hogan, Olive McConnell and Jack Benjamin also earned accolades for their performances.

The Denver reviews (and packed houses) were important indications that Della and her troupe were at least competitive with other performers in a large city market where theatre patrons regularly attended touring Broadway productions with established celebrity stars and noted traveling repertory companies. The many glowing notices and enthusiastic audience she amassed in her tours through small, often remote, towns could be dismissed as flattery by local critics and theatregoers used to performances by second-rate barnstormers. Della had no pretensions of being a star actress, but on those rare occasions when she played in larger cities such as Denver, Salt Lake City, Spokane and Los Angeles before knowledgeable audiences, she more than held her own on stage.

After the successful week in Denver, the Della Pringle Company crossed over the Rocky Mountains, playing at unrecorded towns on the way to a single show at Park City, Utah, on August 30. Della's troupe then opened a week's engagement on September 1 at the Grand Theatre in Salt Lake City. Productions of *The Chorus Girl* and *The Lighthouse Robbery* gained solid, positive notices which cited the acting of Della, Claude Kelly John Hopkins and Laura Laird as "captivating all." The critic felt the "scenic embellishments are all that could be desired."[83] Subsequent notices reported capacity audiences for all performances. Again, Della had done well in a large city.

Leaving Salt Lake, Della's actors headed north into Idaho for a first stand at Pocatello the week of September 9 and a second at Blackfoot on September 16.[84] They presented a single play at Idaho Falls before settling in at St. Anthony with week of September 23. By October 3 they returned to Idaho Falls for an additional three evenings.

Della's company then went to Evanston in northwest Wyoming for a week of performances ending on October 12.[85] From there Della entered into new touring territory with a jump to Elko, Nevada, on October 14 to perform five nights in the Bradley Opera House before large crowds.[86]

As Della entered the gold mining area of Nevada, she increased admission to fifty cents and a dollar. Her first stop, the week of October 20 in Tonopah at the Pavilion Theatre, drew very limited press coverage. In marked contrast her next stand at Goldfield merited almost daily comment in the town paper. The opening performance of *The Chorus Girl* at the Lyric Theatre on October 27 drew a standing-room-only audience. *The Belle of Richmond* on the following evening met with the same as did performances until the engagement ended on November 6. During the run the paper observed that the troupe had made a "record for popularity that has never been approached in southern Nevada."[87]

A miscue during Della's matinee performance of *The Little Detective* in Goldfield on November 2 provided prolonged and unintended merriment for the audience. One scene showed a Brooklyn waterfront where the villain attempted to get rid of his unattractive wife by knocking her out and hauling her heavy body to the river for disposal. Unfortunately, the combined weight of villain and victim proved too much for the flimsily constructed waterfront platform and it collapsed which in turn knock over a ground piece intended to mask the imaginary "river." In great confusion the supposedly unconscious wife scrambled on her hands and knees to the rear of the stage and flopped on a mattress. This was the cue for the stagehands in the wings to pull the platform bearing the mattress slowly offstage by concealed ropes; thereby giving the audience the illusion of a body floating down the river. With only a bare floor and the moving mattress, there was no illusion and the crowd exploded into spontaneous laughter at the spectacle. For the rest of the show, the audience kept giggling in the wrong places.[88]

Tonopah's theatregoers welcomed back Della and her troupe on November 7. The local paper reported that while in Goldfield M.F. Hogan and Olive McConnell had wed, "thus ending an interesting romance."[89] The same item disclosed Della Pringle had had a narrow escape from burning to death. "She, upon retiring for the night, took an electric iron to bed to keep warm and fell asleep, but was awakened by the smoke and flames that partially consumed the bed clothing."[90] Della, unharmed in the incident, had to pay the hotel for the ruined bedding.

Having escaped incineration, Della extended her stay in Tonopah through the week. A local theatre manager offered he an eight-week contract to stay in Tonopah, guaranteeing her $500 per week, but she had to turn down the lucrative offer due to prior commitments.[91] The miners still showed their appreciation by throwing gold nuggets on the stage as they did in earlier times and Della enjoyed a box office bonanza during her stay in the gold mining camps of Nevada, this in spite of hard economic times in the state.

Della's troupe made a long hop into northern Arizona, opening there for a single show at Kingman, Arizona, on November 13.[92] The following day Della arrived in Phoenix to begin a week's stand of *The Chorus Girl*.[93] She paid $410 in railroad fares to get to Phoenix, but more than paid for the jump when she took in $455 on opening night alone.[94] After a successful week in Phoenix, she moved on to fabled Tombstone, performing at Mesa and other small towns en route.[95] Following a single show in the town made legendary by the gunfight at the O.K. Corral, Della moved her company to Tucson for a week's engagement beginning December 1. Initial performances met with poor attendance, but by the rest of the week Della's troupe played to capacity audiences. All shows won positive reviews and M.F. Hogan earned high praise for the lead role in *The Parish Priest*, the reviewer dubbing him the equal of Daniel Sully who originated the part on Broadway.[96]

After a single performance at Prescott, Arizona, on December 8 or 9, Della opened at Douglass, Arizona, for a five-show engagement.[97] On December 15, while on the way to the next stand in Globe, Arizona, the company became involved in a nearly disastrous railway accident. Della described it in a letter to the *Knoxville Express* from Globe, Arizona, dated December 20.

> There came near being no Della Pringle and company. We were all seated in the caboose of the freight train, waiting for them to couple on, and an engine hit us, running at the rate of 20 miles an hour, knocked us all flat on the floor, and threw Mr. Hopkins, who was seated in the cupola, through the window, cutting his head and face. The bump was so hard it tore the stove loose and turned it completely around. I have traveled a long time, and this is the worst accident I was ever in; and to make matters worse, we had to remain on the freight train all day, and we were so scared and nervous that we women all had hysterics when we saw the blood streaming from Mr. Hopkin's wounds, and no doctor to dress them until we got to Safford, forty miles from where the accident occurred. I haven't been able to sleep since, my nerves are so bad from the shock.[98]

After all the trouble of getting to Globe, Della and company had a very successful two-week engagement, playing to big crowds night after night at the Dreamland Theatre. An opening night review noted the low prices of a quarter to half a dollar for "the best repertory company that has played in Globe since the camp has become known as a show town" and added, "Many of the one-night stands are far inferior in plays and players."[99]

Because Arizona lacked a fully developed railroad system, Della's actors had to travel over forty miles in a bone-jarring stagecoach to Kelvin, Arizona, in order to catch a train to Phoenix after they completed the long run at Globe on December 26.[100] On the way to Phoenix, the troupe filled a short engagement on December 30 and 31 at Tempe, Arizona.[101]

At the beginning of the new year (1908), Della leased the Olympic Theatre in Phoenix and began a one-month season. Business was slow the first week; opening night grossed only sixty-four dollars. However, the lure of low admission and the talents of the performers increased attendance and Della could boast in the theatre trade papers of three weeks of standing-room-only audiences.[102]

Good fortune continued to follow Della as she led her company from Arizona to Amarillo, Texas. Booked for the week of January 27, shows drew so well that the local theatre manager held the troupe over for an additional week of full houses. Dalhart, Texas, hosted the Jolly Della Pringle Company for the opening of the town's new Grand Opera House on February 10. A week of SRO houses followed.[103]

For the remainder of February Della failed to report anything to the theatrical trade paper her tour through Texas, but then an item in the *New York Clipper* revealed that Della's 1907–1908 challenging season ended on March 1, presumably in the Fort Worth, Texas, area.[104]

9

Rough Road to a New Home

Following the close of her 1907–1908 season in early March, Della returned to Knoxville, Iowa, for two weeks of rest and to visit her friends there. She also needed to find a buyer for her home, The Maples, which had been on the market and rented out for almost a year. Valued at $3,200, she was willing to sell for $1,800.[1]

Having rested and taken care of real estate concerns, Della began to prepare for her next theatrical venture. By March 14 she placed an ad in the *New York Clipper* looking for actors to be part of a new company. The ad announced Della's plan to tour Texas in a portable airdome theatre and asked potential troupe members to contact her by general delivery in Fort Worth, Texas. In addition, the ad stated that Della would add a ladies' orchestra for this tour.[2] By mid–April she had a troupe ready to open a season at Fort Worth,[3] an opening that never took place.

Della cancelled her Texas touring plan when she received word that her brother, the Rev. J. Elmer Van Winkle, was seriously ill in Colorado Springs. She hastened to Colorado to supervise care for her brother.[4] With her Texas plans in shambles, she indicated in trade papers that she would rehearse a troupe in Colorado Springs with the intention of touring to Trinidad and other Colorado towns.[5]

Within two weeks her brother's health had improved enough for Della to return to theatre business about May 1. At this time in the *New York Dramatic Mirror* she again announced that she would tour in Colorado.[6] Perhaps due to the hectic reorganization of her company, Della did not report the sites of her touring dates in the trade papers as was her practice. She did place an ad seeking performers on May 9 in the *New York Clipper*, listing the contact address of the Curtis Theatre in Denver,[7] but there was no local confirmation of a performance in Denver.

By the middle of May, Della resumed reporting her play dates beginning with the week of May 18 at Fort Collins, Colorado, and the following week at Boulder, Colorado. Local notices in both towns described Della's company as the best ever to perform there.[8] After a week's break, the troupe paid a return visit to Evanston, Wyoming, for the week of June 8.[9]

During Della Pringle's next engagement at Ogden, Utah, events occurred that exceeded any drama she ever presented on stage. While in Denver, she had hired a handsome new leading man, Cecil Van Auker. In the following weeks she fell in love with him and when they reached Ogden she accepted his marriage proposal, donned one of her finest gowns and eloped to marry him in front of a local justice of the peace on June 14, 1908.[10]

On the very same day, sorrow eclipsed the joy of the new bride. Della received the devastating news of her brother's sudden death in Colorado Springs. She immediately abandoned her new husband, cancelled all playing engagements and left for Colorado.[11]

Della attended her brother's funeral at Colorado Springs on June 16. She was joined in mourning by the many friends and associates of Joseph Elmer Van Winkle.[12] In his life he had pursued several careers (teacher, clergyman, excursion train director) before becoming a national lecturer for the Brotherhood of American Yoemen, a noted fraternal insurance group. He had been afflicted with tuberculosis for several years and died of pneumonia. He left behind a wife and a daughter, Grace. Della accompanied his remains to Des Moines for final services and burial on June 17. She made a brief visit to Knoxville, then returned to Utah to resume her theatrical tour.[13]

The time spent away tending her brother's funeral services and burial led to complications in her touring itinerary. She lost a week at Logan, Utah, and had to rearrange dates for other previously contracted engagements. This meant she had to improvise her tour through northern Utah and southeastern Idaho. She also faced the loss of some performers in her company due to their lost income while she was away and the unpredictable future of the tour itself.

Somehow about June 20, Della managed to pull things together and begin a series of one-night stands featuring her popular production of *Faust*, first at Preston, Idaho. She finally appeared at Logan, Utah, but for only one day rather than the week originally scheduled.[14] For the rest of June she toured to the Utah towns of Hyrum, Smithfield and Box Elder.

During the early weeks of July, the troupe appeared in the Idaho communities of Pocatello, Blackfoot, Idaho Falls and Rexburg.[15] Summer business was poor and Della decided to end the season, giving her company members two weeks' notice to close.

Then, fortunately, a newspaper article saved the day for Della and her troupe. At Sugar City, Idaho, about July 9 or 10, Della happened to pick up a July 8 edition of Boise's *Idaho Statesman* and read an article about foreclosure proceedings on an airdome theatre in Boise. Sensing an opportunity to extend her tour, Della sent her agent to Boise to see about arranging an engagement in the airdome facility. By July she had made a deal to play the rest of the summer in the Boise airdome beginning on July 20.[16] In the next eight days her troupe appeared in the Idaho towns Twin Falls, Rupert and Shoshone on her way to Boise.[17]

Boise's Airdome Theatre, built as an open air resort, seated 1,500 people on an inclined floor and side bleachers. It featured a "suitable stage" and a moveable roof in case of rain. A ten foot corrugated iron fence, painted white and illuminated by electric lights, surrounded the grounds at Sixth and Main in downtown Boise.[18] People could eat ice cream or drink lemonade, pop and soda water while watching a show. The facility opened on May 9, 1908, but unseasonably wet and cold weather plagued the variety entertainments offered there through the rest of May and almost all of June. Conditions severely limited attendance that in turn led to reduced income at the box office and eventually resulted in the foreclosure proceedings.

When the Jolly Della Pringle Company opened at the Airdome Theatre on July 20, it made a hit from the very beginning of its run. Press notices for the opening production of *Faust* praised Della for her smooth, quiet method of acting, Van Auker for his acting excellence and the rest of the company for being well balanced and "equal to anything they attempt."[19] In a review of *The Chorus Girl* on July 31, Miss Pringle was described as wearing a fine Paris gown and "bubbling over with mirth the entire evening."[20] Special scenery, accumulated over years of touring, also drew lavish and favorable commentary.

Roughly a dozen actors made up the Pringle troupe that opened in Boise. Della, of course, played the leading female roles. Her husband, Van Auker, possessed all the attributes required of a leading man—a lean body, a handsome face, black hair, dark eyes and a strong voice. He had acted at the well-known summer theatre at Elitch Gardens in Denver, had been part of an eastern repertory troupe for ten years, had been in unnamed Broadway shows for two years and served for several years as understudy to the famous Shakespearean actor, Lewis Morrison. Michael "M.F." Hogan, a versatile actor played both heavy or villainous roles and sympathetic character roles. Baby Emily performed all children's roles. James Hawley, a supporting actor, also served as the troupe's press agent. Eddie

Barnes and Olive Wilkins performed parts in the plays and appeared in specialties between the acts—he as a highly amusing comedian and she as a "champion" cornet player. In addition, Wilkins continued to join with Milo McMinn, the troupe's orchestra leader (formerly with the famed Liberati Band), in the "Olive and Mac" duets of cornet and trombone.

Della added actress Ollie Cook to her company just before the Boise opening. Miss Cook had recently been the leading lady of a Boise repertory theatre that had gone broke.[21] Her talents as a strong supporting actress strengthened Della's already talented troupe. Others named in the Pringle company were Roy Wilkins, Ethel Watson, Benton Hinton and Kittie Edwins.[22]

Although the roster of Della's company changed only slightly over the next year in Boise, by July of 1909 she had replaced some actors with new performers. At that time newspaper items listed actors James Dillon, Riley Meyers, Ed Stanley, former troupe member Fred Stevens and James Wright, a local actor and dancer whose real name was James Cheesewright. New actresses in the troupe of 1909 included Fanny Hammond Stanley and Laura "Babe" Laird, a veteran of several seasons with Della Pringle's companies. At some point La Petite Ruth replaced Baby Emily in juvenile parts.

While there were some changes in the troupe's personnel, Della's repertory of plays, all produced during recent tours, remained the same for the entire Airdome Theatre season. Pringle's company played at popular prices (ten to thirty cents) six nights a week and changed bills twice each week with such proven productions as *Faust, A Parish Priest, California, The Chorus Girl, The Belle of Richmond* and *The Sultan's Daughter,* etc.

The opening night of *Faust* by the Jolly Della Pringle Company on July 20 in the Airdome Theatre thoroughly entertained a standing-room-only audience, making a hit from the very beginning[23] of a successful engagement that would last through the first week in September. Even though hampered by the small stage space and its inadequate equipment, Della and her talented performers turned out a series of high quality productions. The *Idaho Statesman* reviewer, like so many critics before, heaped golden opinions on Della's company, labeling it the best repertory company to ever appear in Boise.[24] Since several esteemed repertory groups such as the Bittner Company, the Clara Mathes Company, Eckhardt's Ideals and the George Noble Company had appeared in Boise since 1900, this was valued praise, indeed.

As Della's season continued in the Airdome Theatre, audiences filled the auditorium for every show. However, press commentary diminished in frequency and detail. One exception was a review of *On the Hills of Idaho*, a play written for Della Pringle presented on August 23–25, which described the work at length and found Della excellent in her role.[25] Otherwise, newspaper items were positive, but brief.

After some forty successful shows in the Airdome Theatre, Della and Van Auker decided to seek a new venue, one that would allow them to make more use of their special scenery and to present matinee performances. About August 25 they purchased a lease for the Turner Theatre located in the Turnverein Building, a relatively new structure erected by a local German social organization.[26] The Turner Theatre, just across the street south of the Airdome Theatre, had a smaller auditorium (estimated seating of no more than 700), but had a large and well-equipped stage better suited for Pringle productions.

When the engagement at the Airdome Theatre ended on September 5, Della and her troupes took only one day to move across the street and prepare for shows at the Turner Theatre.[27] With the change in venue, Della made changes in the operation of her theatre season. Instead of following the usual practice of a traveling repertory troupe that offered two or more changes of bills each week, she established a resident stock company operation that presented seven performance of a single play for six evenings and a Saturday matinee with Sundays off.

Actors must have welcomed the change in management which made their work much easier. When operating as a traveling repertory company, performers had to put up with stressful conditions such as having to sleep in a different room two or more times a week, eating on an irregular schedule or missing meals altogether in order to catch a train on schedule and trying to get laundry done while on the road. All this misery and more disappeared with the establishment of a resident stock company approach. It also made work on stage easier.

Performers could concentrate on remembering lines and pieces of stage business for a single play rather than keeping two or more plays in their heads for a given week. No doubt it added to the quality of a show to have it repeated for seven consecutive performances. The resident stock operation also allowed a week of rehearsals in preparation for the next stage offering by the troupe. The single play per week also helped improve attendance and box office receipts because it allowed word-of-mouth publicity to spread through the community. Even stagehands benefitted since scenery for a production only had to be set up once a week.

From the opening Turner Theatre production of *In the Heart of the*

Hills on September 7, 1908,²⁸ to the closing performance of *All the Comforts of Home* on June 5, 1909, Della presented a different play every week of the long engagement. All were new plays to the company except for three from recent seasons: *Faust, The Sultan's Daughter* and *The Midnight Express*.

The plays certainly entertained Della's audiences at the time, but about all lacked enduring dramatic interest. Spectacular formula melodramas, extended one-joke farces and sentimental domestic dramas replete with scenes of tears and joy appealed to the average playgoer in Boise and across the nation. However, Della made no apologies for the choice of dramas presented to her public and the press agreed. As reported in Boise's *Evening Capital News* for September 18, 1909:

> Comedy is the high feature at the Turner. Miss Pringle reads her patterns aright. Shakespeare is dead. People nowadays don't care for Jacques spouting the "Seven Ages of Man," or Hamlet with his doleful query, "To be for not to be." "Camille" and "East Lynne" are packed away with the red fire of livid melodrama. Present day productions are in demand and Miss Pringle is presenting the goods wanted. Hence her success.²⁹

Out of all the plays produced by Della at the Turner Theatre, only a few might still be recognized. As many of the leading ladies of the time did, Della enacted the role of Marguerite Gauteir in Dumas *fils* famed drama, *Camille*. In Della's performances of the play during the week of October 12, her display of emotion in the concluding death scene no doubt moved the audience to tears.³⁰

Boise audiences had the rare opportunity to see a play that was still running in New York when Della obtained the rights to Ferenc Molnar's hit play, *The Devil*, and presented it the last week in October of 1908.³¹ Two plays presented by her troupe had famous titles: the stage adaptations of *Dr. Jekyll and Mr. Hyde* and *The Adventures of Sherlock Holmes*. No resident stock season would be complete without a production of the most revered soap opera tearjerker, *East Lynne*. The week of December 14, 1908, Della took the drama's lead role of a fallen woman who abandons her family only to return later in disguise as a governess who raise her own children.³²

Della Pringle did more than present entertaining shows at popular prices and plenty of pleasing specialties to draw large audiences. She maintained excellent relations with the press and placed ads for her performances almost daily. She repeated the promotional activities she had offered on previous tours for Boise audiences. On Monday nights ladies were admitted free when accompanied by a paying patron. At all performances audience members were given tickets for the raffle of a silver tea set held on Friday evenings and another drawing for a diamond ring held during the Saturday night shows. Della revived the practice of holding "pink teas" on stage after performances for the women and children attending Saturday matinees. From time to time she sponsored stunt nights with audience participation. Most memorable of these was a stunt night during in which some young boys wrestled and five other lads in blackface flailed around in a very large and shallow pan of flour for a hidden rubber ball.[33]

Years later Della would remember the almost year-long engagement at the Turner Theatre as "some of the best and happiest times of all my years in the show business,"[34] noting her pride in her husband and company and her love of Boise and its people. She would also remember it for some of the best and profitable business she had ever experienced.

Della Pringle's troupe, hailed often as the best stock organization to ever visit Boise, enjoyed a patronage no other company of its kind had ever received there. Audiences packed the theatre for every performance and each day the box office handled large orders for seats, sometimes several days in advance. It became necessary to install a second phone line to handle the requests for tickets.[35] Members of Boise's highest society organized theatre parties to enjoy the productions at the Turner Theatre where the ladies delighted in Della's display of the latest fashionable gowns.

Della's successful engagement at the Turner Theatre was all the more remarkable in view of her competition for patronage from among Boise's population of 17,000 people plus another 4,000 residing in the adjacent urban areas or Meridian, Nampa and Caldwell. At the beginning of her stand at the Turner Theatre she did not have to compete with Boise's largest theatre, the Columbia. It had hosted a variety of road shows and traveling repertory troupes since it's opening in 1893. Boise mayor James Pinney, owner of the Columbia, closed the venue on in April of 1908 before Della arrived in Boise. However, he constructed a large, new theatre, the Pinney, which opened on September 17, just after Della began her Turner Theatre season. Thereafter Della's company still did a good business even when performing opposite Broadway road shows and reputable regional repertory troupes booked into Pinney's theatre.

During the warm weather season between May and September, Della competed with musical comedies and vaudeville presented at the Riverside Park Theatre, an amusement park containing a large outdoor theatre seating up to 1,500. Another competitor in the regular season from September to May was another smaller venue, the Orpheum Theatre, which offered a mélange of vaudeville, stock theatre and motion pictures to the Boise public. Lastly, Della operated in competition with some ten motion picture theatres with names such as the Dime, the Bijou, the Boz, the Lyric and the Isis. In 1908 the developing motion picture business in Boise had little effect on Della's theatre enterprise. However, within less than a decade the film industry would prove to be a devastating force against live theatre productions, including Della's.

At age thirty-eight after touring about the United States for two decades and spending the time between 1906 and 1908 moving to and from Knoxville, Long Beach and Colorado Springs, Della decided to put down roots in Boise. She and Van Auker invested in local real estate, living at various residences during the next few years. An item on December 12, 1908, reported their purchase of an eighty acre fruit tree farm in Meridian, Idaho, a farm community eight miles west of Boise, for $12,000.[36] For a time they lived on the farm and commuted twice a day to Boise in their recently acquired motor car. By June of 1909 Della also owned and operated a rooming house, the Palantine, at 12th and Main in downtown Boise. She advertised that three rooms were for rent for three to five dollars a week. The ad describes the Palantine as the "coolest place in the city; nice lawn and shade; hot and cold water in every room."[37] By September of 1914 the Van Aukers resided at yet another home, 1711 North 18th Street. Although Della left Boise to tour and spent as much as a year out of Boise, the city would remain her permanent home to the end of her long life.

Before the long Turner Theatre season neared its end, Della mounted a production of an old classic, *Rip Van Winkle*, during the week of June 7. In a publicity item for the show Della revealed that she had appeared twenty-six years ago in Fishkill, New York, as one of the village children in a performance of *Rip Van Winkle* starring the fabled Joseph Jefferson. She also declared that she was of Dutch lineage and a descendant of Peter Stuyvesant who supposedly knew the original Rip Van Winkle. She even had a picture of her grandfather printed in the paper.[38] How much of Della's claim was true is open to question. After all she was skilled in creating interest in her shows.

After the first Turner Theatre season finally ended on July 3, 1909, Della and Van Auker took time off from performing. During this vacation period they went on an automobile trip of 130 miles to Twin Falls, Idaho, a trip that ended in disaster. According to an account in the *Idaho Statesman* of July 24, Della "came in on yesterday's afternoon train from Bliss almost a nervous wreck from the frightful auto accident which occurred to her on the steep grade going down to the lower ferry at Twin Falls."[39]

The hill was so steep that Della had chosen to walk down. Only a few moments after she exited the car she saw that Van Auker had lost control of the vehicle. She realized the brake must have broken and nearly fainted from fright. Just when it appeared that the large auto would plunge off the steep embankment down to the precipice at the next turn, Van Auker turned the car up into the side of the hill. This caused the automobile to turn over, the gasoline to explode and the radiator to empty itself. Miraculously, Van Auker crawled out from beneath the debris without serious injury, but the car was severely damaged. Somehow Della and her husband managed to right the car and attempted to drive the damaged vehicle back to Boise, but found the desert heat to be too severe. The water in the radiator had to be cooled every half hour and the damage to the car made it impossible to get up to any speed. The top of the auto was completely demolished and afforded no shelter from the summer sun. After coaxing the damaged vehicle along for about thirty miles to Bliss, Idaho, Della gave up and boarded the train for Boise,[40] presumably leaving Van Auker to arrange for getting the auto repaired so he could drive it home.

Following their automobile incident, Della and Van Auker turned to planning for their fall theatre season. In the August 2, 1909, edition of Boise's *Evening Capital News*, Van Auker revealed a policy change for the Turner Theatre under his lease. Now it would become part of the national Sullivan and Considine vaudeville circuit and feature acts returning from the Pacific coast to eastern bookings.[41] Boise citizens had attended vaudeville entertainment for decades, but this would be the first time that arrangements had been made to furnish the city with two performances each night of high quality, big circuit vaudeville. Della and her husband felt so confident in their new venture that they thoroughly renovated the Turner Theatre, improving the cooling system and installing new scenery, carpets and other furnishings.[42]

At the same time he announced his vaudeville plans, Van Auker told reporters that he and Della would send a company out on the road under the management of troupe member James C. Cheesewright. He and Della would remain at home in Boise and occasionally perform in vaudeville sketches at their theatre.

Evidently, the arrangements with the Sullivan and Considine vaudeville organization fell through immediately after Van Auker had announced his plan to bring big time vaudeville to Boise. On August 7, 1909, he placed an ad in the *New York Clipper* looking for actors to fill *two* companies, one to tour, the other to perform in the Turner Theatre.[43]

Della and Van Auker began a second season of plays at the Turner

Theatre on August 16[44] which lasted until October 4. They sent the road company out on August 30 to tour to Pocatello, Blackfoot, Montpelier and American Falls in southeastern Idaho and Garland in northeastern Utah.

Della opened her second Turner Theatre season with a new production, *In The Shadow of the Cross*. At the first performance a crowded house of avid admirers welcomed her and her company back to the stage. Ovations greeted every company member as they appeared on stage, the applause for Della and Van Auker so pronounced that it was several minutes before the play could proceed.[45] This enthusiasm for Della's troupe continued for the next eight weeks during which time Della offered week long performances of two additional new works, *My Lord in Livery* and *Plain Mary Jane*, and revived previous productions of *Old New England, California, An American Girl* and *The Rose of Virginia*.

Even though they were drawing capacity audiences, Della and Van Auker closed the engagement in early October due to illness. Van Auker had a respiratory condition that developed into pneumonia and Della suffered general ill health related to a continuing stomach problem. They turned the operation of the Turner Theatre over to the Marlowe Stock Company. In spite of ill health, both rallied to play roles in the first couple of the Marlowe productions.[46]

By late November Della and Van Auker, now in much better health, joined their touring troupe for week-long engagements in Twin Falls and Shoshone, Idaho.[47] Shortly after Della reported that the company would celebrate Thanksgiving in Caldwell, Idaho, about twenty-five miles west of Boise. On November 29, Della and her troupe slipped back into Boise for a successful week-long engagement in the city's largest theatre, the Pinney,[48] before continuing the tour at Payette, Idaho, for a week at the Elite Theatre.[49]

Following a rewarding week in Payette, she crossed the border into Oregon and settled in at La Grande's Steward Opera House from December 13 to 26, an unusually long stand for such a small community. The opening night presentation of *In the Heart of the Hills* filled the theatre to overflowing. The evening's review noted Della's "captivating and assured manner" in her part and Van Auker's "clean acting free from clownish antics." The remainder of the company played their parts in an "honest and conscientious manner."[50] Scenery and costume received equally flattering comment. It was also noted that Della had performed in La Grande during December exactly eight years ago and at that time had done the biggest business ever done by a stock company at the Steward Theatre.

Part way through her La Grande engagement Della wrote an article for the *La Grande Evening Observer* entitled "Allurements of the Stage" that defended women in the acting profession and revealed her belief that a stage career had no more pitfalls for women than other vocations. She began her essay by noting the attraction of a stage life that "no matter what its trials, disappointments and delusions, ... continues to beckon irresistibly."[51] She cites the example of a young Yale graduate who lost a parental allowance because he chose to be an actor over his father's objections. He expressed no regrets over his choice and said he would rather be "working for twelve dollars a week with a barnstorming company than to be President Taft." While many warned of the temptations of an actress's life, Della declared that in her twenty years on stage she had seen no confirmation of these temptations. To her the stage was not a type of entertainment offering only "poor music, stupid women and the antics of silly clowns."[52] She saw the people of the stage as no better or worse than those in other occupations. As she wrote: "The wolf seeking to devour lurks outside the factory, the office and on street corners just as frequently as he haunts the slandered stage." She continued with the observation that the high life attributed to popular actresses by preachers and critics of "yellow Sunday supplements" had "no foundation in fact."[53]

She ended her article with her account of the truer life of an actress.

> Year in and year out I have seen plainly dressed women hurrying out the stage door after the performance intent only on an hour of study or fitful sleep just before dawn, or, pale and exhausted from an all day rehearsal, snatching a bite at a neighboring restaurant and hurrying back for the evening performance, performing double work on holidays when other people are resting and enjoying themselves. There is little chance for temptation to show its head there. And suppose it did? The woman of the stage would meet it precisely as the woman who earns her living in other ways meet it.[54]

Della reported to the *New York Clipper* on January 29, 1910, that she and her company had celebrated an "old fashion" Christmas in La Grande with a grand feast and the exchange of many "useful" presents, a revelry that continued past four in the morning.[55] In the same report Della declared her intention to return to Boise after a month in Washington State, but she did not make it back home until early May. The company roster at the end of the report listed only one change in Della's troupe; Zona Wright had become musical director.[56]

At the end of the La Grange stand Della's troupe had to leave comfortable travel on the Oregon Short Line Railroad to take a branch railroad to Enterprise, Oregon, for the week of December 28. Here they encountered the same snow and cold weather that had plagued them during the previous two weeks.

After Della performed with her company during the first two days of the new year, she made a quick trip from Enterprise back to Boise on January 4 to take care of personal business and spend a few days visiting friends.[57] She rejoined her troupe at Joseph, Oregon, to finish a week of shows. Della played the last Oregon engagements at Baker the week of January 11, 1910.

Della continued her tour of small towns, or as she put it "barnstorming the crossroads,"[58] with a visit to Dayton, Washington, the week of January 17 to play at the Weinhard Theatre. According to the local press, the company proved to be "a surprise and a pleasure to the theatre-going public" for both its star and the strength of the supporting actors. The paper characterized Della as "one of the wealthiest minor stars on the American stage." Reviews disclosed that attendance increased each evening. One also quoted Della as saying she saved money to pay the salaries of "a high grade of actors and actresses" by not carrying a street band.[59]

For the next five weeks Della crossed and re-crossed the border between Idaho and Washington in a series of engagements, most for a whole week. After departing Dayton on January 23, the company played a week somewhere between there and Grangeville, Idaho, where they appeared for the week of January 31.[60] Following another week in unknown community, the troupe showed up in the first of two stands at Lewiston, Idaho, on Valentine's Day.[61] At the end of the weeks the company left to play four shows at nearby Pullman, Washington, before returning to Lewiston for a final two performances.[62]

On March 1 the Pringle company opened a short season at Asotin, Washington, before starting out for Colfax, Washington. Unfortunately, Colfax and surrounding country were devastated by "the mightiest flood of water known to white men."[63] Confronted with heavy rains, flooding and railroad bed washouts, the troupe could not fulfill the planned engagement. Della lost ten days of playing time and considered herself lucky that no lives were lost.[64] Frustrated by the weather conditions in eastern Washington, Della and company jumped all the way to Missoula, Montana, and opened for an indefinite period on March 12, 1910, at the Family Theatre.[65]

On opening night of *My Lord in Livery* the biggest audience ever gathered in the Family Theatre welcomed the Della Pringle Company. Every seat was sold and many turned away at the door.[66] No doubt pre-show publicity that stressed Della's enviable reputation in the theatre world helped fill the house. It also explained that Della personally directed and staged every production, insisting the quality of shows be just as good as that of touring New York companies.

The success of opening night continued for most of the Missoula engagement that lasted into late April. Della prospered even with competition from rival stock companies at the Harnois Theatre, vaudeville at the Grand Theatre and motion pictures at two other venues. Her ten- to thirty-cent shows compared favorably with two-dollar road shows such as the one starring Mrs. Leslie Carter, known as the Sarah Bernhardt of America which played Missoula the night before Della arrived in town.

The *Daily Missoulian* of March 12, 1910, printed an article about the "clever people" in the Della Pringle Company. It repeated such information about Van Auker's as his ten years in an eastern company, his position as leading man in Denver's Elitch Garden troupe and his two years on Broadway. Laura Laird, a soubrette from Omaha, was described as a "universal favorite" (especially with the younger populace) whose portrayals were witty and jolly and whose singing drew encore after encore. Olive McConnell, a graduate of the Wheater dramatic school of New York, had spent several seasons with the best companies in the east including those of Julia Marlowe and Minnie Maddern Fiske, major stars of the era. Fanny Hammond Stanley, a pupil of Shakespearean actor Frederick Warde, lived in Ogden, Utah, when not on tour. A strong character woman with ten years of stage experience, she was also the first woman to be employed as an advance agent for a tent show. An actor of the old school from Atchison, Kansas, M.F. Hogan, was a recognized star in villain parts by all stock companies. James C. Wright and Bob Roberts, specialty artists with the Pringle company, had been hired direct from the renowned Orpheum vaudeville circuit. Riley Myers, a two-year veteran of the troupe, was described as another "universal favorite."[67]

Week after week the Missoula paper printed praise of Della and her talented cohorts. There were frequent mentions of Della's fabled wardrobe and the completeness of scenery and stage effects. During this long engagement, Della revived pink teas for matinee ladies. Most plays presented were from her Boise repertory, but near the end of the Montana season she did add a few new shows. The Missoula stand ended the week of April 24,[68] after which Della and Van Auker returned to Boise to work on their farm and recuperate from a long touring season that began in August of 1909.[69]

10

Running Before the Wave

In America at the end of the first decade of the twentieth century, the rapidly growing motion picture industry began to have a decided effect on traditional theatre business. Only twenty years before, short films had been a novelty offered as a between act specialty by repertory companies. Now films had developed into longer and longer features that in time threatened the existence of theatre troupes such as Della Pringle's.

Theatres in large population centers such as New York and Chicago that presented live theatre productions continued to be successful by presenting works with all-star casts. Broadway road shows remained popular, but such presentations toured mainly to large cities that would support extended runs.

People living in America's small cities and towns that had relied on traveling repertory groups for entertainment turned more and more to motion pictures for amusement. Such communities seldom attracted Broadway stage stars, but with the movies patrons could see the same celebrity film stars as anybody in a large city. Would a small town theatregoer pay to see good repertory actors when for the same price he or she could see major star actors in motion pictures? Economics, too, played a part in the decline of the repertory companies. Repertory managers incurred considerable costs in housing, feeding and transporting about a dozen actors while on tour. On the other hand, films could be put in cans and be shipped from town to town almost anywhere in America for a pittance. In effect, repertory troupes like Della's would eventually be washed away by a rising wave of films and motion picture theatres.

In the next few years Della and her performers would be running before the film wave, seeking new audiences in new territories to survive. She may have sensed the change in public support of repertory theatre as early as April of 1910 when she wrote to the *New York Clipper* after ending an eight-month tour that "while business was good it was not big and if there were any companies in the West that did get big box office returns, we failed to find them."[1]

Della and Van Auker spent most of May 1910 vacationing at their Boise home. Walter Mendenhall, manager of Boise's Pinney Theatre, secured their services for a month-long summer season. By June 4, Van Auker advertised in the *New York Clipper* for performers and shortly after began rehearsals for the engagement.[2] The company roster included several new members since some of the old favorites were enjoying summer vacations and would not return until later in the season. The new performers included Mr. and Mrs. Nelson Lawrence, Helen Del Mar, Mr. and Mrs. C.G. Weston, Frank Gallagher and Charles B. Archer (a former member of Della's troupes). Olive McConnell and M.F. Hogan stayed on from last season.[3]

Della opened the Pinney Theatre summer season on June 27 with a play entirely new to the Boise public, *Dolores of Old San Juan*, a comedy drama of gold rush days in the Southwest. The day before the opening her husband told reporters an anecdote that illustrated the popularity attained by Della and her troupe in the western territory. According to Van Auker, an advance agent for Mrs. Leslie Carter, a major star of national fame, arrived in a Washington town and had to locate a piano for the star's performance. He called upon the dealer who had previously supplied instruments for traveling companies. Unfortunately, the last time he had rented out a piano it had been damaged so the Carter agent met with an absolute refusal to supply a piano and the dealer's bad opinion of troupes in general. "But," said the agent, "I represent Mrs. Leslie Carter." "Huh," answered the dealer, "I don't care—you wouldn't get that piano from me if you represented Jolly Della Pringle."[4]

The opening night of the summer season did not draw a full house, but Della and her new troupe received a great ovation following the performance.[5] Della continued the limited engagement with all new plays for the Boise audience. The week of July 4 *The Boys of Jumping Gee* did a good business for all shows.[6] The final two productions, *The Call of the Circus* and *Lies of a Traveling Man* met with equal success for a season without a losing week.[7]

At the conclusion of the Pinney season on July 22, Della made a short tour to the Idaho towns of Twin Falls, Shoshone[8] and Hailey between July 25 and August 17. While in Hailey, company members enjoyed a week of hunting, fishing and visiting the local natural springs in the daytime and playing to big houses each night.[9] She returned to Boise and a week later was back in business in her familiar Turner Theatre.

Della chose a comedy, *The Honeymooners*, to open her season at the Turner on August 22. As in past seasons, show-stopping applause greeted her first entrance on stage.[10] Four months of solid business followed with a change of play ever week and a diamond ring given away each Friday. During that time about the only negative comment in the press alluded to some scenery not being correct due to the smallness of the stage.[11]

The season at the Turner Theatre might have lasted well beyond the new year, but the stomach trouble Della had suffered with since her accidental poisoning in 1906 worsened to the point that she missed two weeks of performances after which doctors recommended surgery for the ailment.[12] In spite of her misery, she returned to the stage to finish an engagement of *The Girl on the Throne* on November 26 before departing the following Tuesday for "sanatorium treatments" in Des Moines. She would undergo two "very severe surgical operations."[13]

Della's troupe continued on at the Turner Theatre without her, but then her husband, manager of the company, developed pneumonia. The company, now without a leader, disbanded after a final performance of *Under the Lone Star* on December 31, 1910. Various members of the company found positions in other companies or went into vaudeville.[14] The *Idaho Statesman* lamented the sudden close of the season, noting that "the company is one of the strongest companies in this section of the country and the members have played to large houses every night throughout the fall and winter season. Those who had the 'Turner habit,' and there were many, will be quite lost for their regular weekly amusement."[15]

By January 17 of 1911 Della returned to Boise after spending six weeks in Des Moines recuperating from her successful surgeries, or, as a Boise paper quaintly phrased it, "Della went to Iowa some time ago for repairs, after being worked over, has returned looking frisky and as good as ever."[16] After suffering for years, Della was at last on the road to good health. Her husband, too, regained his health after his siege of pneumonia.

After overcoming their medical problems, Della and Van Auker lost little time in re-establishing their theatre business. They placed an ad in the *New York Clipper* on January 28 seeking performers for a stock company that would play in a new location during the summer. In the ad Della described herself as "The Clever Little Lady Who Can Come Back." She stressed that prospective company members "must be good looking, possess wardrobe, and … can't be too clever for this company" for the managers "set a pace that is hard to keep up with."[17]

Della and Van Auker assembled and rehearsed their new company within ten days to open a short season at the Turner Theatre on February

9. Except for M.F. Hogan and his wife, Olive McConnell, all the performers were new to the Boise audience. One couple came from Portland, a comedian came from the east and others from the Midwest.[18] Della ran the season as usual with six nightly performances, popular prices, a Friday diamond ring raffle and a Saturday matinee. During the abbreviated engagement she appeared in *The Girl and the Highwayman* and *Paid in His Own Coin*, productions that attracted solid patronage.[19]

Following the brief Turner Theatre engagement, Della began a tour that would cover cities in Idaho, Washington and Montana. Her ten-member troupe first appeared in the nearby community of Emmett, Idaho, for the week of February 27 at the Pleasure Club Hall.[20] The following week found the company paying a return visit to Dayton, Washington, again performing in the Weinard Theatre.[21] On March 13 Della's group began a one-week stand at Lewiston, Idaho's, Temple Theatre, another return engagement.[22]

After the series of one-week appearances, the Pringle company settled in at Walla Walla, Washington, for a lengthy engagement that ran for six weeks, from March 20 and April 30. During this time the local paper, the *Walla Walla Union*, devoted many columns to publicizing and criticizing the Pringle company's various productions, giving a rather complete record of the season.

Altogether Della presented thirteen different productions, changing the bill twice a week. Patrons filled the 500 seats of the Bijou Grand Theatre night after night. Reviews described crowds with such terms as "large attendance," "capacity house" and even "immense throngs." One review stated that with such strong plays the troupe "may never know what it is to play to a small house."[23]

Newspaper items also disclosed the names of additional company members. Former Pringle troupe actors Jimmy Wright and Riley Meyers had rejoined the group. New performers were Arthur Matthews and two actresses, Francis Searth and Margaret Haywood, whose specialty rendition of "Cuddle Up a Little Closer" made a big hit with Walla Walla theatregoers.[24] The company must have had several good dancers for a review of *The Hayseed* refers to an encore for a country dance in the first act.[25]

Della's popular priced theatre offerings compared favorably with the much more expensive Broadway touring shows frequently presented at Walla Walla's Keylor Grand Theatre. They also had to compete with motion pictures and vaudeville at the Rose Theatre. Della's shows, according to the press, featured the winning attributes of "artistic detail, careful delineation of character and natural acting."[26]

Della received most of the critical attention for her acting. A review of *The Parish Priest* singled out Della's portrayal of a school teacher as "delightfully unaffected and sweetly sympathetic." She demonstrated her versatility by playing not only a school teacher, but a jolly soubrette in *The Hayseed*, a college girl mouthing quaint and slangy expressions" in *Lies of a Traveling Man* and a Turkish harem girl in *The Awakening of Zuluana*.[27]

The wardrobe worn by Della also merited mention on occasion. Three costumes won special attention. In *The Honeymooners* she wore "a lounging robe direct from the land of the Mikado," one of two costumes by Oriental designers. She created a sensation in the first act of *The Awakening of Zuluana* "when she appeared clad in the soft, breezy draperies of the Orient and the latest fad—the harem skirt." In the final play of the season, *The Sea Wolf*, she wore "a wondrous gown of shimmering satin" that delighted the women in attendance.[28]

While Della Pringle played heroines on stage in Walla Walla, villainy reigned at her home in Boise—the rooming house she owned there (the Palantine) had been robbed! On Sunday April 9 lodgers at the Palantine notified Della that the woman she had hired to look after the rooming house in her absence had suddenly departed on Saturday. Della left her troupe in Walla Walla and arrived in Boise on April 10 to find the caretaker, Alice Farmer, had absconded with many of the pillows, most all of the linen and some money from the rooming house. The woman and her husband supposedly fled to Portland, Oregon. The city police and detectives still had no clue as to the whereabouts of the couple when Della had to leave Boise to rejoin her company in Walla Walla on April 16.[29]

After Della came back to her troupe, the Walla Walla season continued on for two weeks. When Della announced the departure of her players for Butte, Montana, the *Walla Walla Union* paid Della's company this final tribute:

> The many friends and admirers gained by this capable theatrical organization during their engagement here will regret their going. The high standard plays produced have been a source of delight to amusement lovers who appreciate classy entertainment and the reputation enjoyed by the Pringle company of being the best in the West at popular prices is well deserved.[30]

Traveling to Butte, Montana, and preparing productions for a month-long season occupied the Pringle troupe during the week of May 1. They were booked into the Family Theatre, one of four Butte venues, the others being the Empire and Orion featuring vaudeville and motion pictures and the Broadway, home of road shows.

Before the first show, *Peaceful Valley*, opened on May 7, Cecil Van Auker predicted in the press that Butte audiences "will see a new era in stock theatre circles."[31] The opening performance by the Pringle company fulfilled his rather brash statement. The review of the show in the *Butte Miner* hailed the initial performance as "one of the best stock offerings, if not the best, ever seen in Butte, and the Della Pringle Company, ... incidentally is one of the best aggregations to visit the city."[32] The writer characterized Jolly Della Pringle as "a sparkling fountain of vivacity [whose] radiance seemingly permeates every endeavor of her company."[33] Flattering comments continued with "Miss Pringle impresses as a ray of sunshine, dancing, it may be called, every time she enters.... Versatile, the very essence of grace, possessing a charming stage appearance, her remarkable success in stock causes no wonder."[34]

After such a glowing reception in the press, attendance for the Pringle shows grew steadily. On one night of the next play, *The Parish Priest*, 200 people were turned away at the door. This production and the following offerings, *Faust* (a Pringle staple for almost a decade) and *The Awakening of Zuluana*, gained favorable reviews. *Faust* was praised for its overall excellence, its elaborate staging and electrical effects. Della's skill as a comedienne won attention in *The Awakening of Zuluana* as did her "correct Turkish costume, jeweled headdress, harem trousers, strings of pearls and jeweled ornaments."[35] This costume, allegedly imported from Paris, was claimed to be "the most elaborate gown of its kind ever introduced in the west."[36]

The Butte newspaper reviews also contained additional information about company members, repertoire and performance schedule. As for the company, Francis Searth had sung with the Grau Opera Company, Arthur Matthews had acted for several years in *Faust* with the famed Lewis Morrison and Mr. and Mrs. Charles Newton were new to Della's troupe.[37] According to one article, Van Auker claimed the troupe an amazing twenty-five plays in its repertoire.[38] At Butte one week offerings of a play had nightly performances with matinees on Saturday and Sunday, the usual Wednesday matinee being dropped. Additionally, Della's specialties included some short motion pictures. Films were not new to Della's attractions, but had not been mentioned in conjunction with her shows for several years.

The successful Butte engagement ended the week of June 4 with *What Happened to Jones?* after which time Della disbanded her company and headed for home in Boise with her husband.[39] Following a short stay there, they took off on a five-week vacation trip. First they visited San

Francisco and Los Angeles where they took in shows from vaudeville to productions at the Belasco Theatre. In a note to the *New York Clipper* Della observed, "Los Angeles is the greatest show town I ever saw—every theatre is packed all the time, especially the cheap priced ones, and they are surprisingly good for 10 and 20 cents."[40]

After a short visit to Long Beach, Della's former California home, Della accompanied her husband to San Diego for a visit with his mother who he had not seen in ten years. While in San Diego, Van Auker took a side trip to Tijuana, Mexico, in mid–July, taking his camera with him, but unaware that Mexico had laws against tourists taking pictures. When some Mexican soldiers saw the camera, they immediately arrested Van Auker and confiscated his camera. Determining that no pictures had been taken, the soldiers released him and returned the camera.[41] He had crossed America's southern border and in four months would cross its northern border.

Van Auker rejoined Della in San Diego and they departed for Boise via Los Angeles and Salt Lake City, arriving home on July 22.[42] A week later they advertised for players.

On August 17, while waiting for their troupe to assemble for the new season, Della and Van Auker joined 150 other Boise residents on an Oregon Short Line Railroad excursion to Nahcotta on the southwest coast of Washington State. The trip provided unexpected diversion when a freight train wreck delayed the excursion at the little town of Arlington, Oregon, for twelve hours. It took little time for the passengers to thoroughly explore the little town. They were rescued from boredom by an enterprising Boise businessman, C.B. Samsom, who arranged to rent the only dance hall in Arlington and invited everyone to join him in a dancing party. The dance lasted all the afternoon and well into the night. From time to time refreshments were secured from local stores and a jolly time was had by all, including Jolly Della Pringle.[43]

Della and Van Auker returned from the Washington excursion about September 1 and by the eleventh opened their fifteenth Boise season, this time at the city's biggest theatre, the Pinney. The season lasted only three weeks during which time Della mounted three new plays she had added to her repertoire: *The Blue Mouse, The Lottery Man* and *Pierre of the Plains*. She hired a strong company of players for support of her and Van Auker. Several returned from previous seasons: M.F. Hogan and his wife, Olive McConnell (veterans of many seasons), Riley Myers, Fanny Hammond Stanley and her husband, Edwin Stanley, who doubled as the troupe's business manager. New to the Jolly Della Pringle Company were B.D. Bard, Willie Goodman and Virginia Weaver.[44]

The booking of a road show into the Pinney Theatre on September 24 temporarily interrupted Della's limited engagement. She took advantage of the situation and moved her troupe to nearby Nampa, Idaho, and presented a well-attended performance of *The Blue Mouse*.[45] She returned to the Pinney Theatre to complete the short season after doing the largest business ever done by a stock company in Boise.[46]

After the Pinney season closed on September 30, Della and her players took time to pack up scenery, props and wardrobe before beginning another tour. The troupe first appeared in nearby Caldwell, Idaho for the week of October 3.[47] Then, for the next month, there is no record of the group, an unusual event since Della normally reported her tour dates and plans regularly in the theatrical trade papers.

Finally Della wrote to Boise's *Idaho Statesman* on November 11 that, surprisingly, she had left the United States and had been playing towns in Canada's northern British Columbia, for how long she did not say. However, she had plenty to say about touring in Canada and little was good except its beautiful scenery and good roads. Strikes in mining towns resulted in hard economic times. Della lamented that money was hard to get and the high cost of living made it "ten times worse."[48] She remarked that fuel costs for heating were high while the weather was exceedingly cold, adding, "We have to pay four cents a mile to travel and hotels are double the price of the states."[49]

Della also objected to "this cold, foreign country [where] everything is so different" and found fault with Canadian theatregoers. "Our audiences are made up entirely of English and they don't 'savey' American comedy a little bit and we have had to change our entire repertoire ... and put on melodrama entirely. They all look so stolid and phlegmatic, you couldn't make them laugh or show a bit of amusement."[50]

At last exact dates of Della's whereabouts came from Edmonton, Alberta, Canada where on November 23, 1911, she appeared in a production of *What Happened to Jones?*. Evidently she had been playing in other Canadian towns since an Edmonton newspaper article said about Della's troupe: "In every city played in Canada so far the verdict of the press has been unanimous in saying 'the best plays, the finest costumes, and a real company of comedians.'"[51]

This Edmonton engagement lasted for only three evenings and one matinee at the Empire Theatre. The opening night review of the show, while generally positive, did find fault with a first act that dragged, the selection of scenery and Della being far too matronly to play the role of a twenty-three-year-old girl.[52] On the final evening of the brief season,

Della's specialties were augmented by the appearance of a minstrel group, the Dixie Jubilee Singers.

Ads for the first Edmonton appearance contained the usual information about the title of the show, time, place and admission cost (which had been raised to a top rate of one dollar). The ad also contained a special notice: "The Della Pringle Company has no connection with any other traveling company under a similar name."[53] This disclaimer was prompted after Della discovered her first husband, Johnny Pringle, was also on tour in Canada. He had maintained traveling repertory companies in the Pacific Northwest for many years, but none had gained the same solid reputation enjoyed by Della. Della's ad was in defense of that reputation.

Della and company left Edmonton after November 25 and returned there three weeks later. During that time they may have appeared in Calgary, Canada, since Van Auker placed an ad from there in the *New York Clipper* in late November. It read: "Della Pringle wants / Comedian and soubrette specialties, Clever / Child, Pianist or Musical Act to double in parts. Address C. K. Van Auker, Lyric Theater, Calgary, Alberta, Canada."[54] However, there was no local confirmation of any appearance by Della and her company.

On December 13, 1911, *The Edmonton Journal* reported that Della Pringle and C.K. Van Auker had taken over the Majestic Theatre at the corner of Third and Jasper and after a thorough overhaul of the theatre would install a first-class stock troupe. Della promised an excellent company of ten people reproducing many of the latest New York successes with special attention to all details in the staging of the plays. She planned to offer Wednesday and Saturday matinees and two shows on Friday and Saturday nights. Matinee admission would be ten and twenty-five cents and evening performances would cost thirty-five cents for downstairs seating and a quarter for the balcony.[55]

Della opened her second Edmonton engagement on December 18 with the production of a hit comedy, *The Man in the Box*, before a good-sized audience that took great delight in the performance. Within days of the opening Della placed large ads in *The Edmonton Journal* stating, "Every City of Consequence Has a Stock Company [and] Edmonton Has the Majestic, the Future Home of Miss Della Pringle." The ad featured a picture of Della and phrases such as "Prices That Are Right," "Good, Clean Wholesome Plays," "Excellent Company" and "Della Pringle and her big Company are here to stay."[56] And stay they did—for a year until December 21, 1912!

Della and her company members faced obstacles before they could even open their season. Unable to get bookings from a local theatrical trust, Della resorted to renting the unused Majestic Theatre with its rather poor accommodations. Every vestige of scenery and lighting equipment had been stripped from the theatre. While some troupes would have required several weeks of rehearsals and repairs to get the venue ready for performances, Della and her company readied the theatre in a miraculous fashion. They arrived at the theatre about 9:00 a.m. and from that moment each individual member of the company began to hustle. From scenic artist to leading man, from leading man to soubrette, from soubrette to prop boy, all pitched in. As a result of this prodigious effort the Della Pringle Stock Company opened at 8:00 p.m. that very evening in a clean, well-lighted theatre.[57]

After establishing her first-class stock theatre troupe in Edmonton, Della enjoyed solid support from the community of 50,000 whose citizens filled the small Majestic Theatre night after night as the months wore on. She prospered in spite of competition with six movie houses, a combination house offering road shows almost every night and a musical comedy stock theatre.

The troupe that Della had formed in Boise had the same performers who contributed so much in getting the Majestic Theatre ready for performances. For the most part this group with such veteran members as M.F. Hogan, Olive McConnell, Riley Myers and Nelson Lawrence remained together for most of the Edmonton season. At times during the year Della and Van Auker placed ads for additional performers in the *New York Clipper*. One ad quaintly and with humor stated: "We like married people, children and dogs, if they are clever."[58] From such ads Della added such talents as former troupe member James C. Wright along with Bert Ransome, James H. O'Neill, Lew Shively, Chester McMann, Helen West, Lenore Allen and Verna Warde. In September Thomas Wiggins and Helene Wilson joined Della's company. Della began the Edmonton season with eight actors besides herself and Van Auker. Although several performers joined and left the troupe, the number grew to fourteen as the season progressed.

After seven months of continued success in Edmonton, Della wrote a letter to the *New York Clipper* about her prolonged season. She found her work very easy with one bill a week, no Sunday performances and only one matinee. Following the usual cold Canadian winter, weather had been good for business with only a few really hot days and plenty of rain which drove crowds off the street and into theatres. She noted that being so far north it didn't get dark until 11:00 p.m. and the sun rose at 2:30 a.m.

the next morning, resulting in nights only three and a half hours long.⁵⁹

In her tenth month in Edmonton, Della again wrote to the *New York Clipper* to report that her houses were still fine in spite of "big opposition" from two sources.⁶⁰ The Empire Theatre presented three days of Orpheum vaudeville and completed the week with high priced road attractions featuring such recognized national celebrities as Forbes-Robinson and Minnie Maddern Fiske. On July 9 Canadian theatre manager, Arthur Aylesworth formed a troupe titled the Winnipeg Stock Company which played in the Lyceum Theatre, located within just a few feet of Della's Majestic Theatre. In spite of being nearly identical theatre operations presenting stock theatre at the same popular prices, both rival companies did well until the Winnipeg Stock Company left Edmonton in early October.

Della, age 43, during her year-long season in Edmonton, Alberta, Canada (courtesy the National Society for the Preservation of Tent, Folk and Repertoire Theatre at the Theatre Museum of Repertoire Americana, Midwest Old Threshers, Mt. Pleasant, Iowa).

Della's letter also contained sad news. She had lost her prize winning Boston terrier, Winchester Beauty, "who had sacrificed her life for the sake of a red ribbon."⁶¹ The terrier had been entered into a dog show in August, won a second prize, but caught distemper and died on September 15. Della had been enamored of Boston terriers ever since her experience with her bag-punching dogs in 1903 and would keep one of the breed well into the 1930s.

All through the extended Edmonton season the *Edmonton Journal* printed generous coverage of the Pringle company shows. However, the press items and reviews expressed little judgment about or evaluation of the plays or their production. Mainly they offered a plot synopsis, a cast of characters and general praise for the entire company. Occasionally an item might contain some interesting information such as on September 28 when a review mentioned that Cecil Van Auker had once acted in a German stock theatre in New York, playing various roles from Hamlet to an English butler.[62]

About the only negative commentary about Della's productions centered on the troupe's specialties, suggesting that they be "edited" or improved and objecting that it was inappropriate to present them between acts of a serious play or melodrama.[63] For a time, Della heeded the criticism and eliminated the specialties. However, after securing new talent, she reinstated them and they remained to the end of the engagement.

Only occasionally did a review make any detailed mention of Della's acting. In a production of *Mrs. Templeton's Telegram* she played a "spirited" Mrs. Temple who "laughs and cries, coaxes and storms and acts the temperamental wife to perfection."[64] Della also won praise for the range of emotions displayed when playing the role of Marguerite in her often-repeated production of *Faust*.[65] Her wardrobe warranted attention when she played a dashing young actress in *When We Were Twenty-one* presenting a "dazzling picture of scarlet and gold."[66]

Although Della's troupe performed for a year without interruption, she and Van Auker did not. She took a week off to rest during the last week of May and possibly another short vacation in late August. Van Auker left the company for two weeks in late July to conduct business back in Boise where he purchased some additional real estate.[67]

Della's Edmonton season finally came to an end on December 21, 1912—an engagement of one year and three days—at which time she departed eastward to perform at Winnipeg, Manitoba, Canada.[68] The season there began at the Grand Theatre on December 23 and ended on January 25, 1913.[69]

Unlike the Edmonton press, the Winnipeg papers reported little about Della's productions. Newspaper ads disclosed that Winnipeg, one of the largest cities in Canada's Manitoba province, supported two legitimate theatres, three vaudeville houses and six movie theatres. Della presented a play one week at popular prices of ten to thirty-five cents and fifty cents for box seats. During her time in Winnipeg she presented *The Fortune Hunter, Heir to the Horrah, Arizona* and *My Friend from India*.[70]

Even though the *New York Clipper* reported on January 11, 1913, that "The Jolly Della Pringle Stock Co.. is making good at the Grand, Winnipeg,

Canada,"[71] for undisclosed reasons Della closed her season there on January 25. Her company journeyed westward to Moose Jaw, Saskatchewan, arriving there in late January and opening on February 3 in the Moose Theatre, a converted movie house, with a performance of *My Wife's Family*.[72] Possibly in an attempt to appear as a Canadian troupe, during the Moose Jaw engagement Della changed her group's name and presented plays under the title of the Winnipeg Stock Company.[73]

Evidently some of the fourteen company members didn't want any more of Canada's frigid winter because almost immediately after arriving in Moose Jaw, Van Auker telegraphed a want ad to the *New York Clipper* which appeared in the February 1 issue. His troupe needed a soubrette who could play child's parts, a "heavy" man, a scenic artist who could play parts and "Specialty People."[74] A similar ad on March 15 indicated the soubrette and scenic artist positions had not been filled for six weeks (an unlikely situation) or else those hired thought better about staying on.[75] The company membership remained stable until April 17 when Della advertised for a young and pretty woman for general business and two musicians to play piano, violin or trap drums.[76]

Due to a lack of Moose Jaw newspaper resources, the only information about Della's seventeen-week stay came from her correspondence with Boise's *Idaho Statesman* and the *New York Clipper*. She began a March 13, 1913, letter to the *Statesman* urging Boise business men to consider arranging for shipping Idaho farm produce up to Canada. She explained that people in Moose Jaw were "starved for green stuff" and paid "terrible prices" to buy vegetables imported from Oregon and Washington.[77]

More importantly, her letter described the severe winter conditions in Moose Jaw. She wrote: "It is so cold here that it freezes the tears right out of your eyes. I walked to the post office last night (March 2) about four blocks and my cheeks were frozen when I got home. We all have to bundle up with furs and moccasins ... to 'mush down' to the theatre."[78]

Della also complained about Moose Jaw's poor water system. Moose Jaw's population had rapidly risen to 25,000, but had a water supply inadequate to meet one third of demand. Della explained: "They shut the water off every day at 9:00 a.m. until 6:00 p.m. and sometimes we don't have a drop for three or four days except what we buy from the ice company, which melts the ice and sells the water."[79]

Her final complaints focused on Canada's high cost of lodging and simple amenities:

> We pay $35 for one furnished room which is supposed to have steam heat and hot and cold water. As for steam heat! Did you ever have an

experience with an English janitor? Well, they are enough for me; one would be perfectly justified in murdering them in cold blood because they try to kill you by freezing you to death. As to hot water and baths, "they ain't no such animal" in Canada. If you would pay the highest price known in a hotel in Canada for room and bath, you'd get the room but no water for the bath. This is the absolute truth.[80]

In spite of all her complaints, Della endured Canada's frigid climate, its failure to provide "a few comforts of life" and its humorless theatre patrons. She concluded her letter with a positive note, "but the harvest is rich." Indeed, frequent references in the *New York Dramatic Mirror* to capacity houses and big crowds for Moose Jaw's Winnipeg Stock Company attest to the financial success of Della's troupe.[81]

Della wrote another letter from Moose Jaw on February 22 to the *New York Clipper* which was printed in the March 8 edition. In it she discloses some of the problems associated with doing theatre business in Moose Jaw. "They charge $200 a year license for the city and $300 a year provincial, meaning $500 a year licenses for our little theatre which seats less than four hundred people." She also had to comply with stringent building codes and restrictive city by-laws:

> We have had all the inspectors, aldermen, city council, fire chiefs, health inspectors, etc., coming around every day, ordering the seats to be changed, new wiring installed, new doors and exits, etc., just because the house is changed into a dramatic stock house. It stood as it was and no one paid any attention to it as a picture house, but the moment we came in to start to do business they all got busy.[82]

Della and her troupe also kept busy, presenting a new show each week for over four months. Near the end of the Moose Jaw season the company roster included thirteen members: Della and Van Auker, Lenore Allen and Baby Bobby, Mike Hogan, Al Bridges, Arthur Matthews, Tony West, Riley Meyers, James O'Neill, Olive McConnell and Helen Hartley West.[83]

On May 10, after more than four months of theatrical presentations in Moose Jaw, Della announced initial plans to take a vacation trip from Canada to New York, Chicago, Knoxville, Iowa, Colorado Springs and Boise.[84] She and Van Auker actually left Moose Jaw on May 25 with intentions to return in the summer. By May 30 Boise newspapers reported that they were in town. Della told the paper that she had not decided whether to return to Moose Jaw or a more northern city. She revealed that despite hardships the brisk Canadian air had been beneficial for her company who had all gained weight. She also commented that they hardly knew how to walk in shoes since the Canadian cold and snow made it necessary to wear moccasins when trudging to and from their theatre.[85]

Altering their original vacation plans, Della and Van Auker stayed a short time in Boise before leaving to visit Van Auker's old home in Denver and spending a week in Colorado Springs with Della's niece, Grace Van Winkle. They returned to Boise for a few more weeks during which time they visited with friends and enjoyed driving their automobile into the mountains on fishing trips, at one time catching over a hundred fish.[86]

About July 14 Della and Van Auker departed Boise, again bound for Moose Jaw to renew their season.[87] Shortly after they left the *Statesman* reported two real estate transfers from Van Auker to Della Pringle.[88] It is not clear why this was done, but in view of what happened between Della and Van Auker in 1918, it had definite advantages for Della.

After Della reached Moose Jaw about July 18, there is no further solid information about her activities until August 9. She may have briefly continued presenting plays in Moose Jaw and then moved on. A letter to the *New York Dramatic Mirror*—written earlier, but appearing in the August 6 edition—hints at a season of indefinite duration in Regina, Saskatchewan.[89] The only certainty is that Della and Van Auker had ended their nearly two-year sojourn in Canada in early August, never to return.

11

Off the Stage and Onto the Screen

The first indication that Della's company had returned to the United States came from a *New York Clipper* ad that appeared in the August 9, 1913, edition. Della's husband, placing the ad from Butte, Montana, revealed that she had a year's lease on Butte's Empire Theatre and needed to fill six or more positions in her troupe.[1] Apparently half of Della's Canadian contingent had either remained there or accepted engagements elsewhere.

The opening of Della's season in Butte took place on August 31. The hiring of so many new actors, rehearsing them for a number of productions and a rather complete redecoration of the Empire Theatre occupied almost three weeks from the arrival in Butte to opening night.

The Butte season lasted almost five months, through January of 1914 during which time Della's troupe performed as the "Permanent Players." The opening matinee and evening performances of *The Lion and the Mouse* drew a positive response from the *Butte Miner* critic whose review began with "The 'Permanent Players' at the Empire Theatre made their initial bow before Butte audiences and if the enthusiasm evinced by their audiences is any criterion of judgment they are assured of a long and profitable stay in the city."[2] The critic pointed out the surprise shown by the audience when first seeing the entirely renovated theatre and the pretty girl ushers clad in gray silk Quaker costumes. He found the play well staged with newly painted scenery and an "efficient" company. He singled out Della for her "sincere portrayal" of the female lead.[3]

A second production, *Pierre of the Plains* during the week of September 7, pleased a large audience. Again the paper praised the exciting production for both acting and staging with a particular note of Van Auker's striking portrayal of a "half-breed gambler" and Della's "sweet and appealing" role. This review also listed the names of Della's new troupe: Miss

Fannie Keeler, C.N. Hutchinson, Albert Shellworth, James H. O'Neill, William Hester, Hallie Mitchell, J.C. Wright and Charles Malloy.[4]

After such attention to early productions, the Butte newspaper devoted little space to comments about Della's Permanent Players and their shows except for listing show titles and an occasional note on attendance. No ads or items appeared at all for months after September 21. Finally, in late November the paper briefly renewed coverage of Della's with two items. The first disclosed that Cecil Van Auker had supposedly been offered a job by one of the reigning stars of the American stage, Minnie Maddern Fiske, but had turned it down to continue as manager and leading man at the Empire Theatre.[5] In the other item Della revealed some of the costs involved in producing shows, citing the $100 royalty fee for her current production of *The Wolf*. In a barely hidden plea for public support, she wrote: "We have to pay a roll of $650 a week and it is paid every Saturday night. The money is kept in Butte and not taken away; that's why a really deserving stock company is entitled to consideration and patronage."[6] She boasted, "Miss Pringle has a reputation that is gilt edge. When you see her name connected with any business enterprise, it has to be right."[7]

Della's Butte engagement carried on without her in mid–November when she temporarily left her company to attend to her ranch and home in Boise. She found the ranch in good condition with twenty acres of apple trees and much more in alfalfa. The orchard, now five years old, promised to be a commercial proposition. Before returning to Butte she declared, "Boise itself never looked better."[8] Della arrived back in Butte by November 23 and her theatre business there continued past the new year to the end of January 1914.

The long Butte engagement ended abruptly about the first of February 1914 under unusual circumstances.[9] About mid–January Della had taken a short vacation to visit her old hometown of Knoxville, Iowa, and when she returned to Montana her husband said he was also going to take a vacation. Business had become poor and he was disgusted with show business in general. Della assumed he would go home to Boise.

Then, as Della wrote to Boise's *Idaho Statesman*, "imagine my surprise when I received a letter from him, written in Salt Lake, stating he was on his way to Mexico to accept a commission as captain in the rebel army,"[10] the army of the notorious Pancho Villa! Evidently, Van Auker had had the Mexican war on his mind for some time. Della observed, "He knew if he told me he was going I would make such a fuss he would probably abandon so he kept me in the dark. I heard from him at El Paso."[11]

Although abrupt, Van Auker's rapid change from actor to soldier was not as strange as is seemed. He had graduated from an eastern military college and earlier in his life had served in the Philippines during the Spanish American War with an artillery company, gaining the experience and knowledge sorely needed by Pancho Villa's peasant army. His commission had been secured by fellow graduates from his military college.[12]

Della remained in Boise for most of February attempting to find a new manager for her ranch. On or before the nineteenth she received a letter from Van Auker in Mexico. He let her know that he was having an exciting time educating Pancho Villa's forces how to operate a howitzer they had captured but didn't know how to use. They were mounting it on a high hill overlooking a city they wanted to capture. Van Auker wrote that he had met Pancho Villa himself and described the fearsome rebel as "a decent chap but extremely ignorant—could neither read nor write." He also noted that Villa "has a penchant for standing men up against the wall and firing at them."[13] Van Auker ended his letter with "There is plenty of money here, but precious little grub. Our rations are fierce, a good meal costs about ten bucks."[14]

Della finally found a suitable manager for her ranch and then left for San Diego to join Van Auker's mother in waiting for her son's return from the war in Mexico. She didn't have to wait long. By April 1 he had resigned his commission in the Mexican army and met Della in San Diego.[15] He had been in the thick of fighting and glad to get out alive. Witness to the slaughter of federal troops at Torren by Villa's artillery, he wrote, "Human hearts could not bear the sight of Villa's butchery nor stand the sight of so many dying men."[16] Clearly, the Mexican hostilities had disgusted the Boise soldier of fortune and he gladly returned to a life behind the footlights.

By May 16, 1914, Boise's *Idaho Statesman* reported that Della and Van Auker, now back home, had recently purchased a residence at 1711 North Eighteenth Street and were "busy making it attractive." They announced plans to return to the stage again in the fall. Their new home would be a place to return to after their theatre tours. After putting the house in order, they spent part of the summer in Hailey, Idaho, on the Wood River.[17]

By July 17 Della and husband had returned to Boise and were playing host to his sister, Grace Van Auker, who was also in show business. She had been leading lady in producer William Brady's popular production of *Bought and Paid For* which had been playing all the large cities in the East for the past two years. Following her visit with her brother, she returned to New York to begin rehearsals for another Brady production.[18]

During the time of the sister's visit, Della and Van Auker spent some time conducting their own rehearsals for a new season beginning with an engagement at the Pinney Theatre. They opened there on August 3 with a light comedy, *The Happiest Man Alive*. A crowded house welcomed them and their company which a reviewer deemed "probably the strongest which they have yet had."[19] He noted that Riley Myers, the only remaining member of the previous company, received a special welcome and declared the new actresses (Verna Warde, Kate Stein and Maude Phillips) "all excellent." The men (Harry Dunbar, Joe C. Berry and Fred Tonkin along with Van Auker) he found to be "as good a quartet as any stock company could assemble." Della Pringle and Cecil Van Auker were described as "never in better spirits nor better cast" with their acting "as finished as usual."[20]

The reviewer remarked that the show itself had "all the earmarks from the stage setting to gowns, of a regular $1 production" at picture show prices.[21] A photograph of *The Happiest Man Alive* printed in the paper shows an elaborate, detailed two-level setting with French doors, a large central staircase and two balconies backed by windows. The actors wear formal attire and the actresses are clad in fashionable full-length gowns.[22] The picture makes clear that Della Pringle presented shows of exceptional quality on a par with most touring Broadway productions, all for an admission of no more than twenty cents which included vaudeville specialties between acts.

The Pinney Theatre engagement lasted for fourteen weeks, ending on November 14.[23] During this time sizable or full audiences filled the 1,000-seat auditorium on many evenings and afternoons, a tribute to Della and Van Auker's talents as performers and skills as theatre managers. That they had played in Boise off and on for six years was remarkable in that their popularity never waned in spite of such frequent exposure to their patrons. Of course, promotional stunts such as raffles for diamond rings, silver tea sets and even groceries helped to draw in crowds. One Friday night an astonished woman won a live pig which she led through the audience back to her seat.[24]

Little disturbed the routine of rehearsal and performance during the season. The *Idaho Statesman* reported on September 1 that Van Auker's auto had been stolen on Monday night from in front of the Pinney Theatre and found badly damage a few blocks away.[25] On September 17 Della and spouse made their first attempt to sell their forty-acre ranch with its five bedroom bungalow by placing an ad in the paper's classified section.[26] There were no takers and it remained in their possession until 1918. Late in the season former troupe members Fannie Hammond Stanley, James C. Wright and Ed Stanley rejoined Della's company.[27] Anticipating the end of the Boise season, Della placed an ad in the September 26 *New York Clipper* looking for a tour manager.[28]

Immediately after closing the Pinney Theatre engagement on November 15, 1914, Della's troupe began a twelve-week tour, first performing in nearby Nampa, Idaho, and then heading east to play in the Idaho towns of Mountain Home and Jerome[29] before settling in at Twin Falls on November 25 for a month at the Lavering Theatre.[30] From Idaho, Della moved on into Washington State to appear first in Walla Walla where her troupe gave a daytime performance at the penitentiary on New Year's Day, 1915. Next the American Theatre management in Spokane booked her for the week of January 6 in performances of *The Lion and the Mouse*.[31]

For the roughly five weeks after January 12, there were no indications of exactly where Della appeared. It is assumed that some engagements took place in Oregon for when the troupe returned to Boise about February 20 the paper made reference to a "trip through eastern Idaho and Oregon."[32] During the five weeks Della wrote no letters to the local press as she had done while on past tours. As the motion pictures began to dominate the entertainment business, the theatrical trade papers no longer carried "Dates Ahead" information that had made it possible to locate places visited by touring repertory companies like Della's.

At the time Della arrived in Boise in late February, she announced plans to open a ten week season at the Pinney Theatre in about a week,[33] but for undisclosed reasons the season did not open until March 22. Della's company for the engagement retained dainty Vera Warde and Fred Tonkin and hired four new performers—Hazel Stone, Barron LaPage, Arthur Belasco and Clint Ford. Late in March Charles Breckenridge joined the troupe.[34]

At the season opening performance of *The Spider and the Fly* a full house welcomed Della and Van Auker with a great burst of applause. The show's review noted that they had assembled an "unusually strong company" as supporting players. Arthur Belasco and Barron LaPage were described as "without peer in stock upon the coast."[35] Character woman Hazel Stone earned praise for the laughter she provoked in her portrayal of a spinster aunt. The remainder of the cast and a new lot of between the act specialties drew similar positive commendations.

Della continued her season at the Pinney, offering two productions a week through May 15 with six evening and two matinee performances. Touring Broadway shows booked into the theatre occasionally pre-empted her performances for an evening or two. Attendance was generally good but only a few reviews mentioned crowded houses. One review referred to a "fair-sized but enthusiastic audience" for *The Barrier* and another reported that the opening of *Jim, the Westerner* "was greeted by a smaller audience than it deserved."[36]

Shortly after her season ended in late May, Della wrote letters to the *New York Clipper* and the *New York Dramatic Mirror* expressing her dismay over her declining theatre business. In the *Clipper* letter, printed on June 4, 1915, she wrote:

> We closed a season of thirty-nine weeks at Boise, Idaho, May 25. We have had an excellent company and gave fine satisfaction to the public, but candidly it's the poorest season I ever had financially. I've worked harder and have less money that when we opened Aug. 1. Mr. Van Auker and I will spend the summer in and around Boise. I am raising chickens, turkeys and geese on the ranch. We have a fine apple crop, and have fine prospects for grain..., so we could be worse off.[37]

In the same *Clipper* edition she placed an ad that read "At Liberty. For Stock, Movie, or Anything that Pays Salaries. Jolly Della Pringle, Leads. C. Van Auker, Leads and Heavies. Single or Joint Engagement. Can Join at once."[38]

On June 16 the *New York Dramatic Mirror* printed a similar but longer letter under the heading of "Della Pringle in the Dumps." In it Della wrote:

> We had a season of thirty-nine weeks, part good and some pretty bad. We paid all salaries, and don't owe anybody anything, except the bank and ourselves. Actors who had a job the past season on a salary, and got it, are the lucky ones. Believe me, I know. I talked to some of the biggest managers who came through here this season, and none of them were making it; all had a worried look; so now I don't know whether to look for a job in the show business, or join the Sheepherders' Union: they are the only people I know of making money.[39]

She continued:

> Show business has changed. You can't run a show on the road anymore; the managers won't answer your letters; they don't want traveling "troupes": they have feature films on certain nights and would rather have them than any New York attraction. I can't figure out what's going to become of the actors if we can't get jobs working for the movies. I'm a good cook, and looking for work "stiddy."[40]

Certainly Della had cause to be in the "dumps." Her once lucrative theatre career verged upon extinction. Employment ads in the national trade papers went unanswered. Looking high and low for a job, she resorted to placing an ad in Boise's *Idaho Statesman* beginning on May 5 announcing that she and Van Auker were available to "commercial clubs, high schools, amateur societies wanting to engage these clever people to put on benefits."[41] It, too, went unanswered.

A visit from an old friend brightened Della's summer of discontent when the internationally famous Buffalo Bill Cody came to Boise on June 12 with the Sells-Floto Circus and Wild West Show. Della and her husband hosted a luncheon in her home for Mr. and Mrs. Cody, enjoying a pleasant reunion. Della then took Mrs. Cody for a ride about Boise and afterward she and Van Auker were entertained in the tent at the circus and were pleased and honored when Buffalo Bill personally showed them around the circus grounds. Della complemented Cody on his good looks, telling him he had a pink and white complexion making him as pretty as a girl. He returned the compliment, telling Della that she was never going to get old.[42]

During the few weeks after Buffalo Bill's visit, Della and Van Auker still sought ways to revive their theatrical fortunes. Then they found a solution. They noticed that many automobiles were passing through Boise on the way to an exposition in San Francisco and thought if roads were good enough for transcontinental travel they would serve to support a tour by a small repertory company. So, they came up with a scheme to tour by automobile to Idaho mountain towns and summer resorts in the areas surrounding Boise.[43]

Della and Van Auker put together a company of only five performers—themselves plus Barron LaPage, Hazel Stone and Arthur Belasco from their most recent season at the Pinney Theatre. They reduced their repertory to two small cast plays—*Bought and Paid For* and *Paid in Full*.[44]

The troupe traveled in two automobiles. The Van Auker's Ford touring car carried the actors and the other vehicle hauled special stage properties and costumes.[45] Each actor's clothing was tied up in a bundle, wrapped in a tarpaulin and strapped to a car fender.[46]

Della's small company played two- and three-night stands. She booked engagements by telephone and sent her "paper" (posters, handbills, etc.) by parcel post.[47] Even with a reduced payroll, admission prices of twenty-five and fifty cents along with savings on railroad fares and baggage handling it was still difficult to make the auto tour a financial success.

In theatre parlance, Della was "barnstorming at the cross-roads" or playing in very small towns. Her first "barnstorming" took place in the Boise Basin (the old mining camps of the 1860s gold rush within forty miles of Boise) and the Payette River area of western Idaho between July 27 and early September. In this period of time Della's troupe performed at Placerville, Idaho City, Emmett, Horseshoe Bend, Sweet, Ola, Van Wyck, McCall, New Meadows, Council, Sour Dough and Weiser.[48]

Della's account of this tour sounded like a vacation idyll. She refers to travels through the most beautiful scenery, great pine forests, mountain streams and lakes. She and her companions took time out to fish, hunt and go swimming in hot springs. They enjoyed the dances they held after each performance, dined on grouse and generally shared all the luxuries afforded other tourists.[49]

Of her many experiences on the tour, Della told of a Sunday night at a small town in the Indian Valley.

> The hamlet of Sour Dough consists of an Odd Fellows Hall, two stores, a church and about six houses, and yet we had the biggest house of anywhere on the trip. They came in from all over the valley. It's a rich cattle country and great big cars rolled up to the theatre door. It was a discriminating audience and an appreciative one.[50]

She also expressed high regard for the steaks served at the Hotel Heigho in New Meadows.

About September 4, Della's group returned to Boise to replenish wardrobes and stock up on billboard posters before starting a tour of the eastern part of Idaho. Except for two engagements in Buhl, Idaho, in late September and early October and a three-night stand at Oakly beginning October 7, there were no other details about the tour.[51] There is a hint that the company was in the Twin Falls area in late September.

Della had to interrupt her eastern Idaho auto tour on September 23 to return to Boise and take care of a problem related to her ranch in Meridian, Idaho.[52] Although Della and her husband usually farmed their property in the summers, they had decided that while on their auto tour to sublet the ranch to a man who was to have half of all the produce. While playing in the Twin Falls area she learned the man had left the ranch. When she arrived in Boise she found he had sold all the chickens, turkeys, hay and potatoes before skipping town with all the proceeds. He had also mortgaged the unharvested apple and corn crops to a Meridian grocer. In addition, the man neglected to water the apple trees and Della had a hard time arranging to save them. Before returning to her tour, she consulted with the county attorney to see what steps she could take to protect her rights.[53]

For the month after rejoining her company and filling the engagements at Buhl and Oakley in early October, Della toured through towns in southern Idaho and northern Utah. By early November her troupe was playing west of Salt Lake City, probably the town of Grantsville, Utah. From there she continued westward into Nevada, arriving at Ely on November 11.[54]

On the trip over the great Salt Lake desert to Ely the company lost its way in Utah's Dugway mountain range. They took a wrong turn and ended up in a canyon at an old deserted mine at the end of the road. Night began to fall and the actor's found themselves low on gas and water and hungry, having eaten only sandwiches at noon. They began to search for a cabin to stay in for the night. Fortunately, Van Auker discovered a miner's cabin a half-mile away. It was uninhabited, but he could hear a clock ticking within. The men managed to get the company's auto within walking distance of the cabin. They found the door locked, but forced their way in and found the cabin stocked with provisions and treated themselves to an excellent meal. Shortly after dinner the cabin owner appeared and received a grateful welcome. Far from being indignant at the actor's intrusion, he was pleased to have their company. He turned the cabin over to the company for the night while he slept in his stable. The next morning the cabin owner treated the company to a splendid breakfast and started them happily on their way to Ely.[55]

Della's company enjoyed a successful four evening stand in Ely's Liberty Theatre, drawing larger crowds than expected in spite of having little time to advertise in advance.[56] By this time she had added two more plays to the troupe's offerings: the farcical *Baby Mine* and the domestic comedy *Married Life*.

Leaving Ely, Della went north over a high mountain pass covered in two inches of snow to reach McGill, Nevada, and then dropped southward to appear in the Nevada towns of Ruth, Lund and Preston.[57] She arrived in the gold mining town of Tonopah on November 28. The press welcomed Della back, remembering her as a delightful entertainer in earlier engagements almost a decade ago.[58] Company actor Arthur Belasco also gained notice as a hometown boy who had been a theatre manager in Tonopah and Goldfield.[59]

Della performed for three nights in Tonopah's Airdome Theatre, one of the largest facilities in Nevada. Audiences were good and the press complimented the company, saying, "It was a real pleasure to witness a performance by a capable company" and "one of the best shows in Tonopah for some time."[60]

On December 1 Della moved on to the mining camp of Goldfield, Nevada, for three performances at the Lyric Theatre. Prior to her arrival the local paper reminded readers that "Miss Pringle played an engagement in Goldfield some years ago and needs no introduction to the theatregoers in the camp."[61] All three shows were well attended and enthusiastically reviewed.

After a short engagement at Rhyolite Della's small company left the snow and cold of Nevada behind and motored through southeast California and northern Arizona for the next six weeks. Della halted her five-month auto tour at Phoenix, Arizona, on January 13, 1916. She disbanded her troupe and with her husband set out to visit his mother and sister in San Diego.[62]

Getting to the Pacific Coast became an epic struggle. The Van Aukers began their trek by crossing the sandy desert from Yuma, Arizona, where windstorms had drifted sand into high mountains over the planked road. Their auto got mired in the sand and Della left her husband with the vehicle to walk six miles for help. Three miles out she ran into three government surveyors who, learning of her plight, told her to continue on to their camp while they went to help Van Auker dig out the automobile. It was a long, lonesome hike to the surveyors' camp and Della had to stop frequently to shake the sand from her shoes. She feared that bandits from the Mexican border only a half-mile away might rob her of her jewelry she carried in her bag. Quenching her thirst by sucking on two oranges, she reached the camp just at dark and met a fat male Dutch cook who was surprised to see a woman afoot in such a remote spot. Della never tasted anything as good as the clam chowder and cornbread served up to her by that cook. An hour later the surveyors and Van Auker showed up with the auto. Della and her husband spent the night in a teamster's tent with a dirty old comforter and a smelly tarpaulin for bedding while rain pelted down on their shelter.[63]

The drifting sands of the Yuma desert were only the beginning of the challenge to reach San Diego. The rain in Arizona continued and spread westward all the way to the Pacific coast, resulting in the biggest storm in San Diego for twenty years and causing numerous floods.[64] Della and Van Auker got caught in the worst of them. It took ten days to travel the 110 miles from El Centro, California, to San Diego. Their auto was one of some fifty marooned in the mountains with bridges washed out and roads blocked with boulders and landslides. They helped rebuild bridges and roads all the way and crossed raging rivers pulled by block and tackle. Della walked most of the way and forded streams on horseback. The twenty-five men in her group helped each other out, taking turns hauling stalled vehicles out of wheel deep mud. After such toil, the

Van Auker's auto was the third to make it to San Diego with its passengers glad to escape with their lives.[65]

When they reached San Diego, Van Auker's mother and sister Grace gave them a hearty welcome. Soon Della rented a furnished bungalow at nearby Coronado, California, close to a motion picture studio. In a letter to the *New York Dramatic Mirror* on July 6 she described her idyllic surroundings where she could see the bay with all the warships, hear bands playing and listen to mocking birds singing overhead in the evening.[66]

Della and Van Auker seemed to have adopted a "if you can't beat them, join them" attitude after the movies had negatively impacted their repertory theatre careers. Both of them applied for and gained employment at the Lubin picture studio in Coronado within weeks of arriving in California. Della, in her words, became "camera broke." Once the star of her own troupe, she was relegated to playing minor society lady parts and mainly spent her time keeping house.[67]

Unlike Della, Van Auker's movie career took off rapidly. Within five months after arriving in California he had played major roles in at least eight three reel movies including *Plaything of the Gods, Jack Straws, Ramona, Sons of the Sea* and *Code of the Hills*. In September of 1916 he was living in Los Angeles and left movie work temporarily to be the leading man in a repertory company

Photograph taken in Los Angeles in 1916 when Della turned 46 (courtesy the National Society for the Preservation of Tent, Folk and Repertoire Theatre at the Theatre Museum of Repertoire Americana, Midwest Old Threshers, Mt. Pleasant, Iowa).

at the Belasco Theatre, an engagement lasting only a few weeks. About the same time his first film with the Paramount Company, *Intrigue*, was released.[68] After that he was never able to find another film job he considered worthy of his talent. By mid–December of 1916 he was advertised "at liberty" in the pages of the *New York Dramatic Mirror*.[69]

During the time that Della and Van Auker worked at the Lubin studios in Coronado, Della corresponded with the editor of Boise's *Idaho Statesman* and in a letter printed on May 15, 1916, related some of her husband's varied and painful adventures in the movies. While on location shooting scenes for an Indian movie titled *Romona*, Van Auker and his leading lady were thrown onto rocks when the horse they were riding shied and bolted. He returned to Della with a sprained foot and several cuts and scrapes painted up with iodine.[70]

In a sea picture (probably *Sons of the Sea*) Van Auker played the captain of a battle ship. The script called for him so dive off a ship and swim after some smugglers. It was difficult for him to swim with his clothes and shoes on and he spent so much time in the water that came home blistered from the sun and his eyes so red he could hardly see.[71]

In yet another film, Van Auker had the role of an Indian football player and with other Lubin actors actually scrimmaged with he San Diego High School football team while the cameras rolled. Della did not record any injuries to Van Auker from the game.[72]

Whatever pain Van Auker incurred in filming was partially compensated for by his off camera treatment by the owner of the Lubin studios. Captain Mellville, the owner, and his wife lived on their own yacht anchored in the bay right in front of his studio. He often took his actors for trips around the bay to take pictures of the beautiful scenery.[73]

At Coronado and later in Los Angeles, Della never equaled the short-lived success of her younger husband. Now in her forties, she could never hope to play her accustomed leading lady roles in the movies and had to accept casting in character roles, playing maiden aunts and the like. Although she claimed to have worked in several Lubin pictures, she received no listing in casting credits and may have served only as an extra or as she put it, "society lady."[74]

Although the exact date cannot be determined, by July of 1916 Della had moved to Los Angeles and become a member of the famous Keystone Triangle Company, producer of Mack Sennett's extremely popular Keystone Kops movies. Since it was one of the most poorly documented periods in motion picture history, the time of Della's departure from the

Keystone operation remains unclear. She is credited with Keystone roles up to October of 1916 and by December 9 of the same year was advertising herself "at liberty," indicating she was no longer working at Keystone Triangle. Her hopes of establishing herself in pictures faded when the motion picture business went into an economic slump and Mack Sennett joined with another company, leaving Della out in the cold. Her "at liberty" employment ad listed four films, two with Keystone Triangle and two with the Harry Pollard Company.[75]

Altogether Della Pringle's name appeared in association with nine motion pictures made in 1916 and 1917. She may have had roles in more, but documentation is lacking. On one occasion, a 1917 film entitled *A Finished Product*, she was listed as "Dolly Pringle." Her most important films at Keystone Triangle were *The Social Cub* (July, 26, 1916), starring the very young Gloria Swanson, and the eighteen-minute farce, *Hay Stacks and Steeples* (October 1916), both directed by Mack Sennett. She also appeared in the undated *The Rejected Bridegroom* while still with the Keystone group.

By early 1917 Della performed in two films by the Harry Pollard Company. She played the role of Pep's aunt in *The Butterfly Girl* (January 8, 1917) and another character part in *Madame Trixie* (date unknown). Her other movies included *A Bachelor's Finish* (1917), *The Title Buyer* (date unknown) and a short film, *His Widow's Might* (May 26, 1917).

Della in a playful mood in Los Angeles in 1916 (courtesy the National Society for the Preservation of Tent, Folk and Repertoire Theatre at the Theatre Museum of Repertoire Americana, Midwest Old Threshers, Mt. Pleasant, Iowa).

Della made a great deal of friends at Keystone and other film companies, many of them silent movie stars. Her acquaintances include actors Chester Konklin, the crossed-eyed Ben Turpin, English music hall comedian Charlie Chaplin, the athletic Douglas Fairbanks, Sr., the rotund Roscoe "Fatty" Arbuckle, the amiable Wallace Berry and her favorite Keystone Kop, Charles Murray. She appeared in films with actresses Gloria Swanson, Louise Fanzenda, Bebe Daniels and Mable Normand.[76]

Taking advantage of her position in the Keystone-Triangle Company, Della managed to get her niece, Grace Van Winkle, into the movies. Della sent for her and Grace accepted a contract with Mack Sennett. As Grace later recalled, Della's name was like "magic." "I could walk in anywhere and say Della Pringle was my aunt and I was in."[77]

Della was pleased to be employed as part of the popular Mack Sennett comedy players, but she didn't particularly like acting in slapstick even though circumstances left her little other choice. She said her husband "looked down his handsome nose at slapstick, but pride didn't seem to keep me from feeling hungry."[78] So she brought her talents and elegant wardrobe into the chaotic world of Mack Sennett's zanies.

As Della recalled, the Sennett comedies followed no script and everything was almost entirely spontaneous. Any player was free to do anything to get a laugh. When she went on the set she never knew what was going to happen. In pursuit of

Another portrait of Della at age 46 at the Wetzel Studio in Los Angeles (courtesy the National Society for the Preservation of Tent, Folk and Repertoire Theatre at the Theatre Museum of Repertoire Americana, Midwest Old Threshers, Mt. Pleasant, Iowa).

laughter, even though it hurt her pride and spoiled her fashionable gowns, Della suffered various indignities for her salary of five dollars a day.[79]

She was hit in the face with gooey custard pies, doused with water at unexpected moments, had seltzer bottles sprayed over some of her fanciest gowns, was suspended painfully from the ceiling by wires, floated thru windows on a stream of water, had vases shattered over her head and even put up with ice cream cones being dumped down the back of her low cut dress.[80] Della wrote to the Boise paper that while at Keystone Triangle "she had a fire hose turned on her, a stepladder dropped on her head, and a few other minor details, but was still able to walk."[81]

The "at liberty" ads placed in the *New York Daily Mirror* by Della and Van Auker in early December were repeated several times, his through December 23, 1916, and hers for an embarrassing long period to March 3, 1917. About February 17 Della decided to take a break from making the daily rounds of the movie casting offices and return to Boise to take care

Still photograph from an unidentified Mack Sennett Keystone Kops comedy film. Della is at center. The man with the mustache second from right is a Charlie Chaplin imitator (courtesy the National Society for the Preservation of Tent, Folk and Repertoire Theatre at the Theatre Museum of Repertoire Americana, Midwest Old Threshers, Mt. Pleasant, Iowa).

of some business matters. She had suggested to Van Auker that they might sell the fruit farm in Idaho since they were in dire need of cash and the farm had never been a financial success.[82]

Van Auker saw Della off at the Los Angeles train station; kissed her goodbye and promised to join her at Boise in a few days if something didn't break for him.[83] This was to be the last time she ever saw him.

12

Biding Time in Boise

In Boise on February 23, 1917, Della received a devastating letter from Van Auker in which he branded himself a failure saying she was better off without him, and, most cruelly, he added he no longer cared for her. Della frantically rushed back to Los Angeles only to find that he had joined the United States Army and left for New York for training in the new air corps before going over to engage in World War I.[1] Later Della consoled herself with the thought that "his longing for adventure simply carried him away."[2] She learned after the war that he had married Laura Laird, a former ingénue in one of Della's theatre companies.

After Van Auker's desertion Della remained in Los Angles long enough to get a few months of movie work before returning to Boise in September of 1917. She announced plans to remain in Idaho until the apples were harvested on her ranch and then arrange to go on another theatrical tour.[3]

Understandably disturbed, more likely heartbroken, at her husband's desertion, Della kept the affair to herself for about a year. She acted the role of a dutiful wife and reported on Van Auker's military activities. In February of 1918 she let the press know that he was a captain in an aerial squadron stationed in Camp McArthur, Texas.[4] On March 19 she told a reporter that if her husband, now with the Fifty-first aero squadron, did not sail for France by the next week she would go to see him in Texas.[5]

With these indications of continuing marital accord, Della's friends in Boise were no doubt shocked when she filed for divorce from Van Auker on March 13, 1918, on grounds of desertion over a year ago. By April 28 the paper reported that Van Auker was in default for failure to respond to Della's complaint against him. In the District Court section of the *Idaho Statesman* for June 25, 1918, it was divulged that Della had been granted a divorce from C.K. Van Auker. Mrs. Van Auker was once again Della Pringle.[6]

Shortly before first filing for her divorce in March, Della had finally found buyers for her ranch west of Boise which she had been trying to sell for several years. Two men with adjoining ranches purchased the ranch with its fine stand of apple trees. One bought the twenty-five western acres, including the five-room bungalow, for $5,000 and the other paid $3,000 for the fifteen eastern acres.[7]

Della's husband may have deserted her, but he left her far from destitute. The sale of the fruit ranch for $8,000 represented the equivalent of over $175,000 in modern currency. She still owned her home in Boise's fashionable north end plus at least two other properties in the city. She also owned an automobile in an age when not everyone could afford to buy a vehicle. Importantly, she retained all assets from her repertory theatre business including scripts, scenery, properties, costumes and a large and expensive personal wardrobe.

After the sale of her ranch and before her divorce became final in June, Della decided to make one more theatre tour. Since she made no local announcement about her plans or advertise for actors in the theatrical trade papers, it appears she did not form a company in Boise. More likely she left Boise for Idaho Falls about April 26[8] to play roles in Clyde Waddell's troupe, the Famous Broadway Players.

Following a week of shows in Idaho Falls in late April, Della's seems to have left Waddell's company and formed her own known as Jolly Della Pringle's Original Broadway Players.[9] The first engagement under this title occurred at Pocatello, Idaho, the week of May 10.[10]

For Della's eastern Idaho company, she had recruited M. F. Hogan

Cecil Van Auker years after his divorce from Della (courtesy Albertson Library, Special Collections Department, Boise State University).

and Jim Welch from her previous troupes. The remainder of her performers was identified in the press mainly by their "specialties." Marjorie Randolph sang in Italian character and performed a Grecian classical nature dance. The petite Lottie Ellis appeared in an Irish country dance and one other unspecified act. Le Roy, the Boy Wonder from Montana, played juveniles and sang. Will Drieher entertained with his trombone imitations. No specialties for Helena Shipman and Mr. Mach were noted nor for Jim and Duvall who joined Della on June 3.[11]

After finishing the Pocatello stand on May 18, Della played in small towns on the St. Anthony branch of the railroad and may have appeared in such communities as Blackfoot, Rigby, Rexburg and St. Anthony.[12] Della's company returned to Pocatello's Auditorium Theatre on May 27, this time playing for two weeks.[13] They performed plays from Della's familiar repertoire such as *The Parish Priest, The Chorus Lady* and *The Divorce Cure*. Ads for performances of *Some Baby*, presented May 30 through June 1, humorously warned patrons, "Please Laugh Carefully, Don't Fall Off the Seats."[14] At least one evening a week, Della sponsored a "country store" with a drawing for a bag of groceries.

Della and company left Pocatello on June 9 and played unidentified towns in the southeast corner of Idaho for ten days before arriving in Montpelier, Idaho, for a two-day stand on June 9. The tour ended just across the border in Cokeville, Wyoming, about June 22 and by June 24 Della had returned to Boise.[15]

Della did not disclose whether her eastern Idaho tour had been a success or not, but her subsequent actions indicate that she abandoned plans for any further tours. Within six weeks after her return Della Pringle became a shopkeeper.

Sometime before July 19, 1918, Della started up a business known as The Bonnet Shop at 1005 Main Street in Boise.[16] Here her eye for fashion and skill as a seamstress gained during her many years in theatre production were turned to advantage.

Della's first newspaper ad for her new business appeared on August 19. It offered a five-dollar hat sale with folksy copy like "Ladies, it's time to throw away those old faded, shabby summer hats; they have done their duty." She asserted, "My prices are Right. You can't beat them on the coast."[17]

She had no way of knowing it, but Della had chosen an unfortunate time to begin a new business. Her Bonnet Shop had been open for only about six weeks when Boise, like the rest of the nation, suddenly suffered the outbreak of a devastating epidemic called the Spanish flu. Nationwide,

12—Biding Time in Boise

this deadly epidemic would kill more people in the United States than all those Americans who died in Europe during World War I. Boise was spared the worst of the outbreak, but steps had to be taken to quarantine the disease. All public gatherings were discouraged including church attendance. Theatres and motion picture houses were closed down from October 10 to late November. People were asked to stay off the streets. The wearing of gauze masks when having to go out was encouraged. Under such circumstances, all commerce, including Della's, suffered.

When all the quarantine restrictions in Boise were lifted after November 21, Della took the opportunity to publicize her business with a large newspaper ad, headed with "A Rebuilder of Gowns; Boise's Most Exclusive Dress Making Establishment."[18] The ad copy that followed was a fine example of Della's familiar, almost conversational approach to potential customers. It also disclosed a larger range of merchandise than just millinery and the prices she charged. It read:

> Where a passé gown is really made into a new creation. The legislature will meet this winter. There will be dinners, dances, theatre parties. I want to see the ladies come back to where they left off before the war started. I have purchased some of the most exquisite furs—Seal Coatees, Kolinsky Capes—that make a woman look like a million dollars. They are great bargains. The quarantine will be off Sunday. I'm going to sell the best and any choice of hat in the Bonnet Shop for $10. Think of it. Hats that would ordinarily sell for $20. I also have a beautiful line of Crepe de Chine underwear.... Mme. Gaymore will be associated with me in the dressmaking. I do the planning and she does the work. Together we get results. Don't fail to come down and see the furs.[19]

A Bonnet Shop Christmas ad continued in the same casual vein.

> Only a few more days to do your Christmas shopping. I heard a sweet mother say she would just love some of the beautiful things on display at the Bonnet Shop, but she had spent all her money for others. Let's hope the children and others don't forget mother. She can't have too many waists to gladden her heart by getting her something pretty and dainty. Make her feel that she is not too old to wear pretty things. There is nothing that will cheer like pretty new clothes; they make the world look brighter; create a new interest in life. A new shipment of waists and ladies underwear just received—heavy crepe de chine, warm sweaters, strictly tailored, just the thing for cold weather, prices $8.50 to $10.50. Blouses, handmade lace, silk embroidery. Beautiful things that would sell in larger cities for $18 and $20. At my prices they are bargains. Open evenings until Christmas.[20]

For three decades Della Pringle had been a highly visible public figure. As a leading lady and theatre manager her work was frequently publicized and reviewed. Pictures of her appeared in scores of local papers across Western America and in the most important theatrical publications. She chronicled her professional achievements and personal life in letters to these same publications. Although far from a nationally known celebrity, she was well known and regarded in the many communities in the West where she had performed. Under such circumstances it had once been easy to trace her career and access some details of her personal life.

All changed when she became a clothier in a relatively remote Idaho city with a population less than 20,000. Only glimpses of her life could be seen through advertising for her shop and occasional, brief newspaper items about visits from relatives.

By the end of January 1919, Della was advertising her Bonnet Shop as "The Biggest and Most Exclusive Woman Shop in Idaho." She offered millinery "Just Two Months Behind Paris" that she had seen in *Vogue* and ordered by telegraph. She challenged women of Boise to be in style and "not ashamed when you see how other folks dress."[21]

On April 10 she announced a millinery sale and used her ad to give the following grooming advice to her clientele:

> A few don'ts—don't buy some queer color suit or coat and then run all over town trying to match it in a hat; don't forget to wash your hair at least every two weeks and curl it; use cold cream and powder when making your toilet; use peroxide hydrogen on your face and neck, it won't hurt the skin and is a pleach. With a good complexion and hair nicely pressed you won't have any trouble getting a hat that is becoming, and remember when in doubt buy black.[22]

An ad on June 23 announced that Della had hired an expert seamstress away from a local department store. She stated her specialty would be smocks and fine tailored, beaded blouses made to order.[23]

In her advertising on July 24, Della's introduced her niece, Grace Van Winkle from Colorado Springs, to her patrons, promising them they would find Grace "a most obliging and charming little lady, ready and willing to please all customers."[24] Grace, Della's deceased brother's daughter, was her only living relative and would soon follow in Della's footsteps, pursuing a career in theatre.

Within two weeks of her Boise introduction, Grace Van Winkle was hired to play a role with the Empress Theatre's resident stock company, managed by William Maylon. The play was *The Little Shepherd of Bargain Row*. Although the show's review cited her as being "almost too perfect" in her portrayal of "an insipid young daughter,"[25] Maylon did not use her in any of his subsequent productions.

Grace Van Winkle did get her picture in the September 5 edition of the *Idaho Statesman* even if it was in an ad for Della's Bonnet Shop. Beneath a picture of Grace and the shop's two seamstresses there was a caption written by Della. "I'm not in the picture, some said the Bonnet Shop without Della Pringle would be like Hamlet with Hamlet left out—but Aunt Della is still on the job and everybody in Idaho knows how I look anyway."[26]

Della Pringle came out of her theatrical retirement to appear in the title role of *Mother Carey's Chickens,* presented by the Empress Theatre's stock company on October 9–12, 1919. All advertising for the production emphasized that Della would be in the show.[27] Unfortunately, the sole review of the performances only mentions that Della was in the cast and made no comment on her acting in a character part. The production was a success with the theatre packed for every performance, but Della played no further roles for the Empress company. A week later in one of her business adds Della wrote about her return to the stage: "Believe me, I've been a busy woman for the past four weeks, too busy to write ads, what with studying, rehearsing, playing a part, along with cooking, housekeeping, putting up fruit and running the Bonnet Shop. I call myself the working old fool."[28]

Della continued to work with her niece at the Bonnet Shop until early December. Then Della was instrumental in getting Grace an engagement with a Broadway touring musical comedy company then playing in Boise. One of the production's chorus girls had "jumped" the show and its manager was looking for a replacement. He saw Della Pringle's well-known show business name on her Bonnet Shop and went in to ask her for information about local talent. She, of course, recommended Grace for the job. Grace eagerly accepted an offer and left Boise with the company.[29] She had been preparing for this opportunity for some time. In addition to her work with the Empress Theatre stock company, Grace had been taking private dancing lessons and learning acting skills from Della to prepare for a stage career.[30] Grace would tour in *Chin Chin* for six months.

After the departure of her niece Della kept busy with her millinery and dress-making business which she had expanded in October by adding costume rental. To take advantage of the Halloween celebration, Della created new masquerade costumes and rented them out. This addition to her business proved very successful as demand far exceeded supply, a situation Della promised to correct by creating more costumes for the Christmas and New Year holidays.[31]

Della did more than just run a business in Boise; she took an active role in community affairs. In late December of 1919 she became a member of a newly formed chamber of commerce. Della marked the occasion by writing a newspaper editorial. In it she suggested ways that Boise might grow and improve. To her the biggest issue was roads. She decried the road conditions in Boise and Idaho and pointed out how California and Arizona built better and longer lasting roads. She suggested that penitentiary inmates be employed to improve the roads. Della felt the community needed "a little more work and not so much talk."[32]

She assailed the officials responsible for building and maintaining the roads and challenged citizens to find out why and where their tax money went. Della observed: "The trouble with the people of Idaho—they want to get rich without doing any work; too much politics and graft; nice fat jobs and no work to speak of is the downfall of any community."[33]

Della's editorial went on to suggest that Boise needed apartment houses, some place for people coming to the city to live. She cited women coming into the Bonnet Shop looking for house-keeping rooms or furnished homes. She wrote that if she had any money it would be a good investment to build a California style apartment house.[34]

Della concluded her earnest editorial as follows:

> We are a favored city. Nothing terrible ever happens here, like other places—no race riots, tidal waves, cyclones, earthquakes, droughts, etc., etc., but I sometimes think it needs an earthquake to wake some of these self-satisfied, smug, self-centered into action. The time is now. Let's get busy—more action—"camera," as the movie director would say.[35]

Della turned from concerned community crusader back to her thriving business. Before 1919 ended she contemplated expanding her business into another town. She advertised for a lady partner with $500 to take a half-interest in a millinery store to be established in an unidentified town with a population of 2,000.[36] Despite repeated ads, no partner was found for the proposed expansion.

There was a big change in Della Pringle's life in 1920. On January 17 she wed for the fifth and last time. There was no earlier notice of an engagement and no hint of courtship. A simple statement in the *Idaho Statesman* "Marriages" section read: "At the Oxford Hotel at 8 o'clock Saturday evening the Rev. C.E. Griffith married Mrs. Della Pringle Van Auker and Edward H. Hopper."[37] The city directory listed Hopper as a salesman, but little else is known of him. The marriage would last eleven troubled years.

Roughly a month after her marriage to Hopper, Della surprised her Bonnet Shop patrons by announcing that the business was for sale. In a

February 26, 1920, ad she revealed her reason for selling. "I have worked hard all my life and am entitled to a rest. I want to get out in the open; go camping and fishing this summer."[38] She wrote that the sale would be a great opportunity for an ambitious woman to make a profit in the upcoming spring season. Della declared her bills all paid and the business in good shape. Her conditions for sale were half cash with balance in good security or a trade for ranch property or real estate. She asked $5,000 for the shop including all fixtures, an electric sign, the shop inventory and seventy fine masquerade costumes, a big asset in itself. She emphasized "the location was worth big money."[39]

Nine days later Della announced that she hadn't sold the shop yet, but had prospects and on April 22 her ad revealed a purchaser would take possession of the Bonnet Shop on May 1. Della used most of the ad to promote a big sale to "make all the money I can" and offered hats for a dollar over her cost price.[40] On May 1 the Bonnet Shop was taken over by the owner of an already established Boise clothing store and renamed the Knit Wear and Bonnet Shop.[41]

There was nothing of interest in Della's life for almost three months and then on August 29 her niece, Grace Van Winkle, and her mother, Mrs. J.E. Van Winkle, dropped by to visit. A society page item reminded readers that Grace had joined the *Chin Chin* production in Boise last winter. She had remained with the troupe until it disbanded in June. Grace and mother were on their way to Los Angeles where Grace hoped to get more motion picture work.[42]

After the item about hosting the Van Winkles, Della's name did not appear in the paper until September 15 when she placed an ad to sell her automobile, an Oakland Six sedan, she was willing to consider a trade for land or city property. The ad established that she still lived in her home at 1711 N 18th Street.[43]

During the early months of 1921, Della busied herself making arrangements for one more theatre tour and on March 20 announced she would re-enter theatrical business by opening a road show in the middle of April. She had already purchased a huge exposition tent capable of housing an audience of 1,000. Although it changed later, initially she planned to offer a repertoire of popular farces such as *Fair and Warmer* and *Parlor, Bedroom and Bath* made into musical comedies by adding songs, chorus numbers and specialty acts. Her niece, now performing professionally under the name of Grace Pringle, would be a featured performer.[44]

By April 20 work had started on erecting Della's large theatre tent at

Boise's Eighth and Grove Street in preparation for the opening performance on April 25. The tent, scenery, costumes and performer's salaries represented an investment of $5,000,[45] the equivalent of $100,000 in modern currency.

Della had assembled a company of versatile performers for the new tour. Not all stayed on for the entire tour, but she began with a roster of twenty-five including her husband who acted as advance agent. Grace Pringle played major roles, performed oriental dances and joined six other young ladies to make up the "Pringle Beauty Chorus," described as "Dancing Chicks, All Young and Cute." Della hired Lew Wells, a well-known Orpheum circuit vaudevillian, who was both a comic monologist and "the greatest saxophone artist on the vaudeville stage." Tenor Crawford Eagle, who would eventually marry Grace Pringle, played male leads. Edna Roberts played character roles and specialties. Eight-year-old Baby Helena Pearson charmed with singing sentimental songs and acted in juvenile roles. The Bryan sisters, Beulah and Thelma, danced, made up part of the "Beauty Chorus" as well as performing in harmony singing. In addition Beulah impressed with her skill as a violinist. Della employed a five piece jazz ensemble billed as the Milo Jazz Orchestra. Olive Milo amazed audiences with cornet and piano duos in which she played the melody on a cornet with her right hand and the accompaniment on a piano with her left hand.[46]

Shortly before opening night, Della's troupe, now called "Pringle's Comedians," were asked by the Knights of Columbus to entertain at the Boise barracks community hall. The performance of songs, monologues and stunts pleased a capacity audience of former service men and the medical and nursing staff.[47]

Della faced an extra challenge just the day before opening on Monday evening. The weather had turned unseasonably cold, forcing her to spend Sunday phoning the managers of all the electrical shops in Boise to acquire all the electrical heaters available for installation in her tent theatre. Della declared she was determined that the cold weather wouldn't chill the enthusiasm of the audience.[48]

Despite the unfavorable weather a large audience turned out for the opening performance of *Zeluna, the Turkish Maiden* (an alternate title for one of Della's favorite offerings, *The Sultan's Daughter*). According to the show's review, the merry makers proved popular with the spectators who had paid fifty to seventy-five cents to see hearty comedy that featured a moment when the "Beauty Chorus" sang "Thrill Me" as they danced down and mingled with the audience.[49]

Performances after opening night were not advertised, nor did the *Idaho Statesman* offer further reviews. The other Boise paper, the *Evening Capital News*, did list the week's performances of *Zeluna, The Follies of 1921* and *The Little Mamzelle,* but made no attempt to review the shows.[50]

Pringle's Comedians closed their Boise engagement on May 1 and then made a short twelve-mile hop west to Nampa, Idaho, where they played the week of May 2.[51] Still touring westward, the troupe played a one-night stand at Weiser, Idaho, on May 9. After a week's break Pringle's Comedians showed up in Ontario, Oregon to perform from May 16–19.[52] Nine days later the troupe had reversed directions to appear for two weeks in Pocatello, Idaho. Sometime in that nine days Della's group may have performed in the northern Utah town of Aurora.

All during the tour Pringle's Comedians met with rain and unseasonable snow which discouraged attendance. At the end of six weeks Della had lost $10,000! To raise more capital, she wired her banker in Boise to sell here home for $2,200, money that lasted only two more weeks.[53] Della headed for Ogden, Utah, hoping to regain some of her losses.

Della and company arrived in Ogden on June 13, took two days to erect the large tent at Hudson Avenue and Twenty-second Street and opened on June 15 for an indefinite engagement.[54] Some changes had been made in the troupe. The clever song and dance team of Wheeler and Devere, a married couple, had joined as had black-faced comedian Teddy Bryan. Other new names were Jack Pearson and Adele La Rue. The company had been reduced to twenty and there was no further mention of the Milo Jazz Orchestra.[55]

When Della arrived in Ogden she told the local press she intended to remain through the summer and give Ogdenites stock and musical theatre of a first class order. No doubt her decision to stay indefinitely in the city was influenced by the labor it took by the company to erect and disassemble the theatre tent to meet short engagements. She also made her shows more attractive by lowering admission prices by a quarter, twenty-five and fifty cents.

The opening night of the first play, *The Sultan's Daughter,* made an instant hit with the audience. With their second show, *The Little Mamzelle,* Pringle's Comedians gained even more favor with Ogden theatregoers and filled a long-felt need for a good stock company at popular prices.[56]

Following an encouraging start of a summer season, calamity befell Della and her company. Again rain and cold discouraged patrons from attending and box office receipts plummeted. For the first time in her three decades of theatre management she did not have money enough to pay her actors. As a result, about June 24, performer Mal Wheeler of Wheeler and Devere sued Della to recover $18 in due wages. In turn that compelled the deputy sheriff to attach Della's tent and all stage equipment on June 26 to be held in storage until Wheeler's suit was settled.[57] Pringle's Comedians were out of business.

Broke and with her company disbanded, Della had to make arrangements by phone or telegraph to borrow money from a friend back in Boise to pay fares for her and her niece to get back home. She gathered the remnants of her wardrobe, the one thing her creditors left her, and returned to Boise on July 3.[58]

Della may have been down after the failure of Pringle's Comedians, but she was far from out. She, her husband and her niece did not endure poverty, but certainly lived under reduced circumstances. Since Della had sold her house in Boise's fashionable north end, she moved to a more modest residence on Washington Street shortly after returning to Boise from Ogden.

Della soon resumed her community activities, serving on the entertainment committee for the city's annual Iowa-Illinois picnic held on August 2.[59] About the same time Grace Pringle left Della to join a musical comedy company in Oakes Park, Oregon.[60]

By her own admission Della sat around in a daze after the failure of Pringle's Comedians, unable to eat. To her good fortune, the city of Boise decided to sponsor a big Halloween celebration and costumes would be in great demand. Once more Della's wardrobe and costume collection helped provide her with an income for the city celebrants paid her well for her fine line of costumes. By October 15 she was advertising that in addition to her masquerade costumes she had wigs, makeup, ten sets of musical comedy costumes and 200 scripts available for rent by home talent groups. The ad for the costume business indicated she had no phone and that she had relocated to big stone house at 1601 Washington Street.[61]

Unexpected additional income came to her in the middle of November when the Bonnet Shop business she had sold in 1921 failed and went out of business. As a result, Della got back shop fixtures, the valuable collection of masquerade costumes and an inventory of hats. She sold two handsome showcases and offered the hats for sale at no more than three dollars. At the time she disclosed she had a small millinery shop in her home.[62]

There were no further reports of Della's activities until February 16, 1922, when her classified ad showed that she had moved her costume rental business out of her home to room 9 of the Oxford Hotel on Boise's

Main Street.⁶³ Then on May 18 she advertised another move to room 5 of the Overland Bank building on 10th Street. At this time her residence became room 15 in the same building.⁶⁴

When Della moved into the Overland Bank building she pointed out in a classified ad, "In large cities Parlor Millinery is quite the up-to-date things when rents are high and locations hard to get." She announced she was opening just such a "Parlor Millinery" in connection with her costume rental shop. Her New York and Paris hats would be "about the niftiest hats at reasonable prices in Boise." She invited ladies to visit her nice showroom in the Overland Building.⁶⁵

In the midst of her move to the Overland Building Grace Pringle and her mother arrived for a visit. Grace had just closed a nine-month engagement in Portland, Oregon. Her mother stayed just a short time, but Grace planned to remain in Boise for the summer and support herself by offering dancing lessons.⁶⁶

In early October Della wrote an ad with a message to the women of Boise. It was fairly amusing but indicated some trouble with her millinery business. She began by telling women that the reason they didn't see many really good hats downtown was that most were purchased in "China stores" where people don't know "a good hat from last year's bird's nest." The ad ended with Della all but pleading for business. "Patronize your millinery stores, they are dependent on selling hats for a living. They have rents to pay and other expenses. The laborer is worthy of his hire—don't wait till your merchants go bankrupt, it's a poor advertisement for Boise."⁶⁷

Business may not have been brisk, but Della cleared enough to support at least one civic project. On December 22, 1922, the paper listed her as a contributor to the "Drive Your Stake" campaign aimed at getting the Oregon Short Line Railroad connected directly to Boise.⁶⁸ At the time Boise's only connection to the railroad was a ten-mile spur line from Nampa, Idaho.

As 1922 ended and 1923 began Della had partially recovered from the failure of her 1921 theatre venture. Hats and costumes were keeping a roof over her head and bread on the table. Then halfway through 1923 Della Pringle went into another line of business.

13

"The working old fool"

Della Pringle's life came full circle in June of 1923. In her teens she had been a hotel maid in Iowa. Now in her fifties, she became the manager of a rooming house where she still did maid's work such as cleaning rooms and changing bedding. With a parlor millinery shop, a costume rental business and a rooming house operation, Della was again "the working old fool" she described when she sold her Bonnet Shop in 1921.

Her new rooming house, the Palantine, was quite familiar to Della. She had rented rooms there when she first became a resident of Boise in 1908. Quite often on nights of production she and her husband would stroll the six blocks from the Palantine on 12th and Idaho to perform at the Turner Theatre.[1] By 1909 she had bought the thirty-room building and hired others to run it for several years. It is not clear exactly when she then sold the Palantine, but about June 1, 1923, she acquired the building again through a lease.

On June 3 Della let the public know she was moving her masquerade and theatrical costume business to the Palantine on the corner of 12th and Idaho.[2] A few days later, Della placed a newspaper ad announcing that for ten days a staff of cleaners "had been giving the Palantine the cleaning of its lifetime."[3] The exterior would be painted to make the corner one of the loveliest in Boise. Even though located downtown, the Palantine had a lawn, flowers and shade trees. Rooms rented from $3.50 to $5 per week with a housekeeping suite available for $25 per month. Della also pointed out that the Palantine was a handy location for businessmen.[4]

As to her other businesses, by the end of June Della advertised selling out a line of pattern hats. She needed room for her rapidly growing costume rental business which she expected to double in the next year.[5]

Della achieved success with the leasing and renovation of the Palantine. On July 21 she reported her rooms filled almost every night with "tourists who find the Palatine ... cool and inviting after a long ride over the desert."

Of course, Della did not neglect her other enterprises. In September she promoted a sale of "beautiful cameo pattern hats" at "fifty cents on the dollar." She amused her patrons with an ad containing a reference to a popular song of the period. "'Yes, we have no bananas!' But we have some beautiful Winter Hats we are going to sell for five and seven dollars. Ladies from Cascade, Grandview [Idaho], oh, all around—said they had been reading my ads for years and liked them."[6]

Della was equally enterprising in pursuing business for her costume rentals, adopting at one instance the adage of "if they don't come to me, I will go to them." On November 28 she advertised that she would be in Caldwell [thirty miles west of Boise] on the 28th and 29th "with a full line of costumes for the Odd Fellow's Ball Thanksgiving night."[7] A note appended to the ad requested that everyone return costumes within two days of use or pay an extra rental fee.

Della did little that was newsworthy during 1924. Only occasional classified ads announcing vacancies at her Palantine rooming house indicated that she was still in Boise and still in business. In a self-promoting March ad she wrote:

> You all know Della Pringle. If you don't you haven't lived in Idaho very long. Della is not a fly-by-night—here today and gone tomorrow. She is a real Idaho institution. She has spent a lot of money to make the Palantine on of the nicest places in Boise for genteel folks to live at most reasonable prices. It's clean, close and respectable.[8]

Another March ad by Della described the Palantine as "a clean, homelike place; lawn and trees—where the birds sing and the squirrels play—a touch of nature in the heart of the city."[9]

Although she still maintained her costume rental business, Della did not spend money on advertising it except for a late November display ad aimed at drumming up business for the Thanksgiving and Christmas holidays. It appears she may have closed her parlor millinery business since she didn't advertise it even once in 1924.

The single news item in 1924 involving Della Pringle appeared on August 6. It disclosed that her niece, Grace, had married Crawford Eagle, a member of the 1921 Pringle's Comedians troupe. The couple came to visit Della after a thirteen-week engagement with the Billy Maylon company in Lewiston, Idaho, at the Temple Theatre. After their brief visit with Della in Boise, they had to drive to Spokane to begin a season at the Auditorium Theatre. Della temporarily abandoned her role as "a working fool" to go with them. She spent two weeks in Spokane and while there met with Jimmy Wright, a former member of her companies in Boise.[10]

Della returned to Boise about August 20 to resume managing the Palantine and her costume shop. As Della would observe in later years, "It wasn't easy to run a respectable rooming house in those prohibition days, but that is exactly what I did as long as I remained there."[11] The costume shop, the only one between Salt Lake and Portland, continued to grow. Della remodeled old costumes and added new ones. They were popular at masquerade parties and in demand for amateur play productions.[12]

Della's costume rentals proved a bonanza the week of April 15, 1925, when Boise's public celebrated the opening of a new railroad depot, part of the long awaited direct connection to the Oregon Short Line Railroad. The theme of the celebration was "Pioneer Days" and scores of citizens rented period costumes from Della, earning her a significant profit.[13] It also paid her to furnish makeup for the event, putting fake beards and mustaches on hundreds of men wanting to look like pioneers.[14]

In May of 1925 Della found a new way of making money, breeding and selling Boston bull terriers. She had enjoyed a long association with the breed going back to the time between 1903 and 1905 with a pair of them in a bag-punching vaudeville act. During her years in Canada her Boston bull terrier, Beauty, won prizes in local dog shows. Now she was raising the adorable, black and white coated, bug-eyed, spunky little dogs for profit. Her classified ad under "For Sale Dogs" read: "Della Pringle's Bull puppies, just 5 left; 1 male $25; 4 females $20 each. All beauties and a credit to your family, home and car."[15]

Della could never hope to again amass the fortune she possessed in the best of her theatrical touring days, but with her various business ventures she had a modest, dependable income. Most of the time renters filled all of the of the Palantine's thirty rooms. Even at Della's lowest rate this represented an income of a hundred dollars a week. The costume business, by its nature a less dependable source of steady income, brought in the most money from holiday celebrations, society balls and local theatricals.

Della's costume business benefitted when Boise opened its first airport. She placed an ad urging citizens to "Get Out Your Old Gray Bonnet and Your Pantelettes for the Airport Celebration on April 6" and assured the public she had a lot of costumes to rent if they didn't have one of their own.[16]

Life went on busily and routinely for Della Pringle in 1926. She redecorated the Palantine and declared it "clean as a hound's tooth."[17] Della did most of the work herself but hired a woman to do the heavy cleaning.

The happiest days of the year for Della came when her niece, Grace, secured an engagement with the Taylor Players who began a performance season in Boise beginning April 26.[18] Instead of using her married name, Grace continued to employ the stage name of Grace Pringle in honor of Della. Grace spent a great deal of her spare time with Della until the Taylor Players packed up their show tent on July 5 and departed for a six-month stand in Ogden, Utah.

Sometime in 1927 Della moved her costume shop out of the Palantine to a nearby site at 203 N 12th Street. Apparently her costume inventory had grown too large to be housed in the rooming house.

Boise newspapers printed nothing about Della's husband, Edward Hopper, after he had served as advance agent for Pringle's Comedians in 1921. City directories of the period list him as a salesman and later a clerk for the Overland Trail Stages. It may be assumed that he aided Della in the operation of the Palantine. There was no hint of the Hopper's domestic life, but based on subsequent events, it must have been unhappy and troubled.

The private life of Edward Hopper became embarrassingly public on January 17, 1927, when Hopper was arrested by the police on a charge of disturbing the peace.[19] Shockingly, the warrant for his arrest was sworn by Della Pringle Hopper! Her married life must have been extremely difficult to drive her to have her own husband arrested.

The Hoppers remained together after his arrest, but their marriage which would last four more years, never recovered. For the next two years Della endured Hopper's drunkenness and cruelty. Then on August 28, 1928, she prepared her first filing for divorce.[20] A chastened Hopper must have done the usual begging for forgiveness and promising to reform that led Della to rescind the divorce actions on November 9, 1928.[21] The relationship endured for another two years, but on August 18, 1931, Della again sought a divorce.[22] This time she went through with it and was granted a final divorce. Since the grounds for the divorce were desertion, Hopper must have left her sometime late in 1930. She reclaimed the name of Della Pringle and kept it for the next twenty-one years. Five marriages had been enough.

To Della's credit she maintained an even disposition in spite of her problematic husband and the drudgery involved in running the Palantine. What pleasures she enjoyed were quite simple. She took one day of work off each week to drive around Boise in her fine Essex automobile. And then there were her Boston bull terriers.

A series of newspaper stories in Iowa and Boise briefly brought Della back into the public eye. On October 18, 1928, two Iowa papers, the

Knoxville Journal and the *Des Moines Tribune*, carried identical stories about the demolition of the old Knoxville Opera House with comment about its star performer, Jolly Della Pringle who was a sacred memory to "beau brummells" of 1895.[23] According to the stories "Jolly Della had beautiful blonde hair ... blue eyes and a wonderful figure, combined with a personality which today would be called 'it.' Jolly Della just looked at 'em and made 'em dizzy."[24] The items also commented on her theatrical talents, finding that, in spite of not having dramatic training, she was an accomplished actress with a natural ability for the art.

Boise's *Evening Capital News* picked up on the Iowa stories and on October 29, 1928, published a first page feature about Della headlined as "Boise Costumer Was Once Famous Midwest Actress" with a subhead "Imposing Beauty of 1895 Hears They Are Tearing Down Her Theatre in Iowa."[25] Except for remarking that Della was known as "Jolly" because she laughed so much, the feature echoed the earlier Iowa articles. It did provide a brief overview of Della's career and concluded with:

> She is retired from the world of acting, but the lure of the old days still clings, and there is a secret wish she has that when the "talkies" are perfected, there may be a place for one whose voice was trained for the stage, and who has also been trained to action before the camera.[26]

In appreciation for the Iowa newspaper features, Della wrote a letter to the Des Moines paper on October 31, 1928, thanking the editor for "a very nice tribute to the memory of woman who had been away for twenty years." She expressed a desire to return to Iowa for a visit. The letter ended with "I always told my girlfriends when I died I wanted to be sent back to Knoxville and wanted to be taken to the opera house for the funeral as I would feel more at home there than any place else. Now that's all off."[27]

About the same time Della wrote a letter to a Knoxville friend, Winnie Cotten, that was printed in the *Knoxville Express* on November 15, 1928.[28] In the letter Della fondly remembered good old days in Iowa. She said she had all but forgotten being a chambermaid at the Linden Hotel and was still doing it for her thirty room facility. Della wanted to visit Iowa but was too tied up with running her "cock-eyed" rooming house to get away. She wrote she would like to sell it because she was getting too old to work so hard. Della also commented:

> Am right in the midst of my Halloween costume business. We have been sewing, making new ones, making over, cleaning, pressing for three weeks. Made some cute pirate suits, the girls like them because they can show their shapes, bare legs, etc., the shorter they are the better they rent.[29]

On a more serious note, Della confided: "I have been very sick this fall; had the flu and poisoning of my whole system; couldn't eat or sleep and bloated up like an old cow with alfalfa bloat. Finally found a good osteopath doctor and he gave treatments that helped me."[30]

In the letter Della revealed her political preferences, voicing support for Alfred E. Smith, the Democratic candidate for president. She felt the nation needed a change in leadership. Her letter ended with an invitation to her friend to visit her in Boise. "It is really great, and we have everything but money. We are all so poor and have to work so hard to pay bills and taxes we can't afford a trip anywhere."[31]

Before 1928 ended the *Knoxville Journal* printed one more article related to Della Pringle. In the December 6 edition a reporter speculated, "If Jolly Della's romance with her first husband hadn't ended in divorce court, Knoxville might have added John Gilbert, famous movie star, to the list of famous sons."[32] The article went on to chronicle how Johnny Pringle remarried and fathered the son who would become a Hollywood legend in silent films. After briefly outlining Della's career after her divorce from Johnny the item ended with "Although she has been out of the theatrical game for many years, Jolly Della recently received an offer to enter the talkies, and may accept it."[33]

As a result of all the newspaper exposure, Mr. Keuneman, news editor of the *Knoxville Journal*, wrote a letter to Della on December 2. As a newcomer to the town he had rapidly steeped himself in its lore and history, especially incidents about Della. This led him to write the original stories about the destruction of Knoxville's old opera house. Now he wanted Della to write him a long letter in her "inimitable manner" about her experiences as a stage trouper. He envisioned writing an article for Iowa papers that would be picked up by the national Associated Press and make Della famous again.[34] Evidently, Della did not comply with Mr. Kueneman's request for no such article ever appeared.

In early January of 1929 Della was briefly reunited with an old friend from her movie days. Charles Murray who had been one of the Keystone Kops at the time Della was part of Mack Sennett's Keystone-Triangle company came to Boise's Pinney Theatre in a touring production of the *Marco Revue*. He met with Della and gave her his autographed photo.[35]

After six years Della had had enough of being a chambermaid and attempted to get rid of the Palantine rooming house. It took some time to do so. In March of 1928 she first advertised to sell the Palantine lease and furniture for $3,000. As late as October of 1928 Della advertised that the Palantine was still for sale, admitting in the ad, "I have a costuming business I want to devote more time to, and haven't the health to work so hard. Can't do justice to both."[36]

It is uncertain exactly when Della finally sold the Palantine lease. By early June of 1929 a Boise realty company was listing the Palantine property for sale and there was no further mention of Della's involvement with the rooming house.[37]

Relieved of managing the rooming house, Della was free to travel. She left Boise on June 16, 1929, for Ogden, Utah, to see her niece who had a summer stock engagement with a tent theatre troupe known as the National Players.[38] Della remained with Grace (who had changed her stage name back to Grace Van Winkle) for at least two weeks. On June 27 Della accepted an offer to make a brief return to acting with the National Players. For three evenings she performed with Grace in the domestic comedy, *Wanted*—she in the character of Mrs. Robert Trent and Grace as the ingénue Penelope Martin.[39] The play's review singled out Grace as playing with "fine discrimination and with a delightful charm." Aunt Della received no mention, being lumped along with other members of the company who "were adequately cast and contributed to a swift, finished performance."[40] Della, who once advertised herself in the theatrical trade papers as "the "actress who had made Iowa famous"[41] had become one of the "too numerous to mention."

Following Della's return to Boise she came up with another scheme to make money by using her knowledge of and experience in theatre production. On August 4 her newspaper ad announced that a number of people had requested that she open a "Dramatic School" in connection with her costume business. She planned to teach "clear enunciation, diction, placing the voice for talkies, or radio work, comedy, drama." Della recommended that every boy and girl take part in amateur theatricals because "it gives you confidence, poise and personality."[42] She advised school drama teachers to consult her about selecting scripts since she had contacts with the best play agencies and could save them money on royalties.

At the time Della founded her drama school she held classes in the same building where she had moved her costume shop and residence, the Bristol Hotel building at 207 S 10th Street. She had access to a big basement room which was well equipped for her to teach classes and conduct rehearsals.[43]

Della's drama school may not have lasted more than one term. There were no further ads for it and no mention in the news section. At the end of October the stock market crash led to the beginning of a national depression. Parents may have decided they could no longer afford to pay for drama classes for there was no further mention of the school.

About August 13, Della's first husband, Johnny Pringle, died in Hollywood. At the time she made no public comment on his passing, but kept a copy of his obituary in her scrapbook.⁴⁴

At his death "Old John Pringle" was best known as the father of silent screen star John Gilbert. Theirs was a strange and strained relationship. After leaving Della, Pringle married Ida Adair who he divorced just before his son, Cecil Pringle, was born. Ida remarried a fellow named Gilbert and her son adopted his stepfather's name, later changing his first name to John. Sadly, Pringle never met his son face to face until a few years before Pringle's death at age sixty-seven. Father and son were finally introduced in a rather dramatic manner. It happened on the movie set of Eric Von Stroheim's *The Merry Widow*. Gilbert was the star and Pringle had been hired as an extra appearing as a servant in a big ballroom scene. Gilbert entered, thought he recognized his old father, but went on with the scene, waltzing with his leading lady. Afterwards Gilbert asked Pringle if he was his son. Pringle nodded and father and son were at last reunited. Gilbert had been brought up to feel nothing but bitterness for his father and while the son acknowledged the relationship, he would have nothing to do with him at first. Later, Gilbert changed his mind and went so far as to provide a home for Pringle for the few remaining years of his life.⁴⁵ Vacationing in Europe at the time of Pringle's death, Gilbert did not attend his father's funeral.

Ironically, Della, who was not a blood relative, had more contacts with Gilbert than his father. She had seen him as a young boy in New York and later befriended him when he was trying to get into movies and she was working for Mack Sennett.⁴⁶ She would have more to say of this friendship when Gilbert died in 1936.

During 1930 and 1931 there was little mention of Della Pringle except for notices of her divorce from Edward Hopper. The city directory listed her as a costumer at her residence in the Bristol hotel. A single classified ad indicated that she had hired a seamstress and added a sewing, mending and dressmaking service at her costume shop.⁴⁷

On January 31, 1932, Della had a long feature and her picture printed in the *Idaho Statesman*. For two weeks earlier the paper had printed brief items in its "Pioneer" section about Della's first visit to Idaho in 1902. This prompted Della to write a three column article reminiscing about her first appearance in Boise. She also recalled how the chance reading of a Boise newspaper at Sugar City, Idaho, in the summer of 1908 saved her troupe from disbanding and brought her to Boise permanently. She said that summer and the months following were "some of the best and happiest of all my years in show business."⁴⁸

For her 1902 Boise engagement Della traveled in her own private Pullman car with a company of thirty actors and musicians. She recalled that her Pullman car was parked down in the railroad yard close to the old depot on Tenth Street.[49]

Several paragraphs featured anecdotes about her dog, a Great Dane named Flossie, and how it had won a blue ribbon and four dollars when she entered it in a local dog show. Flossie also marched with the company in its daily pre-show parade through the streets of Boise. Flossie's appearance led some people to assume Della's troupe was an "Uncle Tom" show so Della decided to mount a production of *Uncle Tom's Cabin* since many of her actors had experience in the popular "Tom" shows. The performance of *Uncle Tom's Cabin* went well enough in Boise, but a later show in Sumpter, Oregon, did not and made for an amusing anecdote. Della wrote of the performance:

> We had the house packed and jammed. I played Eliza. When it came time for me to cross the ice, the actors started to bark and twist old Flossie's tail, pinch her ears, trying to excite her to get her to bark but nothing doing. They had to shove her on the stage. I ran screaming, jumping on the cakes of ice with my "cheild" in my arms. Flossie got to the center of the stage, looked down and saw the kids, walked off the stage and laid down out in the audience. I guess the kids wondered where the rest of the bloodhounds were as the actors continued to bark [offstage] till the curtain fell.[50]

Della ended her reminiscence with what she told an Iowa friend about her life in Boise.

> We have everything that makes life worth living; a wonderful healthy climate, lots of sunshine, good water, beautiful scenery right at our door, and we can grow anything there except oranges and bananas and we've got the money to buy them, and we never have to live in fear of anything very terrible happening to us like tornadoes, earthquakes, floods, etc.[51]

For her local audience, she added, "So I guess I am a pretty good booster for Idaho and especially the Boise valley."[52]

Boise's booster again moved her costume shop, to the third location in three years. In 1932 the city directory listed Della's costume and residence as 11 Overland Bank building.

Most of her adult life Della had problems with her health, most of them after surviving an accidental poisoning in Wyoming during her 1906 tour. By 1911 she underwent corrective stomach surgery and didn't report any other ailments until being stricken with the flu in 1929. She recovered and seemed to be quite well, but on June 8, 1933, Boise newspapers reported her to be seriously ill at St. Alphonsus Hospital.[53] Four days later she had gall bladder surgery. Soon after doctors announced that she was showing daily improvement.[54] About June 25 she had recovered enough to be released from the hospital.

Two weeks of hospital care resulted in medical bills that Della did not have the money to pay. Although quite wealthy when she retired from the stage in 1919, she had lost most of her money in the failed tour of Pringle's Comedians and the Idaho properties she had invested heavily in fell in value as the real estate market declined after America's economic depression began in 1929.

To help Della pay her hospital debt, a group of local professional performers led by Della's niece, Grace Van Winkle, organized a benefit performance for her. They announced that a "Mammoth" performance in her honor would be given on June 29 at the Pinney Theatre. The performance consisted of a popular three act farce, *The Elixir of Youth*, three Orpheum vaudeville acts and music by a twelve piece orchestra. No pains were spared by the professional talent of Boise and southern Idaho to make Della's benefit the best local entertainment in years. Grace Van Winkle, her husband (Crawford Eagle) and seven other professional actors made of the cast of the farce. Faye Dietrich led the orchestra. The vaudeville acts featured a comic monologue, musical comedy duets and an accordion medley. The Booster Club of the Woodmen of the World sponsored the benefit, paying for publicity ads and theatre rental, and Mayor John J. McCue gave the curtain speech.[55]

Publicity for the benefit pointed out Della's contributions to the community in the past. One ad hailed her as "the toast of the nineties" and asked the public to "remember Jolly Della's great shows" and show that Boise doesn't forget.[56] A newspaper article reported that Boise's club women were taking great interest in Della's benefit because twenty years ago she had been so generous to all their clubs, giving benefits and making donations.[57] Another item praised her as a "gallant trouper" that "all Boise and most of the towns in southern Idaho knew as Jolly Della Pringle when the stage was no a mellow memory but a living thing."[58]

Della's "Mammoth" benefit performance brought out a large crowd of theatergoers who enjoyed the evening and showed their appreciation for Boise's favorite actress. Because of the hard economic times, benefit organizers charged only "sensationally low prices" of twenty-five and forty-five cents. This meant that the performance probably brought in about $500 which would be enough to cover most, if not all, of Della's hospital obligations.

Ten of the benefit dollars came from Della's old movie friend, Charles Murray, who was half of the then famous Murray and Mack comedy team. He could not attend the performance because of his movie work. Murray sent his check and wrote, "If anyone in this entire world is entitled to a testimonial it is Jolly Della Pringle." He observed that "this is a grand chance for all the town folk at Boise to show their charity and love for Della who in her career as an actress possibly played more benefits than any other actress in the middle west."[59]

In the months after her benefit Della finished her convalescence and went back to work at her costume shop to get ready for busy Halloween season and the holidays that would follow. During 1934 there was no record of her activities except a listing in the Boise City Directory. In December of 1935 she wrote a very informative letter to her old hometown newspaper, the *Knoxville Journal*. The letter was the first of a about a half dozen annual Christmas letters to the paper. Among other things, the letter revealed that Della's health had improved from last year and that she had gained a few pounds.[60]

She reported that her niece and her husband now lived in Salt Lake and that Grace had spent a week with Della in September during which time they had attended some productions by the Taylor Players in their tent theatre. Della commented, "It seems good to see real, live actors and hear the spoken drama again."[61]

Della confessed that she took a short nap every afternoon because it rested her nerves and kept her "peppy" for the evenings which she spent playing cards. She said,

> I still play a lot of pinochle. I believe as my dear old friend Marie Dressler said, all old folks should know how to play cards. You can fit in, and are not left to sit alone or go to bed at 8 o'clock so sorry for yourself you could cry. My friends are nearly all young married couples and do they get a kick out of trying to beat me. I give them plenty of excitement and competition. I didn't get home until 1:30 last night.[62]

Della went on to express her support of Idaho Senator William Borah if he ran for the presidency, but felt he had little chance against eastern money and power. That led her to rant about politicians:

> When I hear some old politician "hemming and hawing," their raucous old voices grate on my nerves so I say shut up you old fool, you don't know what you are talking about. Some old dame announced she would sing, "When I Grow Too Old to Dream." I said, well lady you sure as hell too old to sing, so I shut her off. That's one good thing about radio. We can shut them off and don't have to listen.[63]

Della finished her lengthy correspondence in a folksy manner by sharing her special meat loaf recipe. She also invited readers to write to her since it was so much better than sending "foolish" Christmas cards.[64]

Della came back to public attention when film star John Gilbert died unexpectedly on January 9, 1936. Three days later an *Idaho Statesman* feature disclosed a relationship between the famous matinee idol and Della Pringle. This connection had been hinted at earlier in her life, but the article made it quite clear. In her interview for the article Della first outlined her connection with Gilbert through her marriage to his father, John Pringle. Then she told the reporter that when she and Cecil Van Auker were in Hollywood she was asked to take part in a benefit for the Elks and was paired up with young John Gilbert (known at that time as John Pringle, Jr.) for a sketch, *Hello, Bill*.[65]

> He was nineteen at the time and I told him who I was. No lad could be sweeter than he was to me. He at once dubbed me his "second mother," his own being dead at the time, and he sat next to me all during rehearsals. I saw a great deal of him at Hollywood and I want to say that whatever success John Gilbert made was entirely to his own effort.[66]

Della's interview ended with "Jack was a dear fellow and I feel a personal loss in his death."[67]

The interviewer either omitted or Della failed to reveal that she had seen Gilbert first in New York when he was a young boy. Although Gilbert as a boy spent many years away from home in military schools, it is possible that Della may have seen him when she played in Logan, Utah, where his mother and her family lived. Gilbert may have visited Della in Boise after he became established in films. A book, *Idaho Women in History*, in a section about Della Pringle states that Gilbert "titillated Boise hostesses and reporters by visiting his stepmother several times."[68] However, no local confirmation of the visits to Della has been unearthed.

Months later Della was pleased to receive a letter from Virginia Bruce, a movie star and widow of her "stepson," John Gilbert. Della had written to Bruce when Gilbert had died in January, but she didn't see her mail for months. An old actor friend of Della's in Hollywood made Virginia Bruce aware of the letter and she finally replied, adding another prized letter to Della's souvenir collection.[69]

Occasionally Della contributed her time and talents to help clubs and organizations raise funds for community projects. On February 26, 1936, she directed and appeared in a short play that was part of the University Women's benefit vaudeville show.[70]

On December 11, 1936, Della began her annual Christmas letter to the *Knoxville Journal* by thanking all those who had responded to last year's letter—responses from Red Oak, Iowa to Los Angeles. The cheery opening turned somber as Della related what a hard year she had experienced with her serious sick spells.[71]

She had had a condition in her side ever since her gall bladder was removed in 1931 that caused toxic poisoning. It affected her spine and crippled her back and legs with neuritis so bad that she couldn't get out of bed for week. She was all alone and depended on neighboring tenants for aid. Her condition worsening, the WPA sent a nurse for two weeks and her niece was summoned from Eugene, Oregon. Grace came right away and was spending the Christmas holidays with Della which perked her up and gave her something to live for. Grace's company and a strict diet finally relieved her toxicity and she felt as spry as a two-year-old.[72]

Earlier, in June, Della's niece and husband Crawford Eagle bought a car and came up from Salt Lake City to take Della to the Pacific coast near Eugene, Oregon where Crawford's parents lived. Della had never been to that part of Oregon and marveled at how cool and green it was passing through Baker City and Pendleton. She enjoyed stopping at tourist camps, but found them more expensive than hotels.[73]

Della retuned to Boise in July only to encounter weeks of extremely hot weather with temperatures reaching one hundred degrees day and night. Then Boise had the driest fall in over forty years, causing Della to express concern for farmers facing a lack of irrigation water.[74]

Her letter continued with news about the winter resort being built by the Union Pacific in Ketchum, Idaho, the now famous Sun Valley recreation area. She found it ironic that snow had fallen all over Idaho except at the planned ski resort scheduled to be opened by December 22.[75]

Della describes how she renewed acquaintance with old Hollywood friend Wallace Berry when the star and his family came to Idaho in the summer for fishing and hunting. They stayed over at the Hotel Boise and Della called on them. Because it had been twenty years since their last meeting, Berry did not remember Della right away, but soon he and his charming wife were sharing stories about the old days in Hollywood when Della acted with Gloria Swanson, Wallace Berry's first wife. After their visit Berry showed Della the outfit he used for traveling and camping, an extra long Ford V-8 with a fold-up camping trailer covered in embossed leather. Berry flew to Boise in his own private plane and had his chauffer drive the camping outfit to and from California.[76] Such may have been Della's life had she managed to remain in movies.

Della wrote some amusing paragraphs about her difficulties proving how old she was in order to apply for the federal old age pension, a process made more difficult since she did not have a birth certificate. She presented a family Bible, press notices and pictures, to no avail, She jokingly suggested a doctor be summoned to count the wrinkles on her belly and her surgical incisions. Finally, she called on an old Knoxville resident in Boise who was related to the Idaho governor to sign an affidavit proving Della's age. Della never thought she would have so much trouble proving her age since most folks in Boise had thought her the oldest woman in town for the past twenty years.[77]

Della concluded her letter with comments about Boise at Christmas time.

> Our city of Boise looks very lovely now, all decorated and festooned with evergreens and colored lights. The store windows are full of beautiful things and we won't have any money to buy Xmas presents for anyone but we are so glad to be together this Xmas and that my health is better, and that I'm not crippled in bed. We are happy and grateful we will pool our resources with some other friends, buy a turkey and all have dinner together. I often say to Grace that we don't have much money but we are awful "good looking" and full of fun and have lots of friends, no matter how tragic things are sometimes we make a joke of it and smile through our tears.[78]

As December rolled around in 1937 Della Pringle penned another Christmas letter to her friends in Knoxville. On the eighth she wrote to the *Knoxville Journal* that she was better off financially and in good health.[79]

She told of spending July and August in Pocatello with her niece. While there, friends of her niece treated Della to a tour of Wyoming's Yellowstone Park. At the park she witnessed geysers that belched water and sulfur like miniature version of Hell, thrilled to see wild deer, elk and moose grazing right next to the highway and sat in reverent silence to see incredibly beautiful sunsets which to her resembled the effects of her old calcium lights from theatre days. On the last evening in Yellowstone Della and friends went to a lodge and shared an hour long dinner featuring two fresh caught trout weighing three pounds served with a wide array of garnishes, the dinner made all the more enjoyable by the rustic surroundings decorated with colorful plates, dishes and pottery.[80]

In her letter Della complained about having to relocate her costume rental business. For five years she had operated it out of her residence in the Shaw Building on South Eight Street. In early October the owner had decided to remodel the building into offices and gave Della just ten days to vacate. The housing situation in Boise was terrible with rents sky high. Della read the paper's rental ads, walked miles, peered into basements and climbed long flights of stairs seeking a new location capable of housing heavy wall cases, her costumes and two rooms of furniture.[81] Not being able to find a suitable space, Della decided to quit the business and advertised it for sale on October 3.[82] Early offers to buy didn't pan out and the business did not actually change hands until September 29, 1939.

Faced with having to find new employment, Della boldly went to Idaho's Senator William Borah, told him of her situation and her hope to be part of the national Federal Theatre Project.[83] The project, part of the federal Works Progress Administration, had been created to provide both employment for actors and other theatre workers and cheap entertainment for the public.

Borah's secretaries contacted the right people for Della, but found there was no Idaho Federal Theatre Project. However, they found a place for her as a dramatics instructor in the WPA Adult Education program.[84]

The WPA had taken over Boise's Whittier school to house free Adult Education courses that included typing, sewing, music, painting and Della's theatre classes for all who wanted to improve their minds and qualify for new jobs. Della said she felt like a new woman after she began offering classes for theatre was what she knew and loved. Soon she was rehearsing with her students five nights a week.[85]

In early November Della and her unidentified male co-worker put out a call for stage talent.[86] They were looking for character actors, leading juvenile men, comedians—anyone who had a yen to get behind the footlights. Della let it be known that she was already conducting rehearsals for *The Patsy* and the garden scene from her old standby, *Faust*. She emphasized that there were no costs but people's time and that would be training in acting and public speaking.[87]

Della received word of the death of her fourth husband, Cecil Van Auker, in early February of 1938. After leaving the Army Air Force at the end of World War I, he had returned to the movie profession, making dozens of films (including one in northern Idaho with Nell Shipman). He contracted tuberculosis and retired to Prescott, Arizona, where he died on February 18 at age fifty-three. At the time he was married to Laura Laird, former member of a Della Pringle stock company. Della did not comment about Van Auker at the time of his death, but confessed years later that of all her husbands, he was the only one she truly loved.[88]

Her activities with Boise's version of the Federal Theatre Project quite frequently kept Della's name before the public. After months of preparation, she presented a one-act play, *Yaller Squares*, at the Moose Hall on February 26, 1938.[89] Della directed and made her first appearance on stage in many years. In spite of efforts to recruit men for her shows, she ended up with a cast entirely of women, only one of which was under sixty-five.

The *Idaho Statesman* marked the opening of *Yaller Squares* with a long feature story focused on Della. It found her physically and mentally spry and "getting a good big kick out of playing pinochle."[90] She was described as slightly stout, a bit deaf, wearing quiet clothes and her once blonde hair now a steely gray.

Della recalled the old days "when stock companies roamed the states in stage coaches, reaping gold and plaudits from a stage starved citizenry that thought nothing of riding horseback a hundred miles to whoop a villain, clap for handsome heroes and innocent heroines."[91] Most of her talk of the old days concerned the practical side of trouping and show business—"the one night stands, the big Rochester [kerosene] lamps that gave heat and light and had to be carried from hotel to chilled theatre."[92]

She remembered "the fun of barnstorming when it led to military forts." There "they treated us wonderfully. An officer's house would always be turned over to us: there'd be a bottle of wine at each place for our meals ... and dances. We'd be queens."[93]

Della expressed a modest opinion of her talent. "I was never a great actress, and never would have been—but I did have a good voice, and that's what got me by. I never spoke a line that couldn't be heard all over the house."[94]

She lamented losing so much of her wealth when the motion pictures destroyed the repertory theatre business. "Of course we could see what was happening ... but somehow we just couldn't believe it was over. If I had quit in 1913 I'd still be well off."[95]

When Metro-Goldwyn-Mayer unit director W.S. Van Dyke came to Idaho in late May of 1938 to scout locations in McCall for King Vidor's film, *Northwest Passage*, he dropped off in Boise for a short visit with an old friend, Della Pringle. They had met when he was a boy playing juvenile parts in his mother's stock company. His mother was Laura Winston and her troupe covered the same territory around Walla Walla and Boise that Della's company followed and on occasion they got together on Sunday afternoons. During Van Dyke's hour-long visit he brought Della lots of gossip about old friends and invited her to be his guest on location in McCall when he returned to begin filming and to meet movie stars, Spencer Tracy, Robert Taylor and her old friend, Wallace Berry.[96]

Della, who may not have attended high school, went to college in the summer of 1938. All teachers in Idaho's WPA Adult Education program had to take part in a month of training at Pocatello's University of Idaho, South. Happily, this afforded Della the opportunity to go to college with her niece who was a WPA dramatics instructor in Pocatello. They enjoyed participating in the workshop activities like community singing and listening to lectures about social economics and holding the attention of students.[97]

As their part of the summer workshop, Della and Grace produced two one-act plays. The shows went over well and the boys in the dormitory showed their appreciation by presenting Della a grand bouquet of flowers over the footlights.[98] Della returned to Boise and resumed her work as a drama instructor. Allegedly, she cajoled her students at rehearsals by telling them to get busy, they weren't there just to chew gum.

Della ended 1938 with two December productions of one-act plays, one for the Second Presbyterian Church and the other for the Woodmen of the World, the mutual insurance group that her brother had been so active in before his death.[99] If Della were still "the working old fool," at least she was toiling in the theatre profession she knew and loved, even if her company members were aged lady amateurs.

Della's all-female WPA drama group at Boise in 1938. Della, age 68, is seated third from right (courtesy the National Society for the Preservation of Tent, Folk and Repertoire Theatre at the Theatre Museum of Repertoire Americana, Midwest Old Threshers, Mt. Pleasant, Iowa).

Grace and her husband came to Boise to spend Christmas which made Della extremely happy that she wouldn't be alone for the holiday. Sometime she felt so lonesome she could "weep and howl like my little Boston Bulldog does when I sing."[100] The eleven-year-old dog was Della's company in her loneliness. She confessed that she often spoke to him like a person and fancied he understood.

14

Curtain Coming Down

Nineteen thirty-nine did not go well for Della Pringle; it began badly and got worse. In late 1938 she received notice that her position in the WPA Adult Education program would be eliminated in January. Without the job she faced surviving on an old age pension of twenty dollars a month. The program had run short of money and over a thousand employees in Idaho were slated to be let go. Della remarked that it was a nice Christmas package to hand to old folks.[1]

Always resilient, Della did not give up. She telegraphed Idaho's Senator Borah and he said he would take the matter up and do what he could. Della also had the support of her pupils who all signed a petition to Borah to keep Della on since she had made such a success with her classes and play productions.[2]

The position meant more to Della than money, as important as that was. She never dreamed the position wouldn't be hers as long as she wanted to work at something she knew and loved. The happiness her program gave to others was also of concern. It provided fun and challenges to her cast of older women, making their lives fuller and rewarding.[3]

Della did more than just teach and direct. Without cost she supplied makeup, wigs and costumes from her private stock. Above all she returned to acting in her shows. She found she was a better actress than she ever was and could still memorize lines for sizeable roles. She gloried in knowing Boise audiences thought her the funniest woman they had ever seen.[4]

Her plea to Senator Borah and the students' petition must have been effective, for Della continued to present shows. In 1939 she presented plays much more frequently than in the previous year—nine or more between January and July. Although there was no formal or public announcement, Della's niece (now going by her married name, Grace Eagle) joined her in January as a WPA recreation leader. Both acted and directed plays in Boise and the surroundings communities of Star and Caldwell. Their venues were various schools, grange halls, the Moose Hall and the Boise Junior College auditorium. Local groups such as the Townsend Club, the Rebekah Lodge, the Royal Neighbor Lodge, the Eagle's Auxiliary and Alpha Iota Sorority either sponsored or participated in the shows.[5]

Della's play productions caused both personal amusement and stress. Even professional productions can go awry and Della's amateur shows were not immune. Before one operetta the young lady playing the lead fell out of a cherry tree and had to be hospitalized two days before the show opened; the pastor's wife had to read in her part. At another performance someone lost the prompt book and no one could cue the actors if they forgot a line. They just made up their own lines and there was nothing Della could do about it.[6]

In addition to brief items about her play productions, Della's name showed up in a vacuous *Idaho Statesman* gossip column feature on April 16. Readers had been invited to submit a list of Boise people that they would invite to a party and why. Della Pringle and a John Dunham were chosen by someone because "they can do old-time vodyville [*sic*] ta-ra-ra-boom-de-ay."[7] This silly column elicited a long reply from Della concerning her selection as an interesting party guest and bringing back memories of performing in Iowa at the turn of the century.[8]

She recalled when five or six big repertory companies would spend Sunday at the Hotel Morgan in Des Moines visiting each other's rooms. "All talking, each trying to make himself heard. All boasting about the big business they did in each town. You knew they were lying. But that's actors for you."[9]

A note of regret and sadness was evident in the conclusion of her "party" letter:

> Several years ago I heard a lady say there were two people in Boise who had never been properly appreciated. One was Nick Villeneuve [*Idaho Statesman* cartoonist and amateur theatre participant] and the other was Della Pringle. Well folks, I have no kick coming. Boise has treated me swell. I only regret I wasn't smart enough to hang onto the money I made.... I'm all out of ideas for parties ... it's been so long since I attended one."[10]

Just when it appeared that Della and Grace had built a solid, government sponsored amateur theatre program in Boise politicians in Washington, D.C., eliminated the WPA Adult Education project nationwide. Reduced funding for all WPA projects cost 2,000 Idaho workers their jobs by August 31. Certainly Della and Grace were among those who lost their employment, although the Boise city directory continued to list them as recreation leaders through 1940. However, nothing appeared in the papers about their play productions after July of 1939.

A month before Della's position with the WPA ended, she had a delightful time in McCall, Idaho. Her old friend, W.S. Van Dyke, finally began filming *Northwest Passage* at McCall and Della accepted his invitation to visit him on location. She spent several days in early July visiting old friends at McCall's Payette Lakes and on one of those days watched the arrival of a special train from Hollywood with the movie's stars—Spencer Tracy, Robert Young and Walter Brennan—aboard. Della observed: "It reminded me of bear-feeding time in Yellowstone Park. People came running from every direction to meet that train. When we got there there were about 500 people, and before long there were at least 2000."[11]

Della had as much fun as anybody and freely voiced her opinion about the film's stars. Although she appreciated the talents of leading men Spencer Tracy and Robert Young, she favored character actor Walter Brennan and predicted, "You watch when the picture is released and see if he don't almost steal the show."[12]

Returning to Boise after such a fine time in McCall, Della had to face the reality of being without a job and little prospect of finding other work. Worse yet, she became so ill about August 16 that she had to spend over a week in St. Alphonsus Hospital.

It was the most devastating illness of her life, beginning with an incredibly painful headache that kept her from sleeping for four nights. She tried hot packs, cold, packs and aspirin—nothing stopped the pain. Her niece called the doctor who prescribed stomach and liver medicine which helped her sleep. When she awoke her head was a mass of bumps and water blisters. The doctor returned and determined that Della had the shingles. He immediately sent her to the hospital where expensive serums were administered.[13]

Della had undergone six surgeries in her lifetime, but none more painful than the shingles. The malady affected her head, throat, tongue, ears, neck and eye on her left side. She couldn't bear the weight of her head on a pillow, couldn't sleep longer than a few minutes at a time, lived on liquids for three weeks and couldn't swallow a bit of solid food. As she recovered from the shingles, her sense of humor returned, too. While she was in the hospital, Hitler began the war in Europe and Della said she wished Hitler would get the shingles to keep him quiet and give him something to cry about.[14]

By August 23 she was well enough to receive a few visitors each day.[15] Fortunately, on September 29, 1939, Della finally sold her costume business that had been on the market for almost two years[16] which meant she had enough money to pay for her hospital stay.

Doctors told Della she would have a long illness and could never work again. So she gave up trying to regain the job she loved so well. She also gave up the house she shared with another woman, kept just one room of furniture and moved into an apartment in the Pinney Theatre building, the same building on whose stage she had starred for many years.[17] She would remain there for five years through 1945.

Having no means of support after losing her government appointment, Della availed herself of Idaho's old age benefit. Later she would say, "I wish now that I had taken membership in the actor fund years ago [in Hollywood]. It never occurred to me then that Jolly Della Pringle would ever need it."[18]

In 1940 Della lived quietly and alone in her Pinney Theatre building home and only came into public attention through newspaper articles on three occasions during the year. The first item on January 28 was a brief one about Della attending a play starring the renowned actress, Eva Le Gallienne, and meeting with her after the performance.[19]

The second news item, an amusing feature about Boise Boy, her ten-year-old Boston bulldog, included his picture. Della bragged that "there's at last one dog in Boise with personality" and explained why Boise Boy was it. She recalled how, after she had knitted him a sweater with sleeves and red braid, he refused to wear it, preferring to suffer from the cold rather than be seen in her creation. She claimed he had a listening vocabulary of a hundred words, some in pig Latin. She pointed out that Boise Boy didn't risk his life barking at cars and running loose in the street. He even waited at intersections for someone to carry him across the street. Boise Boy enjoyed automobile rides and friends of Della would pick him up for rides and then take him home for the afternoon, proving (according to Della) how much personality he had. Sadly, Della could not keep Boise Boy in her apartment so he lived at the home of her niece who frequently brought the dog to visit Della.[20]

The last newspaper item about Della in 1940 appeared in the March 22 edition of the *Idaho Statesman*.[21] It covered her presentation at a meeting of the Boise Chapter of the Idaho Writer's League held at the Hotel Boise. She had compiled an autobiography from which she recounted amusing anecdotes from her long stage career:

> Barnstorming in Idaho ghost towns...; her encounter with John L. Sullivan [heavyweight boxing champion] in Omaha in 1904 just before he "licked the leading lady of his troupe"; her Hollywood experiences with

Gloria Swanson when movies were young; [and] her childhood appearances in Iowa.[22]

By October 1 of 1941 Della somehow had gathered enough resources to afford to do some traveling. She had been in poor health and hoped to feel a lot better in the sun and warmth of California where she could visit old movie friends—Bebe Daniels, Mrs. Max Swain and Charles Murray. The newspaper described her departure at the Boise train depot: "The color and drama of the past still cling about the slight figure of Della Pringle, once Idaho's most famous actress, and many eyes sought her Wednesday when she boarded the noon train.... With Della goes the last of the footlight glamour of another era."[23]

In Los Angeles Della saw and visited with many of her old trouper friends. She later commented:

> They took me riding, saw the beautiful places and homes, ate at all the most famous French and Italian places and me with my ulcers. It was a chance for them to spend the money and waste the good food, for I could only peck at a little of it, but did enjoy seeing the places and people.[24]

Della remained in California for two months and returned to Boise just before the United States entered World War II after the infamous Japanese attack on Pearl Harbor.

On June 24 of 1942 *Idaho Statesman* writer Faith Turner wrote a column entitled "Who Is She?" which turned out to be another retrospective of Della Pringle's life. It began:

> She who has always been surrounded by people and bright lights now sits by a sunny window alone—although no one can be alone who can laugh. Her story could fill a dozen zestful books. She has travelled the country over, has been a friend to the famous, the near-famous, the unknown, and many of the living do not forget.[25]

Turner flattered her with "Her blonde beauty, her spry wit, her magnificent gowns 'bowled them over' in the gay nineties."[26] Della told her of performing in a northern Idaho mill town where the seats were just planks laid across cut tree stumps. Della laughingly recalled seeing her orchestra "looking like frogs on those stumps with their long-tailed coats spread out behind them."[27] Turner's article eventually reached the editor of the *Knoxville Express* and was reprinted on September 10, 1942, for the edification of Della's old Iowa admirers.

Della celebrated her seventy-second birthday on August 20, 1942. Boise friends got together on that day at Boise's exclusive Idanha Hotel

14—Curtain Coming Down

and gave a party in her honor—cake, candles and all. Other friends not in attendance sent her jellies, fruits and all sorts of nice presents which pleased her greatly.[28]

Della Pringle had written many long letters to newspapers in Iowa and Idaho during her lifetime. The last such letter appeared in the *Knoxville Express* of January 2, 1943.[29] Of course, Della would give a few more interviews after this, but this would be her last letter. She wrote it as a belated response after the Knoxville paper had reprinted the "Who Is She?" column from the Boise paper. An Iowa friend had informed her of the reprinted article and she was so pleased that old friends still remembered her that she had to write a letter all could read.

Although the letter was written in Della's folksy and friendly style, complaints made up most of it. She began by admitting she could remember things and places from fifty years ago better than something that happened recently. It disturbed her that she didn't see many names in the Knoxville paper that she recognized, attributing this to the passage of time and the rapidly changing world.[30]

Della portrayed Boise as "a strange town to all of the old timers." She wrote: "When I do meet someone I know on the street I waggle my tail like a friendly old dog and just beam all over." She noted the presence of so many soldiers and "everybody so busy with war work, they don't visit or have time for 'duff and dam old' women." The war had been terribly hard on Della and other elderly people who had experienced three wars since the late nineteenth century. Della said she coped with hardships by getting all the laughs she could from listening to the radio comedies of Bob Hope, Fibber McGee and Molly, Jack Benny, Charlie McCarthy and Red Skelton.[31]

She complained about Boise's weather. "We are having the rainiest winter I ever saw, rained all November and every day and night so far in December—foggy and dark, surely not like our usual Boise winters."[32]

Della revealed that her health was very poor. She suffered all the time from stomach and liver ulcers, requiring her to eat a diet of bland food. When she ignored the strict diet she paid for it like when she over indulged at a Thanksgiving meal and had to live on soup for a week after.[33]

Not all the letter was compliant. She wrote: "I am very comfortable, have a nice large room, my own furniture with its familiar look, good friends in the building, who come running if I'm sick of need help."[34]

At the end of the letter Della wished a Merry Christmas to her Iowa friends and invited them to write to her. "Just address me Boise, Idaho, I will get it, they know me better than anybody at the post office."[35]

Della lived in obscurity for the remainder of 1943 and most of 1944. The *Idaho Statesman* did write about her career on October 22, 1944, but the long item revealed nothing that had not been printed several times before. After World War II ended in 1945, Della, who had been ill for some time, left Boise in September to spend the winter with her niece in sunnier and warmer, Dallas, Texas, where Grace and her husband were members of a repertory theatre company.[36] At winter's end Della returned to Boise briefly and then in March went back to visit her niece in Texas, this time at Fort Worth where Grace and Crawford Eagle had an engagement with the Wayne Babb Players.[37]

Della resided in Boise during the months of April and May 1946, before making one last journey, this time to her roots in Iowa. On June 5 she stopped off at Des Moines where the *Des Moines Register* welcomed the slight, bright-eyed little woman after an absence of thirty-eight years. The paper gave a brief review of her career and quoted Della: "I'm sort of footloose now that I have no home of my own" she said wistfully, "and thought I'd come back to Knoxville on a visit before all my friends are gone."[38]

The next day Della arrived in Knoxville, but the town's two weekly papers did not report her presence until June 13. The *Knoxville Express* just reprinted the article about Della from last week's *Des Moines Register*, but the *Knoxville Journal* devoted three columns to her and her acting career. It reported, "Mrs. Pringle, a smart looking, small woman of only 75 years, was happy as she could be visiting the scenes of her girlhood, in and around Knoxville."[39] While most of the article outlined her professional achievements, it ended on a personal and amusing note:

> I's not in the best of health, said Della, for I have stomach ulcers. My doctor told me I should live on thin oatmeal and milk and that is what I have to do. When I told my Boise banker friend about it, he said, "Della, you can live a long time on oatmeal." "Yes, I know I can," I replied, "But who in the hell wants to."[40]

After spending about a week in Knoxville, Della wrote a Boise friend to help her secure her former apartment which she returned to on or before June 19.

When the musical version of *The Perils of Pauline* with Betty Hutton was released in July of 1947, Dell Pringle attended the movie in Boise. Before she entered the theatre, a newspaper reporter recognized her and asked about her interest in the film. Della answered:

> It's going to bring back my days in the Mack Sennett studios forty years ago—and won't that be fun! How well I remember the awful things they

did to me, like cracking teapots over my head, turning the hose on me and floating me out of windows; but the worst of all was being strung up with piano wire until I thought I would break in two. Actually I had to go to the hospital after acting in one of those terrible slapstick comedies.[41]

The reporter used Della's remarks to begin another retrospective of her career.

Earlier interviews with Della had mentioned that she had developed a hearing loss and she had once described herself as a "duff and dam old woman." While hardly a joking matter, on one occasion Della's deafness made for an amusing anecdote that was recorded in the 1976 Winter Edition of *Idaho Heritage* by Nancy Stringfellow.

Della lived in a small room in the Bristol Hotel and Neil Statts had a beauty shop in the same building. As he related, Della, elderly and quite deaf, used to come into his shop and his female assistant would shout, "How are you, Della?" and she would reply, "Ah, I'm so puny." Della had an old alarm clock which she oiled every day to keep it running and then took it into Statt's shop to get the right time of day, dripping oil all over the place. One day Statts grew tired of the mess from the clock and left his shop to buy Della a new alarm clock at a nearby drugstore. He returned and gave Della the new clock and jokingly yelled in her ear, "Della, if you oil this one I'll kill you!" After Della took the new clock and left, Statts dropped the old, oil soaked clock in a wastebasket and went back to work. Shortly his shop was swarming with policemen. It turned out that Della had taken Statts' joke as a threat on her life and gone to the police station to see justice done. Statts fished the sodden old clock out of the wastebasket, showed it to the police and said, "I told her if she oiled the new one I'd kill her." Seeing the clock, the policemen laughed long and loudly. After they got over their hysterics, they escorted Della and her clock out of the shop. She was satisfied; she had seen justice done.[42]

It had been twenty-seven years since Della's last professional theatre season, yet some in the profession still remembered and revered her. Will Locke, a former repertory theatre actor and a contributor to the theatrical trade publication *Billboard* wrote to Della in April of 1948. He was writing reminiscences of the bygone repertory shows and felt his series would not be complete without something about Della Pringle and her once so well-known attractions. Locke requested that Della dig into her memory and send him information about her days on stages across America that he could use in an article. Della sent the requested material and a few months later Locke's article appeared on the pages of *Billboard*.[43]

In his flowery prose, Locke began his tribute to Della Pringle with:

> If the true history of rep shows and that versatile clan we call repsters could be written it would not be complete without the story of one of the best little troupers the West ever knew—that sweetheart of old-time playgoers—Jolly Della Pringle! A story of outstanding interest because for many years this clever little woman toured the Midwest, beloved by thousands. There was not a town of any consequence where she was not a welcome visitor and her name a household word.[44]

Locke followed with a brief biographic sketch of Della's theatre career and concluded his ode to Della in his florid style.

> She had known all the acute trials and vicissitudes that are akin to the actor-life; had known alternate times of plenty and of want; had known the bitter sting of scathing loss, grief and heartache. But to the eyes of her public she was always the true trouper, her griefs and tears hidden behind the gay mask of the artist, living up to that ancient tradition, "away with self—the show must go on!" And thru it all, thru prosperity and thru adversity, she was the same ever-merry, wonderful little trouper—Jolly Della Pringle![45]

Following Locke's hyperbolic tribute, Della lapsed back into obscurity, the only record of her existence a city directory listing of her apartment, room 3 at 720½ Idaho Street. Sometime later in 1950 a prolonged illness, the infirmities of age and a desperate economic situation forced Della to become a ward of the state in the Ada County Hospital, Boise's version of a poorhouse.

Boise friends came to the Ada County Hospital on August 20 with lots of ice cream and cake to celebrate Della Pringle's eighty-second birthday. At the party in her honor she declared herself the oldest living actress, older than Ethel Barrymore at seventy-two. She reminisced about her first appearances in Boise in 1902 and smiled wistfully when she recalled her days in Hollywood. "Gloria Swanson was on the Mack Sennett payroll for eighteen dollars a week. In those days she stood around and admired my beautiful clothes and diamonds. Times certainly do change, but that's show business."[46]

At some time before November of 1952, Maude Cosho Huston visited Della Pringle in the Ada County Hospital to interview her for an article in the *Scenic Idaho* magazine. It would be Della's last interview.

Huston's five full page article covered most of what had already been reported in various sources. However, it gave an inspiring and poignant portrayal of Della Pringle in her final days. Huston found Della to be a little wisp of an old lady, her once golden hair now pure white and her impaired hearing making it difficult to converse. In spite of her eighty-

14—Curtain Coming Down

The final photograph of Della Pringle, age 82, taken in Boise shortly before her death on November 9, 1952 (courtesy the National Society for the Preservation of Tent, Folk and Repertoire Theatre at the Theatre Museum of Repertoire Americana, Midwest Old Threshers, Mt. Pleasant, Iowa).

two years, she still liked to make herself up and wear pretty dresses. The walls of Della's little apartment were decorated with photographs of a younger and very beautiful Della Pringle in theatrical poses along with many autographed pictures of show business friends.[47]

Della kept scrapbooks filled with old newspaper clippings, theatre programs and other mementos which she enjoyed poring over. Her delicate health and her age pretty well kept her confined to her apartment, but from time to time kind Boise friends would drop in and take her out for a much appreciated ride around town. She was also grateful for an occasional letter or postcard from an old Hollywood friend. Because of her hearing problem she could no longer enjoy her old radio programs and occupied most of her time with reading newspapers and magazines supplied by friends which helped keep her informed and up to date with the world outside the Ada County Hospital.[48]

Huston's *The Saga of Jolly Della Pringle* concluded poignantly. "Time has cruelly withered and twisted her once shapely body, but her eyes are still bright and they twinkled almost roguishly as she said: 'I've never once felt sorry for myself. It's been a great life, but sometimes I just wonder if I haven't lived just a little too long.'"[49]

Jolly Della Pringle bowed out of this world on November 9, 1952. She died in the Ada County Hospital of bronchial pneumonia. Her obituary appeared in the *Idaho Statesman* the next day.[50] Sadly, her beloved niece did not attend her aunt's funeral ceremony. Grace Van Winkle, performing her marionette show in Missouri, received the telegram announcing Della's demise several days afterward because she received her messages at general delivery and the telegram did not reach her promptly.[51] However, many Boise show people and community theatre members, contacted by a local newspaper reporter, attended to give a final tribute to the old actress.[52]

Della was buried in Boise's Morris Hill Cemetery (Section J, Block 47, Grave 3) and her funeral expenses of $245 were paid by her niece and Boise friends.[53] Months later Grace had a stone marker placed above her grave. It reads:

> Jolly Della Pringle
> 1870–1952
> A Good Trouper

Epilogue:
A Summing Up

What happened to the people and institutions associated with Della Pringle during her long and eventful life? What endured? How was she remembered?

Della's niece and only living relative, Grace Van Winkle, remained in show business of one sort or other for more than twenty years after her aunt's death. She and her husband, Crawford Eagle, filled engagements with various repertory tent theatres until the decline of that entertainment form after World War II, a victim of the developing television industry. Then they created another way to continue as entertainers by developing and presenting marionette shows. Grace had taken puppetry classes while working in Boise's W.P.A. adult education program. With the skills learned there she designed and built marionettes.

Crawford Eagle worked at various jobs such as motion picture theatre manager and radio announcer before he finally joined with Grace and her marionettes. Their show, titled "Revue in Miniature," featured a line of chorus girls, a juggling marionette and two that twirled batons, all enhanced by recorded music and intricate lighting effects.

They entertained soldiers in hospitals and military camps during the war and after they made a career of touring their puppet theatre to public schools under the National School Assembly program during the school year, sometimes giving as many as fourteen shows in a week. Summers were spent with some of the remaining tent repertory theatres where they acted roles and presented a puppet show as a between acts specialty.

In 1981 Grace and Crawford received honors from The National Society for the Preservation of Tent, Folk and Repertoire Theatre at Mt. Pleasant, Iowa, for their forty-five years in show business. Eventually they retired from performing and spent their final years managing apartment houses in southern California.

Of the two Boise theatres that served as venues for Della's numerous theatre productions, only one structure remains. The large Pinney Theatre that featured Della so often on stage and contained the small apartment Della lived in during her old age served mainly as a movie house after the 1920s. By 1971 the Pinney had been destroyed in the Boise government's

A regal Della Pringle at age 46 in a Wetzel Studio portrait in Los Angeles, 1916 (courtesy the National Society for the Preservation of Tent, Folk and Repertoire Theatre at the Theatre Museum of Repertoire Americana, Midwest Old Threshers, Mt. Pleasant, Iowa).

abortive effort at urban renewal. The smaller Turner Theatre escaped the wrecking ball but ceased to be a venue for theatre productions after the 1920s. Over the years a succession of bars and restaurants occupied the old Turnverein building. Today the inside of the old Turner Theatre has been completely remodeled and under the name of "China Blue" attracts Boise's young people for evenings of drinking and dancing.

Today a branch of the First Idaho Bank occupies the site of Della Pringle's Palantine rooming house where she resided off and on for nearly two decades. A single, large tree still standing on the bank site may have once shaded Della and the tenants of her rooming house in the oasis in the heart of downtown Boise.

Twenty years after Della Pringle died she remained in the memories of some Boise residents. One would remember her wearing flamboyant hats on the street and to community theatre productions. Another remembers as a child having her hair braided by Della at the Palantine rooming house. An elderly newspaper woman recalled how pleased and gratified Della was to have company for an interview in the 1940s. A dance instructor who had known Della through the W.P.A. education program remembered her but had no specific memories, saying only, "It was so long ago." Most older Boiseans, if they remembered Della Pringle at all, probably regarded her as a deaf old eccentric eager to tell endless anecdotes from her theatre career.

According to Betty Penson-Ward in her book of women in Idaho history, Della ended up "like a worn out puppet on the trash heap." Yes, things did not end well for the once jolly actress, but how she lived her life was more important than its end.

Della Pringle should best be remembered for the halcyon days when she and her merry makers boarded her own palace Pullman car in Knoxville, displaying a banner reading "Jolly Della Pringle, $10,000 Invested for Your Entertainment," to skip through Iowa towns headed to entertain in Nebraska communities before reaching the Black Hills of South Dakota and beyond, most of a continent of adoring fans filling crowded houses beckoning her. That was a Della Pringle to cherish, adore and admire—an extravagantly gowned, witty, wealthy, multitalented star of Western stages where she was always a most welcome visitor and a household name.

Chapter Notes

Chapter 1

1. Della Pringle papers, Theatre Museum of Repertoire Americana, Mt. Pleasant, Iowa.
2. *Evening Capital News* [Boise], June 5, 1909, p. 8.
3. *Idaho Statesman* [Boise], October 22, 1944, p. 10
4. *New York Daily Mirror*, June 13, 1903, p. 12.
5. *New York Clipper*, June 18, 1881, p. 206; July 23, 1881, p. 287; April 29, 1882, p. 230.
6. Betty Penson-Ward, *Idaho Women in History*, Vol. 1 (Boise: Legendary, 1991), p. 139.
7. *New York Clipper*, November 26, 1888.
8. *Lincoln Daily Call*, January 27, 1889, p. 4.
9. *New York Clipper*, November 2, 1889, p. 567.
10. *New York Clipper*, November 9, 1889, p. 605
11. *Ibid.*, September 6, 1890, p. 411.
12. *Ibid.*, October 11, 1890, p. 482.
13. *Oskaloosa Daily Herald*, October 21, 1890, p. 3; *New York Clipper*, November 1, 1890, p. 531.
14. *Knoxville Journal*, February 1, 1891, p. 3; April 22, 1891, p. 2.

Chapter 2

1. Leatrice Gilbert Fountain, *Dark Star* (New York: St. Martin's Press, 1988), p. 8.
2. Maude Cosho Huston, "The Saga of Jolly Della Pringle," *Scenic Idaho* 7, no. 8 (1952), p. 11.
3. *Ibid.*
4. *Ibid.*
5. *New York Clipper*, July 25, 1891, p. 331.
6. *Ibid.*, August 15, 1891, p. 384.
7. *Ibid.*, May 14, 1892.
8. *Trenton Morning Tribune*, January 15, 1892, p. 3.
9. *Chillicothe Constitution*, June 26, 1892, p. 1.
10. *New York Clipper*, May 28, 1892, p. 183.
11. *Knoxville Journal*, June 19, 1892, p. 2.
12. *New York Clipper*, July 30, 1892, p. 326; August 6, 1893, p. 343.
13. *Knoxville Journal*, September 21, 1892, p. 3; September 28, 1892, p. 3.
14. *New York Clipper*, November 5, 1892, p. 556.
15. Huston, p. 13.
16. *Ibid.*
17. *New York Clipper*, January 21, 1893, p. 736.
18. *Knoxville Journal*, March 29, 1893, p. 3; *New York Clipper*, April 29, 1893, p. 116.
19. *New York Clipper*, June 17, 1893, p. 231.
20. *Knoxville Journal*, August 1, 1893, p. 3.
21. *Ibid.*
22. *New York Clipper*, September 2, 1893, p. 414.
23. *Silverton Standard* [Colorado], April 28, 1894, p. 2.
24. *Central City Courier* [Nebraska], August 24, 1893, p. 5.
25. *Ravenna News* [Nebraska], August 24, 1893, p. 4.
26. *Crawford Gazette* [Nebraska], November 24, 1893, p. 1.
27. *Cheyenne Daily Leader*, December 8, 1893, p. 3.

28. *New York Clipper,* December 16, 1893, p. 654.
29. *Ibid.,* December 30, 1893, p. 691.
30. *Ibid.,* March 17, 1894, p. 20.
31. Huston, p.13.
32. *New York Clipper,* June 16, 1894, pp. 227, 228; *Knoxville Express,* June 12, 1894, p. 3.
33. *New York Clipper,* July 21, 1894, p. 307.
34. *Knoxville Express,* July 24, 1894, p. 3.
35. *Ibid.*
36. *New York Clipper,* June 8, 1894, p. 509.
37. Huston, p. 26.
38. *Shenandoah Semi-Weekly Sentinel,* August 10, 1894, p. 2.
39. *Fremont Democrat* [Hamburg, Iowa], August 17, 1894, p. 1.
40. Huston, p. 26.
41. *Knoxville Express,* April 30, 1895, p. 3.
42. *Omaha Evening Bee,* January 4, 1895, p. 8.
43. *New York Clipper,* January 12, 1895.
44. *Denver Post,* January 24, 1895, p. 4; *New York Clipper,* March 2, 1895, p. 831.
45. *New York Dramatic Mirror,* April 27, 1895, p. 6.
46. *Knoxville Express,* April 30, 1895, p. 3; May 4, 1895, p, 3; May 14, 1895, p. 3.

Chapter 3

1. *New York Clipper,* June 8, 1895, p. 211.
2. *Knoxville Journal,* June 15, 1895, p. 3.
3. *New York Dramatic Mirror,* August 17, 1895, p. 6.
4. *New York Clipper,* November 9, 1895, p. 578.
5. *Ibid.,* February 19, 1896, p. 821.
6. *Weekly Nashua Post,* February 6, 1896, p. 8.
7. *Nashua Reporter,* February 6, 1896. Cited in *Knoxville Express,* February 12, 1896, p. 3.
8. *Ibid.*
9. *New York Clipper,* February 29, 1896, p. 821.
10. *Knoxville Express,* February 26, 1896, p. 3.
11. *New York Clipper,* June 13, 1896, p. 230.
12. *Knoxville Express,* April 8, 1896, p. 3; May 13, 1896, p. 3.
13. *Ibid.,* May 13, 1896, p. 3.
14. *Knoxville Journal,* June 13, 1896, p. 3.
15. *Knoxville Express,* July 8, 1896, p. 3.
16. *New York Clipper,* July 4, 1896, p. 327.
17. *Knoxville Journal,* June 13, 1946, p. 1.
18. *Knoxville Express,* September 23, 1896, p. 3.
19. *Ibid.,* August 19, 1896, p. 3.
20. *Ibid.,* November 25, 1896, p. 3.
21. *Ibid.,* December 16, 1896, p. 3.
22. *Ibid.,* December 30, 1896, p. 3.
23. *Ibid.,* January 20, 1897, p. 2.
24. *Des Moines Leader,* February 8, 1897, p. 3.
25. *New York Dramatic Mirror,* June 5, 1897, p. 6; *Knoxville Express,* May 26, 1897, p. 2.
26. *Black Hills Daily Times* [Deadwood, South Dakota], April 6, 1897, p. 3.
27. *New York Clipper,* May 8, 1897, p. 153.
28. *Black Hills Daily Times,* March 26, 1897, p. 3.
29. *Evening Call* [Lead, South Dakota], April 1, 1897, p. 4.
30. *Alliance Times* [Nebraska], April 30, 1897, p. 1.
31. *Kearney Hub* [Nebraska], May 31, 1897, p. 3.
32. *Knoxville Express,* July 7, 1897, p. 2.
33. *Knoxville Journal,* June 5, 1897, p. 3.
34. *Idaho Daily Statesman* [Boise], April 30, 1939, Sec. 2, p. 12.
35. *New York Clipper,* July 3, 1897, p. 286.
36. *Knoxville Express,* July 7, 1897, p. 2.
37. Letter from Grace Eagle, Della Pringle's niece, to Dr. Jere Mickel, November 11, 1970. Cited in Jere Mickel, *Footlights on the Prairie* (St. Cloud, MN: North Star Press, 1974), p. 76.
38. *Knoxville Express,* August 18, 1897, p. 2.
39. *Ibid.*
40. *Ibid.,* August 25, 1897, p. 2.
41. *New York Clipper,* November 27, 1897, p. 642.
42. *Knoxville Express,* January 5, 1898, p. 2.
43. *New York Clipper,* October 30, 1897, p. 574.
44. *Ibid.,* October 16, 1897, p. 542.
45. *Knoxville Express,* January 5, 1898, p. 2.
46. *Knoxville Journal,* January 22, 1898, p. 3.
47. *Knoxville Express,* July 27, 1898, p. 2.
48. *Ibid.,* August 17, 1898, p. 2.

49. *New York Clipper*, July 2, 1898, p. 289.
50. *Knoxville Express*, August 24, 1898, p. 2.
51. *Pioneer Grip* [Alliance, Nebraska], September 30, 1898, pp. 1, 8.
52. *New York Clipper*, October 15, 1898, p. 555.
53. *Ibid.*, December 31, 1898, p. 738.
54. *Montrose Enterprise*, January 19, 1899, p. 3.
55. *Knoxville Express*, January 25, 1899, p. 2.

Chapter 4

1. *Knoxville Express*, February 8, 1899, p. 2; March 8, 1899, p. 2.
2. *New York Clipper*, March 11, 1899, p. 26.
3. *New York Dramatic Mirror*, March 4, 1899, p. 15.
4. *Knoxville Journal*, April 29, 1899, p. 5.
5. *New York Clipper*, April 29, 1899, p. 166.
6. *Ibid.*, April 20, 1899, p. 180.
7. *St. Joseph Daily Gazette*, September 18, 1899, p. 5; *Rapid City Daily Journal*, October 22, 1899, p. 1.
8. *Rapid City Daily Journal*, October 27, 1899, p. 1.
9. *Daily Pioneer Times* [Deadwood, South Dakota], November 8, 1899, p. 5.
10. *Moberly Evening Democrat*, September 11, 1899, p. 1.
11. *Knoxville Express*, August 23, 1899, p. 2.
12. *Ibid.*, September 13, 1899, p. 2.
13. *Ibid.*, December 27, 1899, p. 2.
14. *New York Clipper*, January 6, 1900, p. 934.
15. *Ibid.*, December 30, 1899, p. 929.
16. *Knoxville Journal*, January 6, 1900, p. 4.
17. *New York Clipper*, February 17, 1900, p. 1072.
18. *Ibid.*
19. *Knoxville Express*, January 17, 1900, p. 2.
20. *Fort Smith Times.* Cited in *Arkansas Gazette* [Little Rock], February 20, 1900, p. 7.
21. *Arkansas Gazette*, February 20, 1900, p. 7.
22. *Ibid.*, February 23, 1900, p. 5.
23. *Ibid.*
24. *Alton Evening Telegraph*, February 27, 1900, p. 3; March 1, 1900, p. 3.
25. *New York Clipper*, March 31, 1900, p. 101.
26. *Knoxville Express*, March 28, 1900, p. 2; *Knoxville Journal*, March 31, 1900, p. 4.
27. *Knoxville Journal*, April 28, 1900, p. 5.
28. *Ibid.*, May 1, 1900, p. 5.
29. *Ibid.*, June 9, 1900, p. 5.
30. *Ibid.*, July 21, 1900, p. 5.
31. *Knoxville Express*, July 25, 1900, p. 2.
32. *Knoxville Journal*, July 28, 1900, p. 5.
33. *Ibid.*, July 21, 1900, p. 5.
34. *Ibid.*, August 11, 1900, p. 5.
35. *New York Clipper*, September 1, 1900, p. 587.
36. *Ibid.*, November 17, 1900, p. 532.
37. *Knoxville Journal*, July 21, 1900, p. 4.
38. *Knoxville Express*, August 15, 1900, p. 2.
39. *Ibid.*, August 8, 1900, p. 2.
40. *Sidney Telegraph*, September 29, 1900, p. 1.
41. *Laramie Republican*, October 12, 1900, p. 1.
42. *Knoxville Express*, January 23, 1901, p. 2.
43. *New York Daily Mirror*, February 2, 1901, p. 6; February 16, 1901, p. 7.
44. *Lincoln Evening News*, April 5, 1901, p. 5.
45. *Knoxville Express*, July 31, 1901, p. 1.
46. *Ibid.*, May 1, 1901, p. 2.
47. *Ibid.*, May 15, 1901, p. 2.
48. *New York Clipper*, June 1, 1901, p. 295.
49. *Ibid.*, May 11, 1901, p. 252.
50. *Salt Lake Daily Tribune*, December 10, 1901, p. 8.
51. *Knoxville Journal*, June 29, 1901, p. 5.
52. *Knoxville Express*, August 7, 1901, p. 2.
53. *Ibid.*, August 14, 1901, p. 2.
54. *Ibid.*, August 7, 1901, p. 2.
55. *Ibid.*, July 31, 1901, p. 1.
56. *Ibid.*, August 14, 1901, p. 2; July 31, 1901, p. 1.
57. *Ibid.*
58. *Laramie Boomerang*, October 11, 1901, p. 8.
59. *Knoxville Express*, August 21, 1901, p. 2.
60. *Des Moines Daily Leader*, September 1, 1901, p. 20.

61. *Fairfield Ledger*, September 11, 1901, p. 3; *Chariton Herald*, September 12, 1901, p. 5; *New York Clipper*, September 7, 1901, p. 603.
62. *Alliance Times*, October 4, 1901, p. 4; *New York Clipper*, October 19, 1901, p. 726.
63. *Laramie Boomerang*, October 12, 1901, p. 8.
64. *Salt Lake Daily Tribune*, December 10, 1901, p. 8.
65. *Knoxville Express*, December 15, 1901, p. 2.
66. *New York Daily Mirror*, February 27, 1902, p. 2.
67. *Knoxville Express*, March 13, 1902, p. 1.
68. *Spokansman Review*, February 23, 1902, p. 17.
69. *Knoxville Express*, March 12, 1902, p. 1.
70. *Ibid.*, March 26, 1902, p. 1.
71. *Ibid.*, April 2, 1902, p. 4.

Chapter 5

1. *Knoxville Express*, April 2, 1902, p. 4.
2. *New York Dramatic Mirror*, April 19, 1902, p. 28.
3. *Knoxville Express*, May 14, 1902, p. 2.
4. *Knoxville Journal*, May 16, 1902, p. 2.
5. *Knoxville Express*, May 28, 1902, p. 3.
6. *Ibid.*
7. *Ibid.*
8. *Ibid.*
9. *New York Clipper*, August 9, 1902, p. 409.
10. *Ibid.*, August 30, 1902, p. 585.
11. *Knoxville Express*, September 3, 1902, p. 1.
12. *Ibid.*
13. *Ibid.*
14. *Newburgh Daily Times*, August 29, 1902, p. 3.
15. *Ibid.*, September 2, 1902, p. 8.
16. *Knoxville Express*, October 15, 1902, p. 2.
17. *Yonkers Statesman*, October 1, 1902, p. 4; October 2, 1902, p. 10.
18. *New York Clipper*, October 18, 1902, p. 741.
19. *Every Evening* [Wilmington, Delaware], October 14, 1902, p. 6; October 15, 1902, p. 3; October 16, 1902, p. 7.
20. *Hartford Courant*, October 17, 1902, p. 7.
21. *Day* [New London, Connecticut], October 28, 1902, p. 5.
22. *Knoxville Express*, August 20, 1902, p. 1; July 16, 1902, p. 1.
23. *Salem News*, January 21, 1903, p. 6.
24. *Lewiston Evening Journal*, February 13, 1903, p. 7.
25. *Lawrence Telegram*, January 5, 1903, p. 7.
26. *New York Clipper*, November 1, 1902, p. 787.
27. *Knoxville Express*, December 10, 1902, p. 6.
28. *Daily Globe* [Fall River, Massachusetts], November 4, 1902, p. 6.
29. *Brockton Enterprise*, November 18, 1902, p. 4; November 20, 1902, p. 4.
30. *Knoxville Journal*, December 19, 1902, p. 5.
31. *New York Clipper*, December 29, 1902, pp. 973, 976.
32. *Lawrence Telegram*, January 5, 1903, p. 7.
33. *Lynn Item*, January 13, 1903, p. 12.
34. *Daily Eastern Argus* [Portland, Maine], January 27, 1903, p. 9.
35. *Ibid.*, January 28, 1903, p. 6.
36. *Bangor Daily News*, February 7, 1903, p. 4.
37. *Lewiston Evening Journal*, February 12, 1903, p. 7.
38. *Knoxville Express*, February 25, 1903, p. 1.
39. *Haverhill Evening Gazette*, February 18, 1903, p. 11.
40. *Fitchburg Sentinel*, February 24, 1903, p. 6.
41. *Ibid.*, February 25, 1903, p. 6.
42. *Knoxville Express*, March 25, 1903, p. 3.
43. *Ibid.*, April 1, 1903, p. 3.
44. *Ibid.* April 8, 1903, p. 2; April 9, 1903, p. 2.
45. *Meriden Morning Record*, April 8, 1903, p. 2; April 9, 1903, p. 2.
46. *New York Clipper*, May 9, 1903, p. 256.

Chapter 6

1. *New York Clipper*, May 23, 1903, p. 304.
2. *Ibid.*, June 13, 1903, p. 370.
3. *Knoxville Journal*, July 10, 1903, p. 5.

Notes—Chapter 7

4. *Ibid.*, July 31, 1903, p. 5; *New York Clipper*, August 8, 1903, p. 552.
5. *New York Clipper*, September 5, 1903, p. 646; *Morning Appeal* [Carson City, Nevada], December 4, 1903, p. 3.
6. *San Jose Mercury*, December 25, 1903, p. 3.
7. *New York Clipper*, September 5, 1903, p. 646; *Deadwood Daily Times*, September 16, 1903, p. 8.
8. *Knoxville Express*, July 29, 1903, p. 2.
9. *Knoxville Journal*, August 19, 1903, pp. 1, 7.
10. *Alliance Herald*, August 28, 1903, p. 1.
11. *New York Clipper*, October 3, 1903, p. 751.
12. *Ibid.*
13. *Deadwood Daily Pioneer Times*, September 5, 1903, p. 5.
14. *New York Clipper*, October 3, 1903, p. 751.
15. *Knoxville Express*, November 25, 1903, p. 6.
16. *Ibid.*
17. *Ibid.*
18. *Knoxville Journal*, December 11, 1903, p. 2.
19. *Ibid.*
20. *Ibid.*
21. *Ibid.*
22. *Ibid.*
23. *Ibid.*
24. *Ibid.*
25. *Knoxville Express*, January 27, 1904, p. 1.
26. *Ibid.*
27. *Ibid.*
28. *Ibid.*
29. P. H. MacEnery, "Thelma Bungled at the Victory," *San Jose Mercury*, December 26, 1903, p. 3.
30. *Knoxville Express*, January 27, 1904, p. 1.
31. *Ibid.*
32. *Ibid.*
33. *Ibid.*
34. *Ibid.*
35. *Ibid.*
36. *Ibid.*
37. *Ibid.*
38. *New York Clipper*, April 9, 1904, p. 143.
39. *Ibid.*
40. *Ibid.*, May 14, 1904, p. 279.

Chapter 7

1. *Knoxville Express*, April 20, 1904, p. 7.
2. *New York Clipper*, May 14, 1904, p. 279.
3. *Knoxville Express*, May 18, 1904, p. 7; May 25, 1904, p. 7; *Knoxville Journal*, June 10, 1904, p. 5.
4. *Knoxville Express*, June 29, 1904, p. 2.
5. *Ibid.*
6. *Ibid.*
7. *Ibid.*
8. *Ibid.*
9. *Knoxville Journal*, July 29, 1904, p. 2.
10. *Ibid.*, p. 5.
11. *New York Clipper*, July 30, 1904.
12. *Knoxville Express*, August 24, 1904, p. 2.
13. *Ibid.*
14. *Ibid.*
15. *Ibid.*, October 12, 1904, p. 6.
16. *Washington Times*, September 20, 1904, p. 5.
17. *Ibid.*
18. *Ibid.*
19. *Ibid.*
20. *Ibid.*
21. *Ibid.*
22. *Ibid.*
23. *New York Clipper*, October 1, 1904, p. 626.
24. *Knoxville Express*, November 16, 1904, p. 2.
25. *Ibid.*
26. *Ibid.*
27. *Ibid.*
28. *Ibid.*
29. *Ibid,*
30. *Ibid.*
31. *Ibid.*
32. *Ibid.*
33. *Ibid.*
34. *Ibid.*
35. *Ibid.*
36. *Ibid.*
37. *Ibid.*
38. *Ibid.*, December 7, 1904, p. 3.
39. *Knoxville Journal*, November 25, 1904, p. 5.
40. *Ibid.*, December 9, 1904, p. 3.
41. *New York Clipper*, February 4, 1905, p. 1170.
42. *Ibid.*, March 18, 1905, p. 91.

43. *Rapid City Daily Journal*, January 12, 1905, p. 1.
44. *New York Clipper*, February 4, 1905, p. 1170.
45. *Knoxville Express*, December 21, 1904, p. 19.
46. *Knoxville Journal*, December 9, 1904, p. 3.
47. *Chariton* [Iowa] *Herald*, January 5, 1905, p. 3.
48. *Knoxville Express*, January 4, 1905, p. 2.
49. *Alliance Semi-Weekly Times*, January 6, 1905, p. 1.
50. *Rapid City Daily Journal*, January 15, 1905, p. 1.
51. *New York Clipper*, March 18, 1905, p. 91.
52. *Central City Register* [South Dakota], February 8, 1905, p. 1.
53. *Bozeman Chronicle*, March 1, 1905, p. 8. Quoted from *Deadwood Pioneer Times*.
54. *Bismarck Daily Tribune*, March 29, 1905, p. 3.
55. *Knoxville Journal*, May 5, 1905, p. 1.
56. *Ibid.*, April 25, 1905, p. 1.
57. *Ibid.*
58. *Morning Oregonian* [Portland], April 30, 1905, p. 28.
59. *Knoxville Express*, June 7, 1905, p. 7.
60. *Knoxville Journal*, June 9, 1905, p. 3.

Chapter 8

1. *Knoxville Journal*, July 21, 1905, p. 5.
2. *South Dakota Daily Sentinel* [Madison], September 14, 1905, p. 3.
3. *New York Dramatic Mirror*, October 7, 1905, p. 8
4. *Knoxville Journal*, July 28, 1905, p. 1.
5. *Ibid.*, August 11, 1905, p. 5.
6. *Ibid.*, July 21, 1905, p. 5.
7. *Ibid.*, August 18, 1905, p. 1.
8. *Ibid.*, August 25, 1905, p. 5.
9. *Ibid.*
10. *Ibid.*
11. *Madison Daily Leader* [South Dakota], September 23, 1905, p. 3.
12. *Aberdeen Daily* News, September 29, 1905, p. 3.
13. *Pierre Daily Dakotan*, October 7, 1905, p. 4.
14. *Bismarck Daily Tribune*, October 28, 1905, p. 2.
15. *Minot Daily Optic*, December 11, 1905, p. 4; *Williston Herald*, December 14, 1905, p. 1.
16. *Harve Herald*, December 29, 1905. Cited in *Knoxville Express*, January 5, 1906, p. 5.
17. *Dillon Tribune*, January 5, 1906, p. 5.
18. *New York Clipper*, January 13, 1906, p. 1208; January 20, 1905, p. 1234.
19. *Wyoming Press* [Evanston], February 3, 1906, p. 6.
20. *Rock Springs Miner*, February 17, 1906, p. 3.
21. *Knoxville Express*, February 14, 1906, p. 2; *Knoxville Journal*, March 2, 1906, p. 5; *New York Clipper*, March 24, 1906, p. 130.
22. *New York Clipper*, April 14, 1906.
23. *Knoxville Journal*, March 30, 1906, p. 5.
24. *Long Beach Tribune*, April 25, 1906. Cited in *Knoxville Express*, May 2, 1906, p. 2.
25. *Ibid.*
26. *Ibid.*
27. *Knoxville Journal*, May 4, 1906, p. 1. Citing *Long Beach Press*, April 25, 1906.
28. *Long Beach Press*, September 22, 1906, p. 1.
29. *New York Clipper*, July 21, 1906, p. 591.
30. *Long Beach Press*, July 14, 1906, p. 4.
31. *Los Angeles Examiner*, July 14, 1906, p. 6; *New York Dramatic Mirror*, August 18, 1906, p. 13.
32. *Knoxville Express*, August 22, 1906, p. 2.
33. *Los Angeles Herald*, May 23, 1907, p. 5.
34. *Long Beach Press*, May 23, 1907, p. 1.
35. *Knoxville Express*, September 5, 1906, p. 2.
36. *Ibid.*
37. *Ibid.*
38. *Ibid.*
39. *Ibid.*
40. Divorce Decree, Della Pringle Tuttle vs. T.O. Tuttle, October 29, 1906, Marion County Historical Society, Knoxville, Iowa.
41. *Ibid.*
42. *Ibid.*
43. *Ibid.*
44. *Ibid.*
45. *Knoxville Journal*, December 7, 1906, p. 2.

46. *Knoxville Express*, September 5, 1906, p. 2. Citing unnamed Long Beach, California, paper for August 22.
47. *Ibid.*, November 7, 1906, p. 7.
48. *Ibid.*, November 14, 1906, p. 7.
49. *Ibid.*, November 28, 1906, p.7.
50. *Ibid.*, December 12, 1906, p. 11.
51. *Ibid.*, December 14, 1906, p. 7.
52. *Knoxville Journal*, September 7, 1906, p. 1.
53. *Knoxville Express*, December 17, 1906, p. 7.
54. *Ibid.*, December 12, 1906, p. 11; December 19, 1906, p. 7.
55. *Daily Freeman Tribune* [Webster City, Iowa], January 9, 1907, p. 5; January 14, 1907, p. 5.
56. *Knoxville Journal*, January 4, 1907, p. 2.
57. *Daily Freeman Tribune* [Webster City, Iowa], January 11, 1907, p. 5.
58. *Sioux City Journal*, January 14, 1907, p. 8.
59. *Yankton Press and Dakotan*, January 23, 1907, p. 5.
60. *Daily Huronite*, February 1, 1907, p. 4.
61. *Dickinson Press*, March 16, 1907, p. 5.
62. *Enterprise* [Sheridan, Wyoming], March 15, 1907, p. 1.
63. *Custer County Chief* [Broken Bow, Nebraska], April 5, 1907, p. 4.
64. *Long Beach Press*, May 2, 1907, p. 5; May 23, 1907, p. 1.
65. *Los Angeles Herald*, May 23, 1907, p. 2.
66. *Ibid.*
67. *New York Dramatic Mirror*, June 1, 1907, p. 13.
68. *New York Clipper*, June 22, 1907, p. 484.
69. *Colorado Springs Gazette*, June 30, 1907, p. 14.
70. *Ibid.*, July 4, 1907, p. 7.
71. *Ibid.*, June 30, 1907, p. 14; July 3, 1907, p. 5; *Denver Republican*, August 19, 1907, p. 10.
72. *Colorado Springs Gazette*, July 7, 1907, p. 13; June 30, 1907, p. 14.
73. *Goldfield Daily Tribune*, November 2, 1907, p. 8.
74. *Colorado Springs Gazette*, July 5, 1907, p. 5.
75. *Knoxville Express*, July 24, 1907, p. 2.
76. *Leadville Herald Democrat*, July 22, 1907, p. 3.
77. *Salida Mail*, August 2, 1907, p. 4.
78. *Colorado Springs Gazette*, August 2, 1907, p. 5; August 7, 1907, p. 5.
79. *Ibid.*, August 11, 1907, p. 7.
80. *Ibid.*
81. *Denver Post*, August 19, 1907, p. 6.
82. *Denver Republican*, August 19, 1907, p. 10.
83. *Salt Lake Tribune*, September 2, 1907, p. 12.
84. *New York Clipper*, September 21, 1907, p. 14.
85. *Wyoming Press* [Evanston], October 5, 1907, p. 1.
86. *Free Press* [Elko, Nevada], October 15, 1907, p. 1.
87. *Goldfield Daily Tribune*, October 31, 1907, p. 2.
88. Huston, pp. 26, 27.
89. *Tonopah Sun*, November 7, 1907, p. 3.
90. *Ibid.*
91. *New York Clipper*, March 21, 1907, p. 24.
92. *Mohave County Miner* [Kingman, Arizona], November 9, 1907, p. 8.
93. *Arizona Republican* [Phoenix], November 12, 1907, p. 13.
94. *New York Dramatic Mirror*, February 22, 1908, p. 24.
95. *Tombstone Epitaph*, November 24, 1907, p. 4.
96. *Arizona Daily Star* [Tucson], December 6, 1907, p. 6.
97. *New York Clipper*, December 21, 1907, p. 41.
98. *Knoxville Express*, January 1, 1908, p. 1.
99. *Daily Arizona Silver Belt* [Globe], December 17, 1907, p. 1.
100. *New York Clipper*, February 15, 1908, p. 1422.
101. *Arizona Republican* [Phoenix], December 28, 1907, p. 8.
102. *Ibid.*, January 2, 1908, p. 5.
103. *New York Clipper*, February 15, 1908, p. 1422.
104. *Ibid.*, March 28, 1908, p. 153.

Chapter 9

1. *Knoxville Express*, January 29, 1908, p. 7.

2. *New York Clipper*, March 14, 1908, p. 117.
3. *Ibid.*, March 28, 1908, p. 153.
4. *New York Dramatic Mirror*, April 18, 1908, p. 8; *Colorado Springs Gazette*, April 16, 1908, p. 10.
5. *New York Clipper*, April 18, 1908, p. 256.
6. *New York Dramatic Mirror*, April 18, 1908, p. 8.
7. *New York Clipper*, May 9, 1908, p. 325.
8. *Fort Collins Weekly Courier*, May 20, 1908, p. 12; *Boulder Daily Camera*, May 25, 1908, p. 2.
9. *Wyoming Press* [Evanston], June 6, 1908.
10. *Ogden Standard*, June 15, 1908, p. 6
11. *Knoxville Journal*, June 26, 1908, p. 2.
12. *Colorado Springs Gazette*, June 16, 1908, p. 7.
13. *Knoxville Express*, June 24, 1908, p. 1; *New York Dramatic Mirror*, July 11, 1908, p. 13.
14. *Logan Tri-Weekly Journal*, June 29, 1908, p. 8.
15. *Current Journal* [Rexburg], July 2, 1908, p. 1.
16. *Idaho Statesman* [Boise], January 31, 1932, p. 1.
17. *Twin Falls News*, July 10, 1908, p. 5; *Shoshone Journal*, July 10, 1908 p. 1.
18. *Idaho Statesman*, April 26, 1908, p. 1; May 1, 1908, p. 1.
19. *Ibid.*, July 21, 1908, p. 2.
20. *Ibid.*, July 31, 1908, p. 2.
21. *Ibid.*, April 22, 1908, p. 5.
22. *New York Dramatic Mirror*, August 8, 1908, p. 7.
23. *Idaho Statesman*, July 21, 1908, p. 2.
24. *Ibid.*, July 24, 1908, p. 5.
25. *Ibid.*, August 23, 1908, p. 4.
26. *Ibid.*, August 25, 1908, p. 4.
27. *Ibid.*, September 8, 1908, p. 2.
28. *Ibid.*
29. *Evening Capital News* [Boise], September 18, 1909, p. 9.
30. *Idaho Statesman*, October 11, 1909, p. 2.
31. *Ibid.*, October 25, 1908, Sec. 2, p. 1.
32. *Ibid.*, December 13, 1908, Sec. 2, p. 1.
33. *Evening Capital News*, April 15, 1909, p. 5.
34. *Idaho Statesman*, January 31, 1908, p. 1.
35. *Evening Capital News*, September 5, 1909, p. 3.
36. *Ibid.*, December 12, 1908, p. 4.
37. *Ibid.*, June 24, 1909, p. 7.
38. *Evening Capital News*, June 5, 1909, p. 8; *New York Dramatic Mirror*, June 24, 1908, p. 21.
39. *Idaho Statesman*, July 24, 1909, p. 5.
40. *Ibid.*
41. *Evening Capital News*, August 2, 1909, p. 8.
42. *Ibid.*
43. *New York Clipper*, August 7, 1909, p. 669.
44. *Evening Capital News*, August 17, 1909, p. 2.
45. *Ibid.*, August 17, 1909, p. 6.
46. *Idaho Statesman*, December 4, 1909, p. 5; *Evening Capital News*, October 2, 1909, p. 2.
47. *Twin Falls News*, October 29, 1909, p. 11; *Shoshone Journal*, November 6, 1909, p. 4.
48. *Idaho Statesman*, November 11, 1909, p. 2.
49. *Payette Enterprise*, December 2, 1909, p. 1.
50. *La Grande Evening Observer*, December 4, 1909, p. 6.
51. *Ibid.*, December 18, 1909, p. 6.
52. *Ibid.*
53. *Ibid.*
54. *Ibid.*
55. *New York Clipper*, January 29, 1910, p. 1281.
56. *Ibid.*
57. *Evening Capital News*, January 4, 1910, p. 6.
58. *New York Daily Mirror*, January 1, 1910, p. 30.
59. *Columbian Chronicle* [Dayton, Washington], January 12, 1910, p. 2.
60. *Idaho County Free Press* [Grangeville, Idaho], January 20, 1910, p. 3.
61. *Lewiston Morning Tribune*, February 7, 1910, p. 2
62. *Ibid.*, March 3, 1910, p. 5.
63. *Colfax Commoner*, March 4, 1910, p. 1.
64. *New York Clipper*, April 16, 1910, p. 234.
65. *Daily Missoulian*, March 12, 1910, p. 5.
66. *Ibid.*, March 13, 1910, p. 12.
67. *Ibid.*, March 12, 1910, p. 5.
68. *Ibid.*, April 24, 1910, Sec. 3, p. 3.

69. *Idaho Statesman*, June 19, 1910, Sec. 2, p. 2.

Chapter 10

1. *New York Clipper*, April 16, 1910, p. 234.
2. *Ibid.*, June 4, 1910, p. 425.
3. *Idaho Statesman*, June 19, 1910, p. 2.
4. *Ibid.*, June 26, 1910, p. 7.
5. *Evening Capital News*, June 28, 1910, p. 7.
6. *Ibid.*, July 5, 1910, p. 7.
7. *Ibid.*, July 9, 1910, p. 5; July 21, 1910, p. 8.
8. *Shoshone Journal*, August 5, 1910, p. 5.
9. *Idaho Statesman*, August 15, 1910, p. 2.
10. *Ibid.*, August 23, 1910, p. 3.
11. *Ibid.*, September 30, 1910, p. 3.
12. *Ibid.*, November 24, 1910, p. 3.
13. *New York Clipper*, February 4, 1911, p. 1260.
14. *Ibid.*, December 27, 1910, p. 3.
15. *Idaho Statesman*, January 17, 1911, p. 3.
16. *New York Daily Mirror*, January 25, 1911, p. 17.
17. *New York Clipper*, January 25, 1911, p. 1249.
18. *Idaho Statesman*, February 5, 1911, Sec. 2, p. 7.
19. *Ibid.*, February 19, 1911, Sec. 2, p. 3.
20. *Emmett Examiner*, February 23, 1911, p. 1.
21. *Columbia Courier* [Dayton, Washington], March 4, 1911, p. 4.
22. *Lewiston Morning Tribune*, March 16, 1911, p. 8.
23. *Walla Walla Morning Union*, March 21, 1911, p. 5.
24. *Ibid.*, April 6, 1911, p. 3.
25. *Ibid.*, March 30, 1911, p. 7.
26. *Ibid.*, March 24, 1911, p. 6.
27. *Ibid.*, March 24, 1911, p. 6; March 23, 1911, p. 2; March 26, 1911, p. 11; April 27, 1911, p. 11.
28. *Ibid.*, April 6, 1911, p. 3; April 27, 1911, p. 11; April 30, 1911, p. 2.
29. *Idaho Statesman*, April 11, 1911, p. 10.
30. *Walla Walla Morning Union*, April 28, 1911, p. 7.
31. *Butte Miner*, April 30, 1911, p. 16.
32. *Ibid.*, May 8, 1911, p. 8.
33. *Ibid,*
34. *Ibid.*
35. *Ibid.*, May 22, 1911, p. 3.
36. *Ibid.*, May 28, 1911, p. 17.
37. *Ibid.*, May 29, 1911, p. 3.
38. *Ibid.*, May 14, 1911, p. 16.
39. *Ibid.*, June 5, 1911, p. 3.
40. *New York Clipper*, July 22, 1911, p. 23.
41. *Evening Capital News*, July 21, 1911, p. 2.
42. *Ibid.*
43. *Idaho Statesman*, August 22, 1911, p. 5.
44. *New York Clipper*, October 14, 1911, p. 2.
45. *New York Dramatic Mirror*, October 11, 1911, p. 17.
46. *New York Clipper*, October 14, 1911, p. 2.
47. *Caldwell Tribune*, October 6, 1911, p. 3.
48. *Idaho Statesman*, November 14, 1911, p. 7.
49. *Ibid.*
50. *Ibid.*
51. *Edmonton Journal*, November 22, 1911, p. 5.
52. *Ibid.*, November 24, 1911, p. 10.
53. *Ibid.*, November 22, 1911, p. 5.
54. *New York Clipper*, November 25, 1911, p. 21.
55. *Edmonton Journal*, December 13, 1911, p. 6.
56. *Ibid.*, December 23, 1911, p. 9.
57. *Idaho Statesman*, September 14, 1912, p. 6.
58. *New York Clipper*, October 12, 1912, p. 15.
59. *Ibid.*, June 29, 1912, p. 15.
60. *Ibid.*, October 9, 1912, p. 10.
61. *Ibid.*
62. *Edmonton Journal*, September 28, 1912, p. 24.
63. *Ibid.*, April 9, 1912, p. 16.
64. *Ibid.*, September 17, 1912, p. 3.
65. *Ibid.*, September 24, 1912, p. 2.
66. *Ibid.*, September 10, 1912, p. 5.
67. *Idaho Statesman*, July 28, 1912, p. 2.
68. *Edmonton Journal*, December 21, 1912, p. 30.
69. *Winnipeg Tribune*, December 21, 1912, Sec. 2, p. 2.
70. *Ibid.*, December 23, 1912, p. 2.
71. *New York Clipper*, January 11, 1913, p. 15.

72. *Ibid.*, March 8, 1913, p. 23.
73. *New York Dramatic Mirror*, February 26, 1913, p. 23.
74. *New York Clipper*, February 1, 1913, p. 23.
75. *Ibid.*, March 15, 1913, p. 23.
76. *Ibid.*, April 17, 1913, p. 22.
77. *Idaho Statesman*, March 14, 1913, p. 4.
78. *Ibid.*
79. *Ibid.*
80. *Ibid.*
81. *New York Dramatic Mirror*, March 5, 1913, p. 4. Weekly notices through June 11, 1913, p. 20.
82. *Ibid.*
83. *Ibid.*, May 10, 1913, p. 5.
84. *Ibid.*
85. *Idaho Statesman*, May 30, 1013, p. 7.
86. *New York Clipper*, July 26, 1913, p. 4.
87. *Idaho Statesman*, July 16, 1913, p. 3.
88. *Ibid.*, p. 8.
89. *New York Dramatic Mirror*, August 16, 1913, p. 3.

Chapter 11

1. *New York Clipper*, August 9, 1913, p. 17.
2. *Butte Miner*, September 1, 1913, p. 5.
3. *Ibid.*
4. *Ibid.*, September 9, 1913, p. 7.
5. *Ibid.*, November 22, 1913, p. 8.
6. *Ibid.*, November 23, 1913, p. 17.
7. *Ibid.*
8. *Idaho Statesman*, November 26, 1913, 7.
9. *Anaconda Standard* [Montana], February 5, 1914.
10. *Idaho Statesman*, February 6, 1914, p. 1.
11. *Ibid.*
12. *Ogden Standard*, April 17, 1914, p. 10.
13. *Idaho Statesman*, February 19, 1914, p.10.
14. *Ibid.*
15. *Ibid.*, April 19, 1914, p. 7.
16. *Ogden Standard*, April 17, 1914, p. 10.
17. *Idaho Statesman*, May 16, 1914, p. 7.
18. *Ibid.*, July 17, 1914, p. 3.
19. *Ibid.*, August 4, 1914, p. 9.
20. *Ibid.*
21. *Ibid.*
22. *Ibid.*, August 2, 1914, p. 10.
23. *Ibid.*, November 13, 1914, p. 7.
24. Nancy Stringfellow, "The 43rd State," *Idaho Heritage*, Vol. 1 (Winter 1976), p. 2.
25. *Idaho Statesman*, September 1, 1914, p. 7.
26. *Ibid.*, September 17, 1914, p. 11.
27. *Ibid.*, October 18, 1914, p. 12.
28. *New York Clipper*, September 6, 1914, p. 11.
29. *Lincoln County Times* [Jerome, Idaho], November 26, 1914, p. 6.
30. *Twin Falls Times*, November 17, 1914, p. 1; December 25, 1914, p. 1.
31. *Spokane Daily Chronicle*, January 2, 1915, p. 5; *New York Dramatic Mirror*, January 10, 1915.
32. *Idaho Statesman*, February 21, 1915, p. 5.
33. *Ibid.*
34. *Ibid.*, March 23, 1915, p. 5.
35. *Ibid.*
36. *Ibid.*, April 27, 1915, p. 7; April 13, 1915, p. 7.
37. *New York Clipper*, June 4, 1915, p. 6.
38. *Ibid.*
39. *New York Dramatic Mirror*, June 16, 1915, p. 11.
40. *Ibid.*
41. *Idaho Statesman*, May 5, 1915, p. 11.
42. *New York Clipper*, July 17, 1915, p. 7; *Idaho Statesman*, June 13, 1915, p. 12.
43. *New York Dramatic Mirror*, September 15, 1915, p. 6.
44. *Idaho Statesman*, July 27, 1915, p. 3.
45. *Ibid.*
46. *New York Dramatic Mirror*, September 15, 1915, p. 6.
47. *Ibid.*
48. *Idaho Statesman*, September 4, 1915, p. 2.
49. *New York Dramatic Mirror*, September 15, 1915, p. 6.
50. *Idaho Statesman*, September 4, 1915, p. 2.
51. *Buhl Herald*, September 23, 1915, p. 5; October 7, 1915, p. 1; *Oakley Herald*, October 1, 1915, p. 1.
52. *Idaho Statesman*, September 21, 1915, p. 5.
53. *Ibid.*
54. *White Pine News* [Ely, Nevada], November 3, 1915, p. 4.
55. *New York Dramatic Mirror*, January 29, 1916, p. 7.
56. *White Pine News*, November 14, 1915, p. 4.

57. *Ibid.*
58. *Tonopah Daily Bonanza*, November 25, 1915, p. 1.
59. *Ibid.*, November 27, 1915, p. 4.
60. *Ibid.*, November 24, 1915, p. 1.
61. *Goldfield Daily Tribune*, November 29, 1915, p. 2.
62. *New York Dramatic Mirror*, July 1, 1916, p. 11.
63. *Ibid.*
64. *San Diego Union*, January 19, 1916, p. 1.
65. *New York Dramatic Mirror*, July 1, 1916, p. 11.
66. *Ibid.*
67. *Ibid.*
68. *Los Angeles Examiner*, September 14, 1916, p. 4.
69. *New York Dramatic Mirror*, December 16, 1916, p. 35.
70. *Idaho Statesman*, May 12, 1916, p. 9.
71. *Ibid.*
72. *Ibid.*
73. *Ibid.*
74. *New York Dramatic Mirror*, July 1, 1916, p. 11.
75. *Ibid.*, December 9, 1916, p. 30.
76. *Ibid.*, September 9, 1916, p. 32.
77. Letter from Della Pringle's niece, Grace Eagle, to Dr. Jere Mickel, November 11, 1970. Jere Mickel papers, Special Collections Library, Texas Tech University.
78. Huston, p. 27.
79. *Ibid.*
80. *Ibid.*
81. *Idaho Statesman*, September 25, 1916, p. 7.
82. Huston, p. 27.
83. *Ibid.*

Chapter 12

1. Hutson, p. 27.
2. *Ibid.*
3. *Idaho Statesman*, September 27, 1917, p. 5.
4. *Ibid.*, February 22, 1917, p. 5.
5. *Ibid.*, March 19, 1917, p. 3.
6. *Ibid.*, March 13, 1918, p. 10; April 28, 1918, p. 10; June 25, 1918, p. 5.
7. *Ibid.*, March 9, 1918, p. 3.
8. *Ibid.*, April 27, 1918, p. 5.
9. *Billboard*, June 1, 1918, p. 23.
10. *Pocatello Tribune*, May 9, 1918, p. 6.
11. *Ibid.*, May 10, 1918, p. 6; May 11, 1918, p. 8; May 13, 1918, p. 6; June 3, 1918, p. 6.
12. *Ibid.*, May 18, 1918, p. 6.
13. *Ibid.*, May 25, 1918, p. 8.
14. *Ibid.*, May 30, 1918, p. 31.
15. *Idaho Statesman*, June 24, 1918, p. 5.
16. *Ibid.*, July 19, 1918, p. 3.
17. *Ibid.*
18. *Ibid.*, November 21, 1918, p. 3.
19. *Ibid.*
20. *Ibid.*, December 12, 1918, p. 6.
21. *Ibid.*, January 19, 1919, p.10.
22. *Ibid.*, April 10, 1915, p. 5.
23. *Ibid.*, June 23, 1919, p. 3.
24. *Ibid.*, July 24, 1919, p. 3.
25. *Ibid.*, August 9, 1919, p. 5.
26. *Ibid.*, September 5, 1919, p. 7.
27. *Ibid.*, October 9, 1919, p. 5.
28. *Ibid.*, October 23, 1919, p. 2.
29. Letter from Della Pringle's niece, Grace Eagle to Dr. Jere Mickel, November 11, 1970. Jere Mickel papers, Special Collections Library, Texas Tech University.
30. *Idaho Statesman*, December 7, 1919, p. 7.
31. *Ibid.*, October 23, 1919, p. 2.
32. *Ibid.*, December 30, 1919, p. 2.
33. *Ibid.*
34. *Ibid.*
35. *Ibid.*
36. *Ibid.*, p. 6.
37. *Ibid.*, January 18, 1920, p. 5.
38. *Ibid.*, February 26, 1920, p. 5.
39. *Ibid.*
40. *Ibid.*, March 7, 1920, p. 13; April 22, 1920, p. 5.
41. *Ibid.*, May 2, 1920, p. 3.
42. *Ibid.*, August 29, 1920, p. 5.
43. *Ibid.*, September 15, 1920, p. 6.
44. *Ibid.*, March 20, 1921, p. 2.
45. *Ibid.*, April 20, 1921, p. 2; April 12, 1921, p. 5.
46. *Ibid.*, April 23, 1921, p. 5; April 24, 1921, p. 4; *Ogden Standard Courier*, June 16, 1921, p. 8.
47. *Ibid.*, April 24, 1921, p. 4.
48. *Ibid.*, April 25, 1921, p. 5.
49. *Ibid.*, April 26, 1921, p. 7.
50. *Evening Capital News*, April 26, 1921, p. 7.
51. *Nampa Leader-Herald*, May 6, 1921, p. 1.
52. *Ontario Argus*, May 12, 1921, p. 3.
53. *Knoxville Journal*, June 13, 1946, p. 8.
54. *Ogden Standard Examiner*, June 13, 1921, p. 6.

55. *Ibid.*, June 14, 1921, p. 9; June 15, 1921, p. 7; June 16, 1921, p. 8.
56. *Ibid.*, June 16, 1921, p. 8; June 17, 1921, Sec. 2, p. 4.
57. *Ibid.*, June 28, 1921, p. 10.
58. Huston, p. 29.
59. *Idaho Statesman*, July 31, 1921, p. 5.
60. *Ibid.*, August 7, 1921, p. 4.
61. *Ibid.*, October 15, 1921, p. 9.
62. *Ibid.*, November 17, 1921, p. 9.
63. *Ibid.*, February 16, 1922, p. 8.
64. *Ibid.*, May 18, 1922, p. 6.
65. *Ibid.*
66. *Ibid.*, May 18, 1922, p. 5.
67. *Ibid.*, October 6, 1922, p. 4.
68. *Ibid.*, December 22, 1922, p. 12.

Chapter 13

1. *Idaho Statesman*, November 11, 1909, p. 7.
2. *Ibid.*, June 3, 1923, p. 15.
3. *Ibid.*, June 12, 1923, p. 4.
4. *Ibid.*
5. *Ibid.*, July 21, 1923, p. 8.
6. *Ibid.*, September 8, 1923, p. 2.
7. *Ibid.*, November 26, 1923, p. 6.
8. *Ibid.*, March 24, 1924, p. 8.
9. *Ibid.*, March 20, 1924, p. 11.
10. *Ibid.*, August 8, 1924, p. 4.
11. Huston, p. 29.
12. *Ibid.*
13. *Idaho Statesman*, April 19, 1925, p. 8.
14. *Ibid.*, March 29, 1926, p. 4.
15. *Ibid.*, May 17, 1925, p. 7.
16. *Ibid.*, March 19, 1926, p. 4.
17. *Ibid.*, March 28, 1926, p. 14.
18. *Ibid.*, April 18 1926, p. 7.
19. *Ibid.*, January 17, 1927, p. 5.
20. *Ibid.*, August 25, 1928, p. 9.
21. *Ibid.*, November 9, 1928, p.11.
22. *Ibid.*, August 18, 1931, p. 2.
23. *Knoxville Journal*, October 18, 1928, p. 1; *Des Moines Tribune*, October 18, 1928, p. 17.
24. *Ibid.*
25. *Evening Capital News*, October 29, 1928, p. 1.
26. *Ibid.*
27. *Des Moines Register*, October 31, 1928, p. 6.
28. *Knoxville Express*, November 15, 1928, p. 1.
29. *Ibid.*
30. *Ibid.*
31. *Ibid.*
32. *Knoxville Journal*, December 6, 1928, p. 1.
33. *Ibid.*
34. Della Pringle papers, Museum of Repertoire Americana, Mt. Pleasant, Iowa.
35. *Idaho Statesman*, January 6, 1929, p. 6.
36. *Ibid.*, March 14, 1928, p. 5; October 10, 1928, p. 2.
37. *Ibid.*, June 7, 1929, p. 15.
38. *Evening Capital News*, June 14, 1929, p. 10.
39. Play program of National Players, June 17, 1929. Della Pringle Papers.
40. *Ogden Standard Examiner*, June 24, 1929, p. 8.
41. *New York Clipper*, October 24, 1903, p. 30.
42. *Idaho Statesman*, August 4, 1929, p. 4.
43. *Ibid.*
44. Della Pringle papers.
45. *Ibid.*
46. *Idaho Statesman*, January 12, 1936, p. 1.
47. *Ibid.*, September 9, 1930, p. 9.
48. *Ibid.*, January 31, 1932, Sec. 2, p. 1.
49. *Ibid.*
50. *Ibid.*
51. *Ibid.*
52. *Ibid.*
53. *Ibid.*, June 8, 1933, p. 8.
54. *Ibid.*, June 16, 1933, p. 9; June 18, 1933, p. 2.
55. *Ibid.*, June 24, 1933, p. 5; June 27, 1933, p. 3; June 29, 1933, p. 6.
56. *Ibid.*, June 27, 1933, p. 5.
57. *Ibid.*, June 26, 1933, p. 2.
58. *Ibid.*, June 27, 1933, p. 3.
59. *Ibid.*, June 24, 1933, p. 5.
60. *Knoxville Journal*, December 13, 1935, p. 1.
61. *Ibid.*
62. *Ibid.*
63. *Ibid.*
64. *Ibid.*
65. *Ibid.*, January 12, 1936, p. 1.
66. *Ibid.*
67. *Ibid.*
68. Betty Penson-Ward, *Idaho Women in History*, Vol. 1 (Boise: Legendary, 1919), p. 139.
69. Jere Mickel papers, undated, circa 1936.
70. *Idaho Statesman*, February 6, 1936, p. 7.

71. *Knoxville Journal*, December 11, 1936, p. 1.
72. *Ibid.*
73. *Ibid.*
74. *Ibid.*
75. *Ibid.*
76. *Ibid.*
77. *Ibid.*
78. *Ibid.*
79. *Ibid.*, December 8, 1937, p. 1.
80. *Ibid.*
81. *Ibid.*
82. *Idaho Statesman*, October 3, 1937, p. 6.
83. *Knoxville Journal*, December 8, 1937, p. 1.
84. *Ibid.*
85. *Ibid.*
86. *Idaho Statesman*, November 6, 1937, p. 6.
87. *Ibid.*, February 26, 1938, p. 5.
88. Huston, p. 29.
89. *Idaho Statesman*, February 26, 1938, p. 5.
90. *Ibid.*
91. *Ibid.*
92. *Ibid.*
93. *Ibid.*
94. *Ibid.*
95. *Ibid.*
96. *Ibid.*, May 27, 1938, p. 8.
97. *Knoxville Journal*, December 10, 1938, p. 1.
98. *Ibid.*
99. *Idaho Statesman*, November 24, 1938, p. 6; December 13, 1938, p. 7.
100. *Knoxville Journal*, December 10, 1938, p. 1.

Chapter 14

1. *Knoxville Journal*, December 10, 1938, p. 1.
2. *Ibid.*
3. *Ibid.*
4. *Ibid.*
5. *Idaho Statesman*, January 20, 1939, p. 9; January 29, 1939, p. 7; March 13, 1939, p. 5; May 2, 1939, p. 12; June 9, 1939, p. 8.
6. *Knoxville Journal*, December 11, 1939, p. 5.
7. *Idaho Statesman*, April 16, 1939, Sec. 2, p. 12.
8. *Ibid.*, April 30, 1939, Sec. 2, p. 12.
9. *Ibid.*
10. *Ibid.*
11. *Ibid.*, July 7, 1939, p. 8.
12. *Ibid.*
13. *Knoxville Journal*, December 11, 1939, p. 5.
14. *Ibid.*
15. *Idaho Statesman*, April 23, 1939, p. 6.
16. *Ibid.*, September 29, 1939, p. 18.
17. *Ibid.*
18. Huston, p. 29.
19. *Idaho Statesman*, January 28, 1940.
20. *Ibid.*, March 12, 1940, p. 7.
21. *Ibid.*, March 22, 1940, p. 16.
22. *Ibid.*
23. *Ibid.*, October 2, 1941, p. 8.
24. *Knoxville Journal*, January 7, 1943, p. 1.
25. *Idaho Statesman*, June 14, 1942, p. 12.
26. *Ibid.*
27. *Ibid.*
28. *Ibid.*, August 21, 1942, p. 6; *Knoxville Journal*, January 7, 1943, p. 1.
29. *Knoxville Express*, January 7, 1943, p. 1.
30. *Ibid.*
31. *Ibid.*
32. *Ibid.*
33. *Ibid.*
34. *Ibid.*
35. *Ibid.*
36. *Idaho Statesman*, October 22, 1945, p. 10.
37. *Knoxville Express*, June 13, 1946, p. 2.
38. *Des Moines Register*, June 5, 1946, p. 6.
39. *Knoxville Journal*, June 13, 1946, p. 1.
40. *Ibid.*, p. 8.
41. *Idaho Statesman*, July, 1947.
42. Nancy Stringfellow, "The 43rd State," *Idaho Heritage* 1, no. 3 (Winter 1976), p. 2.
43. *Billboard*, August 21, 1948, pp. 33, 45.
44. *Ibid.*
45. *Ibid.*
46. *Idaho Statesman*, August 20, 1952.
47. Huston, p. 29.
48. *Ibid.*
49. *Ibid.*
50. *Idaho Statesman*, November 10, 1952, p. 11.
51. Article by Jere Mickel, Mickel papers.
52. *Ibid.*
53. Mortuary record from Summer's Funeral Home, Boise, Idaho.

Bibliography

Books

Agnew, Jeremy. *Entertainment in the Old West*. Jefferson, NC: McFarland, 2011.
Fountain, Leatrice Gilbert. *Dark Star*. New York: St. Martin's Press, 1985.
Mickel, Jere C. *Footlights on the Prairie*. St. Cloud, MN: North Star Press, 1974.
Penson-Ward, Betty. *Idaho Women in History*, Vol. 1. Boise: Legendary, 1991.

Articles

Hiatt, Richard G. "Lady Troupers Along the Oregon Trail." *Theatre West: Image and Impact*. Atlanta: Rodopi, 1990, 132–135.
Huston, Maude Cosho. "The Saga of Jolly Della Pringle." *Scenic Idaho* 7, no. 2 (1952), 11–12, 26–27.
Lauterbach, Charles E. "Western Actress on Eastern Stages." *The American Transcendental Quarterly*, New Series 103 (September 1996), 245–264.
Locke, Will, H. "Jolly Della: Great Repster." *Billboard*, August 21, 1948, 33, 45.
MacEnry, P.H. "Thelma Bungled at the Victory." *San Jose Mercury*, December 26, 1903, 3.
Stringfellow, Nancy. "The 43rd State." *Idaho Heritage* 1, no. 3 (Winter 1976), 2.

Letters

Eagle, Grace. Letter to Jere C. Mickel, November 11, 1970. Jere C. Mickel Papers, Special Collections Library, Texas Tech University.
Keuneman, William N. Letter to Della Pringle, December 2, 1928. Della Pringle Papers, The Theatre Museum of Repertoire Americana, Mt. Pleasant, Iowa.
Locke, Will H. Letter to Della Pringle, April 12, 1948. Della Pringle Papers, Theatre Museum of Repertoire Americana, Mt. Pleasant, Iowa.

Miscellaneous

Della Pringle Papers. The Theatre Museum of Repertoire Americana, Mt. Pleasant, Iowa.
Divorce Decree, Della Pringle Tuttle vs. T.O. Tuttle, October 29, 1906, Marion County Historical Society, Knoxville, Iowa.
Mortuary record for Della Pringle's funeral. Summer's Funeral Home, Boise, Idaho.
Play program of National Players, Ogden, Utah, June 17, 1929. Della Pringle Papers.

Newspapers

United States Newspapers

ARKANSAS
Arkansas Gazette, Little Rock

ARIZONA
Arizona Daily Star, Tucson
Arizona Republican, Phoenix
Daily Arizona Silver Belt, Globe
Mohave County Miner, Kingman
Tombstone Epitaph, Tombstone
The Tucson Citizen

CALIFORNIA
Daily Morning Union, Grass Valley
Long Beach Press
Long Beach Tribune
Los Angeles Daily Times
Los Angeles Examiner
Los Angeles Herald
Sacramento Bee
San Diego Union
San Jose Mercury

COLORADO
Boulder Daily Camera
Colorado Springs Gazette
Creede Candle
The Daily Sentinel, Grand Junction
Denver Post
Denver Republican
Durango Herald
Fort Collins Express
Fort Collins Weekly Courier
Gilpin County Observer, Central City
Gunnison Tribune
Idaho Springs News
Lake City Times
Leadville Herald Democrat
Mancos Times
Montrose Enterprise
Ouray Herald
Rocky Mountain News, Denver
Salida Mail
Silverton Standard

CONNECTICUT
The Day, New London
The Hartford Daily Courant
Meriden Morning Record

DELAWARE
Every Evening, Wilmington

IDAHO
Buhl Herald
Buhl News
Caldwell Tribune
Council Leader
Current Journal, Rexburg
Elmore Times, Mountain Home
Emmett Examiner
Evening Capital News, Boise
Idaho County Free Press, Grangeville
Idaho Falls Register
Idaho Falls Times

The Idaho Statesman, Boise
The Idaho World, Idaho City
Lewiston Morning Teller
Lewiston Morning Tribune
Lincoln County Times, Jerome
Nampa Leader-Herald
Oakley Herald
Payette Enterprise
Pocatello Tribune
Preston Standard
Shoshone Journal
Twin Falls News

ILLINOIS
Alton Evening Telegraph
The Daily Journal, Freeport

IOWA
The Advocate Tribune, Indianola
Atlantic Daily Telegraph
Burlington Daily Hawkeye
Carroll Sentinel
Chariton Herald
Creston Daily Advertiser
Daily Freeman-Tribune, Webster City
Daily Gate City, Keokuk
Daily Iowa Capital, Des Moines
The Daily Nonpareil, Council Bluffs
Decorah Republican
Des Moines Daily Leader
Des Moines Daily News
Des Moines Register
Des Moines Tribune-Capital
Emmet County Republican, Estherville
Estherville Democrat
The Evening Herald, Oskaloosa
Evening Times-Republican, Marshalltown
Fairfield Ledger
Fremont Democrat, Hamburg
The Greenfield Transcript
The Guthrian, Guthrie Center
Indianola Weekly Herald
Iowa State Register
Knoxville Express
Knoxville Journal
Missouri Valley Daily Times
Mount Pleasant Free Press
Muscatine Daily News Tribune
Nashua Reporter
New Hampton Tribune
The Newton Journal
The News, Sigourney

Oskaloosa Daily Herald
Ottumwa Daily Democrat
Pella Chronicle
Sheldon Mail
Shenandoah Semi-Weekly Sentinel
Sioux City Journal
Washington County Press, Washington
Waukon Democrat
Weekly Nashua Post

KANSAS
Atchison County Journal, Atchison
Holton Weekly Signal
Kansas Democrat, Hiawatha

MAINE
Bangor Daily News
Daily Eastern Argus, Portland
Lewiston Evening Journal
Lewiston Morning Journal

MASSACHUSETTS
Brockton Enterprise
The Daily Globe, Fall River
The Evening Standard, New Bedford
Fitchburg Daily Sentinel
Haverhill Evening Gazette
Lawrence Telegram
Lynn Evening Item
Salem News
Taunton Daily Gazette

MISSOURI
Atchison County Journal, Rockport
Butler County Record, Butler
Chillicothe Constitution
Maryville Daily Democrat
Moberly Daily Monitor
Moberly Evening Democrat
St. Joseph Daily Gazette
Trenton Morning Tribune

MONTANA
Anaconda Standard
Billings Gazette
Bozeman Chronicle
Butte Miner
Daily Missoulian, Missoula
Dillon Tribune
Havre Herald

NEBRASKA
Alliance Herald
Alliance Times
Central City Courier

Chadron Journal
Crawford Gazette
Custer County Chief, Broken Bow
Dawes County Journal, Chadron
Evening Call, Lincoln
Fall River Journal
Fremont Daily Tribune
Grand Island Daily Independent
Hastings Daily Republican
Kearney Daily Hub,
Lincoln Daily Call
Lincoln Daily Post
Lincoln Evening News
Omaha Evening Bee
Osceola Record
The Pioneer Grip, Alliance
Ravenna News
Schulyer Herald
Semi-Weekly Telegraph, North Platte
Sidney Telegraph
Tecumseh Chieftain

NEVADA
Carson City Morning Appeal
Daily Silver State, Winnemucca
Daily Territorial Enterprise, Virginia City
Free Press, Elko
Goldfield Chronicle
Goldfield Daily Tribune
Reno Evening Gazette
Tonopah Daily Bonanze
Tonopah Sun
Virginia Evening Chronicle, Virginia City
White Pine News, Ely

NEW MEXICO
The Daily Citizen, Albuquerque

NEW YORK
The Billboard, New York City
Newburgh Daily Times, Newburgh
New York Clipper
New York Dramatic Mirror
New York Times
Yonkers Statesman

NORTH DAKOTA
Bismarck Daily Tribune
Dickinson Press
Minot Daily Optic
Williston Herald

OKLAHOMA
Daily Oklahoman, Oklahoma City

Oregon
Blue Mountain American, Sumpter
Eastern Oregon Observer, La Grande
La Grand Evening Observer
Morning Oregonian, Portland
Ontario Argus
Oregon Journal, Portland
Portland Evening Telegram
Pullman Herald
Wallowa County Chieftain, Enterprise

South Dakota
Aberdeen Daily News
Belle Fourche Bee
Black Hills Daily Times, Deadwood
Custer Weekly Chronicle
Daily Huronite
Daily Pioneer Times, Deadwood
Dakota Republican, Vermillion
Evening Call, Lead
Lead City Daily Tribune,
Lead Daily Call
Lead Daily Pioneer Times
Madison Daily Leader
The New Era, Parker
Pierre Daily Dakotan
Queen City Mail, Spearfish
Rapid City Daily Journal
The Register, Central City
South Dakota Daily Sentinel, Madison
Sturgis Weekly Record
Watertown Public Opinion
Yankton Press and Dakotan

Texas
Daily Morning Times
El Paso Herald
El Paso Times

Utah
Garland Globe
Lehi Banner
Logan Tri-Weekly Journal

Ogden Standard Courier
Ogden Standard Examiner
Park Record, Park City
Salt Lake City Tribune
Springville Independent
Wasatch Wave, Heber

Washington
Colfax Commoner
Columbia Courier, Dayton
Columbian Chronicle, Dayton
Spokane Review
Spokansman Review
Waitsburg Times
Walla Walla Morning Union
Walla Walla Statesman

Washington, D.C.
The Washington Times

Wisconsin
Manitowoc Pilot
Republican and Leader, La Cross
Watertown Gazette

Wyoming
Bill Barlow's Budget, Douglas
Carbon County Journal, Rawlins
Cheyenne Daily Leader
Cheyenne Daily Sun-Leader
The Enterprise, Sheridan
Laramie Boomerang
Laramie Republican
Natrona Tribune, Casper
New Castle News-Journal
Rock Springs Miner
Sheridan Post
Wyoming Press, Evanston
Wyoming Tribune, Cheyenne

Canada Newspapers
Edmonton Daily Bulletin
Edmonton Daily Journal
Winnipeg Tribune

Index

Numbers in *bold italics* indicate pages with photographs.

Aberdeen, South Dakota 83
accidents 24, 25, 58, 84–85, 96, 105–106
Ada County Hospital (Idaho) 180, 182
Adams, George Faith 20, *22*, 70–72, 86, 90
Adams, Professor J.D. 75
The Adventures of Sherlock Holmes 103
Airdome Theatre (Boise, Idaho) 100, 101, 102
airdome theatres 90, 98, 134
all female WPA drama group 169, *170*, 173
Alliance, Nebraska 24, 41, 44, 60, 76
"Allurements of the Stage" 108
Arbuckle, Roscoe "Fatty" 4, 139
Archer, Charles 9, 39, 59, 79, 112
Ardmore Hotel 85, 86
automobile tour 132–134
Aylesworth's Winnipeg Stock Company 121

Baby Estelle 39, 48, 58, 59
Baby Gail 32
bands and orchestras 42, 74, 75
barnstorming the cross roads 109, 132
Barrett, Grace 14, 16
Barrett, Little Toots 14
Barrymore, Ethel 180
Beery, Wallace 139, 166, 169
Belasco, Arthur 130, 134
Ben Warner Company 14
benefits 22, 47, 163, 164, 165
Bill and Bob (bag punching bulldogs) *50*, 55, 56, 59, 81, 86, 88
Bishop, Louis (violinist) 15, 16
Bismarck, North Dakota 78, 83–84
Bittner Company 101
Boise, Idaho 177
Boise Boy (dog) 175
Bonnet Shop 144, 145, 146, 148, 149, 152
Borah, Sen. William H. 164, 168, 172
Brennan, Walter 174
Brooklyn, New York 47, 48, 49, 72

Bruce, Virginia 165
Bruno, William 74, 80
Butte, Montana 32, 33, 41, 115, 116, 126

calcium lights 27, 59, 167
Caldwell, Idaho 107, 118
Callicote Comedy Company 9
Campbell, Mrs. Patrick 72
Canadian audiences 118
Carter, Mrs. Leslie 110, 112
Centerville, Iowa 47, 70
Central City, South Dakota 77
Chaplin, Charlie 4, 139
Cheesewright, James C. 106, 110, 114, 120, 127, 130; *see also* Wright, Jimmy
Cherry Sisters 26
The Christian 75, *81*
Christmas in Boise 167
Clara Mathes Company 101
Cody, William F. "Buffalo Bill" 4, 18, 29, 43, 85, 132
Colorado Springs, Colorado 90, 93
Comedy Ideals 14, 15, 16, 18, 26
Composton Dramatic Players 20
Congress, Arizona 66
consumptives 65–66
Cook, Ollie 101
Corse Payton Comedy Company 14
Corse Payton Road Company 49, 53, 55, 57, 58
costume rental business 152, 154, 156, 157, 158, 160, 162, 167–168, 174–175
costumes and wardrobe 35, 52, 53–54, 55, 75, 115, 116, 122

Daniels, Bebe 130, 176
Deadwood, South Dakota 15, 16, 24, 60, 77, 78
death: of Della's mother 82; of Reverend Van Winkle 99; of Della 182
The Della (Pullman car) 68, 70
demolition of Knoxville opera house 158
Denver, Colorado 93–94, 98

205

The Devil 103
divorce: from Cecil Van Auker 142; divorce from Edward Hopper 157; divorce from George Faith Adams 70–72; divorce from Johnny Pringle 19; divorce from T.O. Tuttle 86–87
Dr. Jekyll and Mr. Hyde 103
dog breeding business 156
dramatic school 160
Dressler, Marie 164
Dyer, Lillian 16–17

Eagle, Crawford 150, 155, 163, 166, 172, 183
Eagle, Grace 155, 166, 172, 183; *see also* Pringle, Grace; Van Winkle, Grace
East Lynne 44, 103
Eckardt's Ideals 101
Edmonton, Alberta, Canada 118–119, 120, 121, 122
El Paso, Texas 67, 85, 86
Elitch Gardens 100, 110
Ely, Nevada 134
Empire Theatre (Butte, Montana) 126
Empress Theatre Stock Company 146

Fairbanks, Douglas, Sr. 4, 139
Famous Broadway Players 143
Farnum, Dustin 72
Faust 35–36, 37, 40, 116, 122, 169
Federal Theatre Project 168
fire dance 26, 80
fires 60, 62, 66, 95
Fisk, Minnie Maddern 110, 127
Fitzimmons, Robert (heavy weight champion) 73
floods 17, 109, 135
Flossie (Della's Great Dane) 44, 45, 54, 162
fruit tree farm (Meridian, Idaho) 105, 127, 129, 143

George Noble Company 101
Gilbert, John Cecil 74, 159, 164, 165
Globe, Arizona 96
Goldfield, Nevada 95, 134–135
Greenwall Circuit 67

The Half Breed 86
Halloween costumes 147, 152, 158
Harry Pollard Company 138
Haystacks and Steeples (film) 138
Hiawatha Gardens 91, 92, 93
Hogan, Michael F. 91, 92, 94, 95, 100, 112, 114, 117, 120, 124, 143
homestead sites 83, 85
Hopper, Edward 148, 157
Huston, Maude Cosho 180

illnesses and surgeries 102, 113, 159, 162–163, 166, 174, 175, 177, 182
illustrated songs 27, 80
Indians 61

Jerome, Arizona 66–67
J.G. Pringle's Chicago Comedy Company 9
Jolly Della Pringle's Original Broadway Players 143–144

kaleidoscope dance 59
Kelly, Claude 90, 91, 94
Keystone Kops 137, *140*
Keystone Triangle Company 137–138, 140
Knoxville Opera House 82, 158, 159
Konklin, Chester 139

La Grande, Oregon 107, 108
Laird, Laura "Babe" 89, 90, 91, 101, 110, 142, 160
Lamont, Eddie 80
LaPage, Barron 130
Le Gallienne, Eva 175
Lewis and Clark Exposition 78
Locke, Will 179, 180
Long Beach, California 85, 86, 90, 119
Los Angeles, California 117, 136–137, 176
Lubin (studio) 136–137

Madison, South Dakota 83
Majestic Theatre (Edmonton, Alberta, Canada) 119, 120
"Mammoth" benefit performance 163
The Maples (home in Knoxville) *30*, 34, 58, 88, 98
Marlowe Stock Company 107
marriage: to Cecil Van Auker 99; to Edward Hopper 148; to G. Faith Adams 22; to Johnny Pringle 13; to T.O. Tuttle 75–76
Marsden, Richard 24, 28, 31, 37
Marsden, Violet 24, 28, 31
Martin, James H. 24, 25, 49
Matthews, Arthur 114, 116, 124
McCall, Idaho 169, 174
McConnell, Olive 80, 83, 88, 89, 91, 94, 95, 110, 112, 114, 117, 120, 124
Mendenhall, Walter 112
Mexican War 127–128
military forts 169
mining camps 66–67, 93, 95–96, 134–135
Missoula, Montana 109, 110
Moose Jaw, Saskatchewan, Canada 123, 124, 125
Morosco, Oliver 86
Morrison, Lewis 36, 37, 100
Mother Carey's Chickens 149
motion pictures 111
Murray, Charles 139, 159, 164, 176
Myers, Riley 110, 114, 117, 120, 124

National Players 160
Neuville Company 24
Normand, Mabel 139
Northwest Passage (film) 169, 174

Oakley, Annie 4, 43

Index

Ogden, Utah 61, 99, 151–152, 160
Ole Olson Company 17
Oregon Short Line Railroad 45, 108, 117, 152, 156

Palantine rooming house 105, 115, 154, 155, 156, 159–160, 185
Parlor Millinery business 153
Payton, Corse 9, 14, 47, 48, 72
Perils of Pauline (film) 178
Permanent Players 126
Peter McCourt's Silver Circuit 28
Phoenix, Arizona 96, 97, 135
pink teas 51, 104, 110
Pinney, James 104
Pinney Theatre (Boise, Idaho) 104, 112, 117, 129, 163, 175, 184
"Pioneer Days" 156
Pocatello, Idaho 94, 99, 143, 144, 151, 167, 170
poem about Pringle Company 83–84
poisoning 85
Pringle, Grace, 149, 150, 152, 155, 156–157; *see also* Eagle, Grace; Van Winkle, Grace
Pringle, Ida Adair 73–74
Pringle, Johnny 9, 11, 12, *13*, 18, 119, 161
Pringle-Kellogg Company 11
Pringle's Comedians 150, 151, 152
promotional activities 51, 56, 92, 93, 103–104, 113, 129
Pullman car 42–43, 45, 47, 162

Rapid City, South Dakota 15, 16, 18, 60, 77
Reed. Etta 14, 47, 48, 72, 73
Reno, Nevada 63
Rentfrow's Jolly Pathfinders 18, 23
resident stock company 102
Resurrection 59
Rigg's Opera House (Knoxville, Iowa) 88
Rip V an Winkle 7, 105
Riverside Park Theatre (Boise) 104
Robert Neff Chicago Comedy Company 8
Rochester (kerosene) lamps 62, 169

Salt Lake City, Utah 94
San Diego, California 117, 128, 136
San Francisco, California 64, 117
scenery 24, 25, 31, 32, 35, 36, 39, 43, 81, 94, 100, 129
Searth, Francis 114, 116
Sennett, Mack 4, 137, 138, 139, 161, 178, 180
serpentine dance 26
silent films with Della Pringle 138
Simm's *Modern Dromio* Company 11
skirt dancing 15, 18
slapstick comedy 139–140
Social Cub (film) 138
Sour Dough, Idaho 133
Spanish flu epidemic 144–145
specialties 5, 39, 44, 49, 59, 80, 89, 91, 101, 150
Spokane, Washington 45, 78, 130, 155

Spooner Comedy Company 9, 13
Stanley, Ed 101, 117, 130
Stanley, Fanny Hammond 101, 110, 117, 130
Stevens, Professor Charles 75
Stone, Hazel 130
Stroheim, Eric Von 161
subway 74
Sullivan, John L. (heavyweight champion) 175
Sullivan and Considine vaudeville circuit 106
Sun Valley, Idaho 166
Swain, Mrs. Max 176
Swanson, Gloria 4, 138, 139, 166, 176, 180

Taylor, Robert 169, 174
Taylor Players 157, 164
Thelma 59, 64
Tonapah, Nevada 95, 134
Tracy, Spencer 169, 174
train travel 62, 63, 77
Trilby 25
Turner Theatre (Boise, Idaho) 102, 104, 107, 113, 185
Turpin, Ben 3, 139
Tuttle, T.O. 74, 75, *76*, 78, 85
Twin Falls, Idaho 100, 130, 133

Uncle Tom's Cabin 44, 45, 162

Van Auker, Cecil 99, 100, 106, 107, 110, 112, 113, 116, 117, 122, 126, 127, 128, 136–137, 141, 142, *143*, 168
Van Auker, Grace 128
Van Dyke, W.S. 169, 174
Van Winkle, Cora Della 7
Van Winkle, Grace 70, 139, 146, 147, 149, 153, 160, 163, 182, 183; *see also* Eagle, Grace; Pringle, Grace
Van Winkle, the Reverend J. Elmer 22, 33, 34, 98, 99
Van Winkle, Sadie 23, 29
vaudeville 78
Villa, Pancho 127, 128
Virginia Harned Company 61

Wadsworth, Nevada 62
Walla Walla, Washington 114, 130
Walsh, Blanch 56
Wayne Babb Players 178
Winnipeg, Manitoba, Canada 122–123
Winnipeg Stock Company 123, 124
Winston, Laura 169
World's Fair, St. Louis 68–69
WPA Adult Education Program 168, 170, 172, 173
Wright, Jimmy 155; *see also* Cheesewright, James C.

Yellowstone Park 167
Yuma Desert, Arizona 135

www.ingramcontent.com/pod-product-compliance
Ingram Content Group UK Ltd.
Pitfield, Milton Keynes, MK11 3LW, UK
UKHW021845140426
5217IPUK00022B/1602